MICHAEL WILFORD

WITH MICHAEL WILFORD AND PARTNERS, WILFORD SCHUPP ARCHITEKTEN AND OTHERS

ESSAYS BY ROBERT MAXWELL, ANTHONY VIDLER AND MICHAEL WILFORD

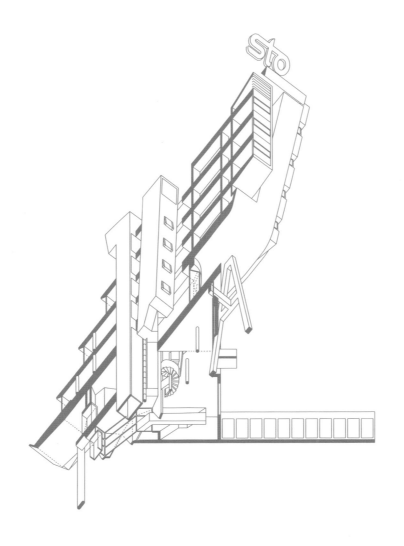

SELECTED BUILDINGS AND PROJECTS 1992–2012

FOR ANGELA, KARENNA, CARL, PAUL, JANE AND ANNA

CONTENTS

AN EVOLVING DESIGN PHILOSOPHY

MICHAEL WILFORD

ARCHITECTURE

Man has always built with aesthetic intention, not only to provide shelter. Representing the tastes and attitudes of generations, architecture forms the built stage for human activity and invests man's constructed realm with meaning. It influences every human being, however subconsciously, and expresses individual and collective culture as well as society's priorities and values. I believe it is a spiritual mission similar to art, music and literature and a fundamental aspect of civilised society.

I have always practised architecture as an art, a social art. By reconciling parallel obligations to client and society, we seek to fulfill the profession's responsibility to increase public awareness of high quality architecture. I believe buildings should establish meaningful relationships with both users and observers and liberate them from any ambivalence towards architecture and the city. They should raise awareness of their surroundings and engender respect for and ownership of the environment of which they form a part.

Working with intuition, imagination and as many ideas as we can muster, we seek to achieve an architecture of order, proportion, balance and stability which provokes exploration, creative interaction and in the process provides aesthetic pleasure. It is an architecture which is intended to stimulate a wide range of experiences by contrast in form, lighting, colour and materials, all within a choreographed spatial organisation and circulation system. As well as satisfying physical, social and psychological needs, we regularly ask ourselves what does the building want to be and what is its animating spirit?

The arts of literature, drama, music and painting can make individual and personal statements but the architect is more constrained, depending upon a collective inter-disciplinary team of people to realise a building. I believe a building should be the equivalent of a profound musical composition containing point and counterpoint, themes and melodies with various overlapping strands of sound woven into a harmonic whole and be equally emotionally rewarding. Our buildings are designed to achieve an interlocking pattern in which all parts come together without compromise to their individual integrity or the resulting geometrically disciplined whole.

Achieving an appropriate balance between the dramatic changes urged upon us by science and technology, the need for stability in our current environment and our sense of history is as critical now as it has ever been. I believe architecture should be a bridge across time, recognisably rooted in the past while optimistically facing the future. History tells us who we are and what we have achieved. It provides a rich resource of precedents and types to study. Appreciating, and learning from, the past is a life-long endeavour and becomes easier with one's advancing years. However, it is critical that contemporary architecture relates to the past and evokes history through an informed and intuitive understanding without compromising authenticity. We strive to interpret by analogy rather than by imitation, thereby transforming and re-charging the meanings of the past. We believe architecture can achieve a contemporary sense of place and time as part of a continuing tradition and our objective is to transform pre-existing situations into a rich dialogue between past and present.

It is essential that every building should, in its own way, advance the body of architectural knowledge and architects should continuously innovate and develop their understanding of the aesthetic, social and scientific aspects of the art of architecture.

URBANISM

I believe urban design is architecture and not a separate activity mediating between planning and building. Similar to architecture, it should be the physical expression of society's hopes and intentions involving areas of endeavour and concern which do not recognise boundaries between public and private domains. Currently architecture deals primarily with individual owners and properties and, unfortunately, rarely crosses ownership boundaries. Planning is concerned with land use and public expenditure policy and rarely involves three-dimensional physical proposals. The ongoing challenge and opportunity for architecture is to integrate design with the power of policy-making and provide a clear physical expression of the community's hopes and intentions for the future of the large-scale public/private environment as well as manage its growth and change. To facilitate this process and protect the public interest I believe the public sector must provide stimulating design direction and formulate appropriate incentives to inspire the private sector to respond with initiative and creative energy.

In our projects we resist the ongoing disintegration of the street and organised public space arising from the making of isolated buildings and the resultant discontinuous and residual open space between them. We aim to reverse the trend in which the public realm continues to shrink to a pale shadow of its former self, and the private realm, although correspondingly increased in extent, is not significantly enriched in either invention or meaning.

To me there are, as in architecture, disparate standards of value apparent in urban architecture exemplified by a concern with problem solving as demonstrated by the application of science or a concern for the common good as demonstrated in populist empiricism and proclamations such as "give the public what they want".

I believe strategies which disregard context by destroying the established physical and social fabric or employ blanket neutral grids or stress methodology and systems are shallow and hopeless as a means of producing a meaningful city.

I also disagree with the belief that the collection and analysis of factual information (programme) will alone lead automatically to a credible synthesis, a proposition in which the future is to be merely an extrapolation of the present. In many cases it seems to me these are merely props and ends in themselves—"we can't act until we have the facts and then we don't need to act since the facts will automatically arrange themselves". Propelled by the rationalist upsurge, the contention that the typical or precedent (paradigm) is alone the starting point for investigation also has gained considerable credence a proposition in which both the present and future are to be an extrapolation of the past. Both doctrines commit us to mere repetition and do not allow or encourage invention and originality. Hypothesis should precede empirical investigation, working with programme and precedent to produce a hybrid of all researches.

It is sad that Disney World and other theme parks thrive in the vacuum of a weak public realm and a dull monotonous environment. They attempt to satisfy a strong human psychological craving for distinctive objects and places but avoid the complexities and realities of life. They fail to provoke the imagination and stimulate speculation.

Notions that either science or the public should design buildings and the city are neurotic and sterile and demonstrate a lack of confidence by the architectural profession. Both play their part but in themselves are not sufficient. Consultation to solicit views and opinions from the public as the 'collective client' is essential to the briefing process but such input must be understood as a constituent part of the analysis of all aspects of the opportunity presented by the project. This input must be combined with the architect's ideas and vision to produce a complete synthesis, a means to an end rather than an end in itself. Careful presentation of the design solution and patient response to feedback is equally essential. I believe the process must be led and inspired by the architect. Throughout the history of city design, the most satisfactory urban solutions have been those which, whilst recognising and fulfilling the necessary pragmatic objectives, have been inspired by philosophical ideals supported by imagination and original ideas.

STYLE

Architecture as a pragmatic art cannot be about style. The battle of style arises substantially from a deep suspicion of change with which modern architecture has been associated, particularly negative change. Confusion between style and quality continues to undermine the development of a truly contemporary architecture and I believe a distinction has to be made between them in the architectural debate. For example, the war of words between architects, historians and conservationists over the respective merits of Modernism and Classicism seems to me to be one of extremes and polarities. I believe it is possible to combine elements of both and achieve a richer, inclusive architectural language relevant to the twenty-first century which synthesises historical precedent with modern abstraction, one which avoids let-it-all-hang-out,

flash-in-the-pan, 'high-tech' modernism, narcissistic, superficial postmodernism, monotonous minimalism and the scale-less biomorphic and crystalline forms of parametric architecture.

We use the best of all periods in our search for a rich architectural language relevant and appropriate to our time. The fundamental values of utility, continuity, authenticity and sustainability are what characterise significant architecture rather than a particular aesthetic or style. We have always striven to enrich contemporary architecture with a vitality that fuses the Modern Movement's ideals of abstraction, functionality, clarity, integrity and economy with the more traditional qualities of form, space and representation to convey a sense of historical continuity.

Modernity is not the enemy of history but by definition can be nothing but evolutionary. Much modern architecture over-emphasised the objective aspects, the logical and the intellectual, at the expense of subjective experiential concerns, such as place, meaning and memory. In retrospect it may prove to have been an important transitional phase in shedding irrelevant cultural baggage and encouraging experiment. Although it has been destructive of cities and communities, its innovations have left a potent legacy for reappraisal.

'High-tech' as an important constituent of modern architecture gave equal meaning to both aesthetics and technology to create purely technological solutions to social and business needs but, fortunately, it later became apparent that the functional and technological programme did not translate in some objective way into a design. It was realised that an architectural language was required to mediate in this process of translation and that good design was aesthetically motivated.

Postmodernism's original impulse had been to ameliorate modern architecture's failures by reconnecting with history, people and the city. But in most cases it became an opportunistic camouflage for the mean spirited and cheap utilitarianism into which much modern architecture degenerated. As Peter Buchanan has written "With objective reality increasingly untenable as a notion, the pendulum perhaps swung too far towards the subjective. Reality is now deemed personal and arbitrary and has become a shallow subjectivity concerned merely with surface and representation. Grand narratives, universals and hierarchies are rejected, leading to a mix of tolerance and nihilism in which every point of view is equally worthwhile or worthless. The inevitable outcome is an array of narrow approaches founded on different arbitrary realities."

The first post-industrial information age, characterised by objective production, technology and work has been followed by the 'conceptual age' which prioritises human skills that the machine or computer cannot replicate such as creativity, establishment of meaning, aesthetic discrimination and emotional response. The new age is characterised by people engaged in, and making their living from, many forms of creativity and cultural pursuits. These depend on empathy to sense and make connections between social, ecological and intellectual/emotional issues and to achieve a more balanced relationship and synthesis between 'doing', as exemplified in work and production and 'being', concerned with the subjective, the experiential and aspects of meaning in human life.

QUALITY

Architecture is a very broad discipline integrating many areas of concern. Design is an invisible process and we understand that the public can have difficulty in comprehending the evolution of the design of a building and the architect's potential contribution to society. His or her power and responsibility are often confused in the public mind with developers, planners and other parties over whom the architect often has marginal influence and no control.

In the United Kingdom architects practise with the knowledge that, with a few noticeable exceptions, buildings are undervalued and the quality of our living, working and recreational environment is low on the list of properties in our materialist society. Clients in other European countries expect to pay more for their buildings and public spaces, to use better materials and are aware that it is necessary to invest in their maintenance.

Quality can mean different things to different people. It is not necessarily about the amount of money invested or quality of materials used but the manner in which they are employed. In the UK it is a term cynically manipulated by politicians. Government ministers repeatedly preach the importance of high quality design in their social building programmes echoing words used by architectural and design organisations in representations to the government regarding the poor design quality produced by these programmes. Such sermons imply that the design professionals alone have the power and influence to ensure high quality design. Politicians follow public opinion through focus groups and other market research devices and habitually abrogate their responsibility to inspire and give a genuine lead on design as in so many other areas of 'responsible government'.

It continues to amaze me that the general public's sense of an appropriate contemporary architecture can be so heavily influenced by manifestations of earlier aristocratic and autocratic societies. This anachronism is made most striking by the simultaneous acceptance of contemporary automobile, aeronautical and communication technologies alongside the popular appeal of pseudo-Georgian homes and Tudor hypermarkets. Unfortunately truth and significance are not provided by the conventions of appearance.

Much current architecture seems to rely on a cacophony of elements and materials and is the product of a 'design' process which has been called "typing and shopping" a collection of elements taken from manufacturers' websites and bundled together in no apparent order or relationship to their surroundings; a mix of ingredients which do not blend, as in the culinary arts, into a satisfactory cuisine. They lack any expression of activities within the building,

its beginning and end, or relationship to the ground. They are a stiff conglomeration of individual objects in which the whole is no greater than the sum of its disparate parts. Often in recognition of the problem the 'designer' resorts to barcodes and other graphic devices and patterns in an attempt to instil character. Conversely another design approach is to distil out building elements and details which can provide a rich architectural vocabulary and produce monotonous grids devoid of any human scale and emotional character.

Historic institutions that contribute to the rich complexity of life are clearly distinguishable by their size, location and architectural language. They provide a clear reading of the city or rural environment in which they are situated. Today imbalance and confusion between the significance of activities and their architectural expression is blighting both individual buildings and the general environment. By our interventions we seek to counter this negative trend and restore an appropriate clarity and balance.

An increasing homogeneity of ambience and experience in current hospital, hotel, airport and railway station design, makes them appear cloned and interchangeable. All take on the appearance of commercial retail centres, some with train platforms, or aircraft gangways attached. The floors, walls, ceilings and lighting are the same wherever you go. The architecture is bland, neutral and subservient to brand names.

The trivialisation of history, sadly typical of recent buildings in most of our cities, undermines rather than advances our culture. It does nothing to enhance the reputation of the architectural profession and makes little contribution towards bridging the ever-widening gulf between public opinion and professional design judgment. It is an irony that, as architects are increasingly marginalised from significant involvement in building design, their perceived responsibility for the poor quality of the resulting environment is increasing.

A popular misconception is that high quality design is prohibitively expensive. In fact it represents only approximately two per cent of the lifetime cost of a building. The social benefits of high quality design in housing, schools and hospitals have been demonstrated in the UK and elsewhere. Enlightened developers and entrepreneurs, in commissioning rare exemplary projects, recognise that well designed buildings achieve higher returns, inspire a more productive and satisfied workforce as well as convey a positive impression of their company to customers and the community in which they operate. Meanwhile, the general environment degenerates, leaving the populace nothing more profound than 'theme' entertainments and 'heritage' shopping centres for something approximating a cultural experience. What legacy are we providing for future generations?

STRATEGIES AND OBJECTIVES

We believe our process of working generates designs which have a simple and inevitable logic. We employ different compositional strategies in response to the particular requirements of the brief and demands of the site and location. The buildings incorporate a series of interlocking strategies and priorities of concern which can be summarised as follows:

The individual expression of the primary functional activities in three-dimensional compositions of geometric forms.

Incorporation of coherent circulation patterns to provide legible routes and connections between functions in and around the buildings.

Provision of internal spatial sequences to reinforce functional activities and circulation patterns.

Articulation of urban spaces around the buildings in formal compositions which enhance the public realm.

Use of solid and void, opacity and transparency, light and shade, colour, texture and a limited palette of materials in support of the formal and spatial objectives and to mitigate against visual complexity and confusion.

Subordination of structure and systems to formal and spatial objectives.

The majority of our urban projects involve the insertion of public buildings into established physical contexts and movement patterns. Our design solutions are intended as a fresh reading and commentary on these complex patterns and textures. They derive their form and character, not merely from immediate functional and physical constraints of the brief and site, but also through the incorporation and definition of new promenades, plazas, courtyards and other open spaces to enrich the character of the public realm and provide appropriate settings for the new buildings. Our intention is to transform pre-existing situations into rich dialogues between past and present and stimulate fresh interpretations and commentary on the complexities of the cities in which they are located. It is usually possible, with careful analysis of history and fabric, to enhance what appears to be, at first reading, even the most desperate urban situation.

As the scale of urban projects becomes larger, so the risk of producing amorphous inappropriately scaled buildings increases. To counter such risk we accommodate the major elements of the brief within individual forms which are assembled into three-dimensional compositions containing a clear hierarchy. In urban situations, dependent upon the number and comparative size of these forms, architectural order is either inherent in the manner of their combination or achieved by the introduction of smaller, supplementary, organising elements, such as loggias and arcades. In this approach the dominant figures establish the identity of the project while the supporting elements respond to the scale and geometry of adjacent structures or spaces in order to integrate the new buildings into their context. In parallel with these interstitial projects, we have also made other urban designs which stand alone as powerful formal compositions. In contrast to the condensed urban solutions, a more open expression is given to suburban and 'green field' projects. Rather than using abstract planning grids, a clear architectural figure is employed to provide an appropriate hierarchy and overall integrity.

Another compositional strategy is that of collage in which major elements of the brief are accommodated in a variety of architectural forms. To respond to objective functional criteria these are positioned within an informal composition and interlocked as required in either plan or section, or both, to provide the necessary connections between them.

The fragmentation of buildings into assemblies of individual forms could, if not carefully controlled, result in visual complexity and confusion. We therefore employ basic geometric figures and use a limited palette of materials to ensure compositional clarity and architectural integrity. Elaborations to suit particular aspects of the brief are developed within the basic enveloping forms rather than as additions to them.

Frequently the requirement for phased construction is a significant factor in determining the basic organisation of a project. We are often asked to make designs which can accommodate either planned or unpredicted future additions. In such circumstances we establish an overall organisational diagram (a masterplan) which provides functional integrity and a clear architectural character on completion of the first stage of construction and facilitates later additions without disrupting that functionality and character. Strategies include the use of incremental linear and radiating systems designed to allow expansion from fixed central cores by addition at the extremities. Alternatively, all-embracing matrices are established, incorporating voids for subsequent infilling. The degree of initial and ultimate integrity required between original and added parts and the extent of re-organisation which can be tolerated at each stage of expansion determines which strategy is adopted.

Pedestrian circulation is a dynamic and motivating element common to all our projects and is articulated in a spatial sequence of richness and subtlety—the opposite of the free plan approach in which activity and circulation are mixed together within a neutral enclosure. The form and scale of the spaces are developed to suit functional and experiential criteria and punctuate the circulation routes. We use arcades, promenades, ramps and staircases to allow pedestrian approach, entry and internal movement to unfold and flow smoothly through level and direction changes and assist the eye and general mood to adjust to controlled interior environments.

Integration of new and pre-existing accommodation in our additions to established buildings often involves the insertion of new spaces and circulation routes into their interstices. Our designs clearly express the interventions by contrasting the new elements against the original fabric. This process is very similar to that used in teasing new buildings into established city fabrics.

We believe a building should be so rich in its form and detail that a viewer on a third, fourth and fifth visit discovers new aspects which were not initially apparent: a series of layers that the viewer can progressively work through. In response to lower building budgets and deteriorating standards of craftsmanship, the various materials we have explored such as brick, glass and metal have generally been used as veneers, detailed as such and expressed as interlocking planes overlapping the structure.

Flexibility in structural systems, building envelopes, internal space division and servicing are regularly debated in the office and with clients. These discussions focus on the extent to which it is appropriate to invest scarce resources in elaborate demountable/reusable systems to accommodate unpredictable changes in activity. Unless there is a very strong argument in their favour, we do not include neutral flexible spaces. We find figural and identifiable volumes can be designed to accommodate the different activities required by the client without compromising their specific character.

Whilst enjoying use of the most inventive and advanced structural, constructional and environmental control systems, we do not believe these constituents, although important to an integrated architecture, should necessarily be the primary, and in some cases the only, determinant of the form and character of the building. Formal and spatial considerations should always be paramount.

DESIGN PROCESS

We strive to develop an original architecture that is convincing on every level.

Each of our buildings emerges from an intense painstaking process as the unique product of a fresh search. We do not believe in waiting for a blinding flash of inspiration. For me, design evolution is an explicit, sequential and reiterative exploration based on priorities and the timely consideration of pertinent factors to ensure that input is valuable rather than an impediment to the design process. In preference to being overwhelmed with detailed requirements at the outset, our ideal initial brief is as concise as possible, providing only key information such as site details, room sizes and functional relationships. Salient issues can be discerned from such basic information which, together with discussion to appreciate and understand the client's objectives, is usually sufficient to commence design work and can be supplemented later in stages, as necessary, to develop it.

To establish the full potential of the project we review all aspirations and constraints upon it with the client. A wide ranging diagrammatic exercise is then carried out by the design team to establish all possible ways of configuring the building (or group of buildings) within the constraints of the brief and site. The diagrams are generated through freehand sketches and discussion. If they are thought to have validity they are summarised in basic plan, section and three-dimensional sketches to enable us to check sizes, critical relationships and assess the relative merits of each option by comparison. Each alternative is critically analysed to achieve, through integration and elimination, a progressive narrowing of the range of options, until a basic concept is established which satisfies the brief and which we are confident has architectural potential. The concept is the result of a myriad of ideas generated by the design team, prioritised under the guidance of the partners. Decisions taken at each stage of this thorough systematic process are fully informed and firm. It is not necessary to review or adjust them unless in rare cases there are modifications to the brief or site by the client. We move forward without back-tracking.

Participation by the client in editing the options enables us to better understand their needs and aspirations for the project. It also allows an insight into the potential opportunities and involves the client in the critical choice of a concept which will form the basis of the design. Functionality is always a fundamental consideration in generating the options because it is essential that the building performs the required task efficiently. We have no interest in foisting architectural solutions on to clients which are inappropriate to their needs.

The selected concept is then developed through a series of abstract drawings to indicate the organisation and massing of the project and form the basis of an architectural proposition which will be developed during the schematic design and design development phases. Such drawings provide few clues as to image and detail. Patience is required by the client to await later production of more informative drawings which will reveal the character of the building.

ARCHITECT/CLIENT RELATIONSHIP

No architect, however imaginative, should pursue values that are not shared by his client and the community. Significant architecture can only develop from a joint commitment to quality and an understanding of the constraints within which architects have to work. In our experience an informed and enthusiastic client can make a significant contribution to the design process. Behind each of our buildings is a particular individual or group who have taken the time to involve themselves in our work, made the effort to comprehend our ideas, supported us by taking risks at difficult times and, above all, maintained their confidence during the inevitable crises associated with the difficult process of turning initial ideas and diagrams into architecture. Our most successful and highly regarded buildings have been those based on mutual trust and respect between client and architect. Our preference is to involve the client in the design process as early as possible as part of a systematic approach in which the brief and design are developed in parallel.

Close client contact is obviously precluded in design competitions and, despite colloquia and question/answer sessions which often form part of the procedure, it is not possible to establish any form of dialogue or rapport with the users of the building. Competition designs tend, therefore, to be developed in a vacuum and become 'hit or miss' affairs. Nevertheless, competitions are ever more common for major public projects and commercial buildings, particularly now that many institutional and developer clients have realised they can obtain a selection of designs by the best architects from around the world for minimal or no financial outlay.

We have been fortunate to develop on-going relationships with several clients resulting in repeat commissions and consultations over any necessary later functional modification to their buildings. However, it is unfortunately becoming more and more common for changes to be made without consulting the original designers—an indication that often the integrity of a building as a work of art is not appreciated and respected.

There is also an increasing tendency for clients to commission a 'concept architect' to produce a design and image for the building and a second 'executive' architect to work up the concept into a detailed design, produce tender documentation and supervise construction. The former chosen to achieve planning consent and the latter to ensure the project is completed on time and within the budget. This often results in a schizophrenic architecture in which the big gesture appears more important than the quality of the detailing of materials and building elements essential for comfort and tactility. I believe that in order to ensure integrity and quality in all aspects of a project it is essential for us to remain involved through all stages and retain design control from beginning to end. I have therefore consistently refused to accept commissions solely for the concept stage or be novated to the contractor for the later executive stages.

DRAWINGS AND MODELS

We communicate our ideas through the medium of drawing because graphic exploration and analysis is fundamental to our design process. We believe drawings allow the best appreciation of a building's intellectual and spatial order because they focus attention on the essence of a design. We draw everything, usually in several alternative versions, to enable comparison and decisions to be properly informed. Because we think and invent as we draw we do not use computers during this creative stage. We use computers later in the process for technical development and the preparation of construction documents once the basic design is established.

The drawings used to illustrate the projects in this monograph are a selection from the variety of images developed during the design and presentation stages. They comprise up and down axonometrics, isometrics, perspectives as well as orthographic plans, sections and elevations. Most are hand drawn, in black ink-line and their appearance is consciously restrained to convey relevant information.

Overlays are used to progressively pare down the scope and detail of the image and that which remains is the minimum necessary to convey the maximum information with the greatest clarity. The drawings are made to the minimum scale capable of conveying the desired information in order to allow the eye to encompass the image without scanning and to eliminate the temptation to incorporate extraneous information. The drawings represent an architectural understanding of the building as distinct from an impression of how it might look in reality. Despite the apparent consistency of style and technique they are the product of many hands.

Axonometric drawings demonstrate the spatial and volumetric composition of a design in one image without distortion and give an accurate reading of a building because the vertical and horizontal planes are represented at the same scale. A single image of this kind conveys the essence of an idea in a manner which orthographic projection can only achieve with several images and often with less clarity. In addition to general compositional and spatial drawings, components and special elements are also developed and reviewed through exploratory three-dimensional drawings. Although some 'axos' have assisted explanation of complex organisations to clients, they are not regularly used as presentation drawings.

To avoid distortion and misrepresentation, our use of perspective drawings is limited. Generally models are used in place of exterior perspectives. Interiors are represented by one-point perspectives, prepared during the later stages of design. They enable us to study the surfaces enclosing the space and ensure that lighting, air-conditioning and other details are properly integrated. Sometimes such perspectives are subsequently elaborated and used for presentation purposes, incorporating shading, hatching or dotting to communicate form and surface. They are always free of gratuitous and fictitious embellishment ('rendering').

Our use of massing models to assist in the editing of initial design options and to explain them to clients has increased in parallel with the size and complexity of the projects. We regularly produce large-scale working models of interiors to study, for example, museum gallery lighting and auditoria acoustics. Detailed models are used primarily for presentation purposes and are commissioned from specialist firms working from drawings prepared by us.

WORKING ABROAD

Facilitated by developments in communications, architecture is now globalised as part of the international cultural exchange. We are working abroad in several countries simultaneously, and hope we are open in our impressions and reactions to the host country, able to transcend local preconceptions and established agendas and offer fresh, unexpected solutions, seizing opportunities to respond uniquely to particular climatic, social and physical conditions.

The European Economic Community regulations allow professionals from member countries to practise throughout the Community. However, outside Europe, state registration is a pre-requisite for the architect of record. In our experience this legal requirement coincides with a need for the client to have local architectural representation to deal immediately with problems arising and compensate for the differences in time zone and distance from our office. To satisfy these requirements we form associations with appropriate architectural firms based in the city in which the project is located. Masterplanning, schematic design and design development work is carried out by our staff in our office. They are assisted by architects on secondment from the associate firm, who contribute their local experience of climate, codes, construction techniques, material availability and other relevant matters. Following their involvement in the evolution of the design and its detail development, the local team members return to their office to form the nucleus of the group which then prepares construction documentation and supervises construction of the project. They are assisted during these work stages by visiting members of our staff who work alongside them to respond to queries and provide design supervision through to completion of the building. We retain design control through all stages of the project by this arrangement and the exchange of staff between the two offices facilitates a seamless and stimulating working relationship. It also ensures efficient and accurate realisation of our architectural objectives.

COLOUR

I believe much of the poverty of contemporary architecture stems from its lack of sensuality. Colour contributes to sensuality and generates a richer more interesting architecture. Our use of colour is more fundamental and carefully considered than mere decoration because I believe it can contribute significantly to the integrity and coherence of a building. Colour has artistic and emotional dimensions and is a key ingredient in the palette of materials and textures available to provide the essential detail and tactility on the internal and external surfaces of a building. We use colour to:

Assist in establishing the individual identity of significant parts of a building and create a visual 'dialogue' between them.

Reinforce the formal hierarchy and its comprehension within the architectural composition.
Identify different functions and public/private zones.
Provide individual identity within repetitive spatial and formal sequences.
Unify disparate formal elements into a cohesive whole.
Emphasise entrance and vertical/horizontal internal circulation.
Provide transitional layers and reinforce spatial sequences.
Heighten contrast in the collage of new and old/natural and manufactured materials.

We use bold, bright contrasting primary hues which vibrate rather than harmonise to stimulate and engage. I consider our ideas to be part of the ongoing tradition of use of colour in buildings throughout history. However, whilst recognising the unique characteristics and associations of each of the primary and secondary colours, the choice of hue within the strategies employed is personal and subjective.

Modern products and application technologies provide ever increasing colour and textural possibilities. We explore alternative colour combinations through two- and three-dimensional drawings in a similar process to that used to establish the basic concept of a building. We select final hues and surface finishes through trials and samples together with paint manufacturers and applicators. Large-scale mock-ups are also used to present our ideas to clients because we always obtain their prior approval before our colour schemes are incorporated into a building.

Each colour scheme is an experiment and I find that clients, users and the general public respond positively to them. They are rarely ambivalent and always express an opinion.

Above all, our use of colour is intended to bring joy and delight to all who use and experience our buildings.

As John Ruskin pronounced:
"The purist and most thoughtful minds are those which love colour the most."

CHARACTER AND COMPOSITION II

ANTHONY VIDLER

The work of James Stirling and his partners between 1956 and 1992 has been famously characterised as stylistically eclectic. Educated at Liverpool University School of Architecture in the years following World War II, Stirling was, the critique goes, introduced to architecture as a stylistic playground through the influence of a former Beaux-Arts school and a culture that had only belatedly accepted the premises of modernism. Throughout his career Stirling retained a relationship to history and precedent that informed his mercurial designs, leading to what some critics detected as a lamentable shift towards postmodernism. James Gowan, Stirling's first partner proclaimed that what was important was determining the "style for the job", and Stirling himself acknowledged in retrospect that his projects seemed to evolve according to more or less distinct stylistic phases.

Yet with hindsight, examining the continuing practice of Michael Wilford, an associate and partner from the beginning, major continuities, hitherto obscured by the "style debates" of the 1970s and 1980s, become evident. A recent exhibition of drawings and models from the Stirling/Wilford fonds at the Canadian Centre for Architecture demonstrated a strong *fil conducteur* through projects of apparently divergent styles, one that emerged as a consistent manner of approach, a way of tackling each design task that, in its formal traces, marked the result as an undeniably characteristic work. We might, using a word that has gone out of fashion in the new digital era, call this approach "compositional".

For most of the nineteenth and twentieth centuries, the word "composition" served to indicate the process, if not the rules, by which a work of architecture was designed. Appropriately enough, the word "composition" came into full service at the same moment that the curriculum of architecture became established in schools—from the École des Arts of Jacques-François Blondel, through the long reign of the École des Beaux-Arts and surviving in the Modern Movement at least to the middle of the twentieth century. The teacher and Encyclopedist Blondel devoted an entire chapter to it in his magisterial *Cours d'architecture* of 1774; the polytechnician JNL Durand systematised its rules for his two-year students, the École ratified it until, ossified, it came under attack from outsiders like Viollet-le-Duc. But, as Jacques Lucan has pointed out in a recent study, *Composition, Non-composition. Architecture and Theory in the Nineteenth and Twentieth Centuries*, even the radical introduction of "Gothic reason" could not dispense with its procedures, and, as Le Corbusier was to demonstrate, its ghost lay behind the elaboration of the free-plan, in the modes brilliantly re-formulated in his celebrated but under-theorised by critics, "Five Compositions". At the height of its usage the notion of "composition" demanded a rigorous approach of the student and architect that enabled the formulation of an *a parti*, or starting-point, appropriate for each programme and site, however awkward.

"Composition" was thus, a fundamentally French idea, but the French system spread to Britain (the University of Liverpool) and to the United States (MIT, Columbia, the University of Pennsylvania, and with the appointment of a Beaux-Arts architect, Jean Labatut, to Princeton). As Colin Rowe observed in his ground-breaking article, "Character and Composition; or Some Vicissitudes of Architectural Vocabulary in the Nineteenth Century", (written in 1953–1954, though first published in *Oppositions* 2, 1974), "the shelves of any representative architectural library in the United States or Great Britain might suggest that between 1900 and 1930 the major critical interest of the architectural profession throughout the English speaking world lay in the elucidation of the principles of architectural composition".[1]

Rowe was, of course, one of Stirling's instructors at Liverpool, himself trained in the attenuated Beaux-Arts curriculum of Liverpool in the late 1930s and early 1940s and one who became a long-lasting friend and it might be fairly conjectured that the combination of the faint echoes of the Beaux-Arts still heard at the school together fueled by the intense and inventive design criticism of Rowe, formed Stirling's own compositional approach from the outset. Rowe, the architect-trained architectural historian, fresh from his course of study at the University of London with Rudolf Wittkower, was ever delightfully oblivious to questions of overt style in favour of an analytical penetration of the underlying forces that shaped buildings and urban spaces, whether it was the "mathematics" of a plan, the parti of the work, or the collage effect of its juxpositioning in the city.

For Rowe, the belated traces of Beaux-Arts pedagogy at Liverpool were there to be activated as the instrument of an enquiry that excavated family relationships among works as diverse as Palladian and Corbusian villas, Mannerist facades and Miesian plans, and, yes, Butterfield's eclecticism and Stirling's, with respect to his critique of Stirling's Thesis project, modernism. Among the tools inherited and put to work by Rowe from the Beaux-Arts kit, were two related concepts: "character" and "composition". And in an equally catholic manner, Rowe saw these two ideas as intertwined in their British evocation with the strange ideological and formal dance between the Picturesque and the Neo-Classic, that dominated the nineteenth century from John Soane to Lutyens.

As Lucan writes, "composition is antecedent to 'styles', or, to put it another way… a given composition can be dressed in several different 'styles'." A question of "syntax" rather than "vocabulary" the idea of composition at any moment in the nineteenth and twentieth centuries is intimately bound to the idea, or theory of architecture itself. Shifting from the eighteenth century theory of the arrangement of interior rooms, to the volumetric organisation of irregular plans in the Picturesque movements of the early nineteenth, thence to the disposition of identifiable elements of the program in the Beaux-Arts, to the rational organisation of structure and ornament in the Gothic Revival, and operating as an abstract technique of manipulating what Rowe called "an architecture of pure form" from 1900 to the 1950s, "composition" emerges once more as the primary key to the revival of modernism in the architectural thought of the immediate post-war period.

Which explains why in this monograph devoted to the work of Michael Wilford and his Partners, Wilford makes reference in his essay to what he calls "compositional strategies". And while not all of his categories might be accurately classified as "compositions"—"Urban and Rural Pavilions" for example might more properly be seen as "Typologies"—certainly "Dense Urban Assemblies", "Orthogonal and Radial Patterns", and "Collage" are compositional at root.

If composition represents the process by which a design is iterated, the result, as Rowe points out, is the "character" that marks the building as special of its kind. "Character", to those who believed in compositional strategies in the nineteenth and early twentieth centuries, represented the "symbolic content" of the building—that which properly displayed its "attributes" as, for example a factory versus a library or, as a supplement, conveying its appropriate "mood", from serious to jovial. In this sense the idea of character had a theoretical history deeply embedded in Neo-Classicism. Blondel in his 1774 treatise insists on defining the means by which a composition determined character: "[the architect] should avoid in his compositions everything that only displays a sterile abundance; he must learn to husband his means so as not to confound the special character appropriate to each building", going on to list 25 "characters" of architecture from male and virile, elegant and delicate, to naïve and frivolous, licentious and barbarous, sterile and flat, a theory that Quatremère de Quincy was to adumbrate at great length in the first volume of his *Encyclopédie methodique. Architecture* of 1788.[2]

In Britain, however, by contrast, the idea of character was captured not by Neo-Classicism but by the Picturesque; in Rowe's terms, "as being particularly applicable to the new, free, asymmetrical organisations which could not be comprehended within the aesthetic categories of the academic tradition".[3] Indeed, the demand for expressed as opposed to embodied character was a major force in undermining the hierarchical academic system itself. The "cult of character", as Rowe terms it, was in the terms of the Picturesque, fundamentally against all ideal typology, and for the specific, the local, the contextual.

Now, while Rowe's long essay may be interpreted as an elegy to what Frank Lloyd Wright called the "death" of composition and thereby of character, "the leitmotif of an era gone beyond recall", it is also clear in retrospect, that strong echoes of both ideas resonate throughout his own critical writings, and especially in his observations on the work of Le Corbusier, in which he found a powerful dialectic at work between the individual "picturesque" gesture and the overall "academic" order. And my own two-year experience of Rowe's design critiques over

the desk at Cambridge reinforces the impression that the dialogue between composition and character had not ceased to animate his insatiable appetite for continuous thematic iteration.

Certainly, as Michael Wilford remarks in his "Introduction" to *James Stirling, Michael Wilford, and Associates: Buildings and Projects 1975–1992*, (and as demonstrated once more by the projects in this new monograph) something of the dramatic dialogue between the formal and the informal remained as a continuous preoccupation of the office: "a strategy of breaking down each building into a number of discrete parts, each expressed separately and clearly; clarity and dramatisation of pedestrian circulation within and between these separate parts; an interest in the contrasting relationships between solids and voids (i.e. between "mass and membrane"); the exploration of non-rectilinear, oblique, and curvilinear geometries … and especially, the predominance of formal and spatial objectives over structural and technological systems". A characterisation of the design process that would not be out of place in a nineteenth-century handbook of Picturesque design, with a modicum of classical elementarism added for good measure, but which, as integral to the continuation of the modernist project begun by Stirling and Gowan in 1956, and continued by Michael Wilford and his Partners, is as relevant today as it ever was.

1   Rowe, Colin, "Character and Composition; or Some Vicissitudes of Architectural Vocabulary in the Nineteenth Century", *The Mathematics of the Ideal Villa and Other Essays*, Boston: MIT Press, 1976, p. 60.
2   Blondel, Jacques-François, *Cours d'architecture*, seven volumes, 1771–1774, volume one, Paris: Deaint, 1771, p. 172.
3   Rowe, "Character and Composition", p. 65.

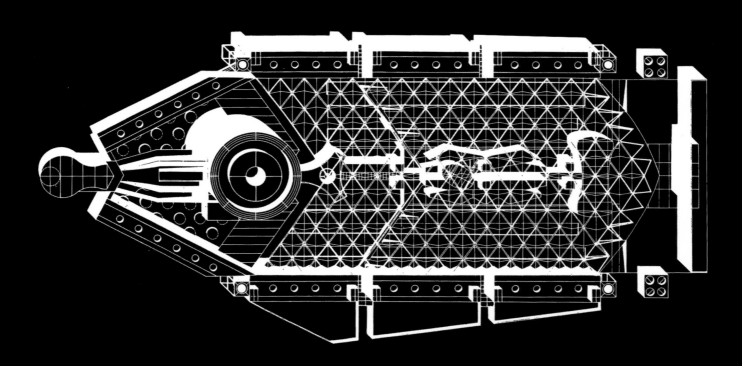

INFRASTRUCTURE

Aerial photograph of the existing station   Context plan

ABANDO PASSENGER INTERCHANGE
BILBAO, SPAIN, 1992–1993

Michael Wilford & Partners

Although strategically located, the existing Abando Railway Station and its elevated plateau separate the Medieval and nineteenth century quarters of the city and contributes little to the amenity of adjacent neighbourhoods. The new Abando Passenger Interchange will weave together the two halves of the city at numerous locations with a network of pedestrian routes to assist revitalisation of the central area.

The Interchange comprises a central bus station for suburban and intercity bus services together with two new railway stations, in a multi-layered organisation linked directly to the Metro and adjacent streets to provide convenient passenger access and connections. It also contains a retail concourse, Trade Centre, offices, hotel and housing. Relocation of the railway stations to the centre of the site allows construction of a new public plaza with covered car and taxi drop-off as the forecourt of the Interchange.

The new RENFE Station situated along the centre of the site contains 12 platforms for long and short distance trains, including the new high speed AVE. Trains will emerge from a tunnel into the grand station hall, flooded with daylight from the vaulted roof above, providing a dramatic entry into the city. Lifts and escalators connect platforms to all levels and facilities. Situated between the Bus Station and RENFE Railway Station levels, the new FEVE Railway Station is the focus of the retail concourse linked by arcades to adjacent streets. The concourse is a place for passengers to buy tickets, shop and relax whilst waiting for a bus or train. Buses enter the Interchange into a large hall at plaza level via ramps from a dedicated motorway connection.

The Interchange establishes a vibrant new heart to the city and the dramatic vaulted roof and Trade Centre Tower registers its central presence on the city skyline.

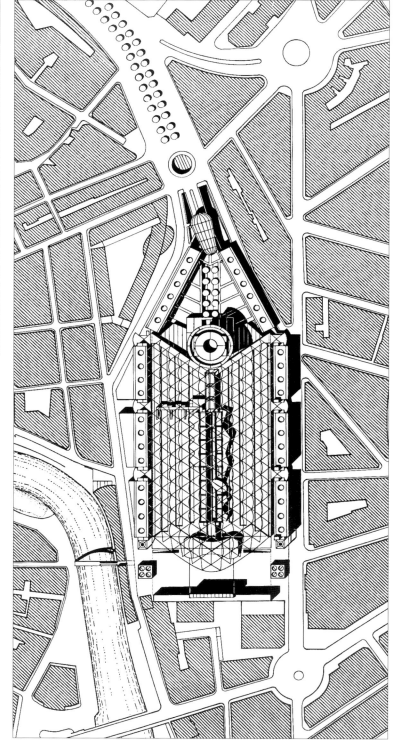

Site plan

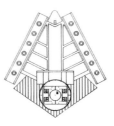

Tower levels three to nine

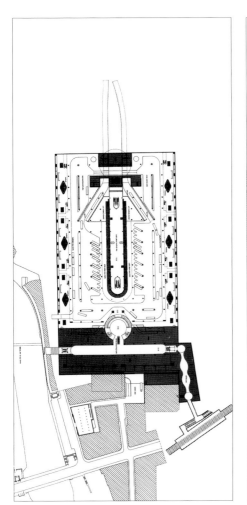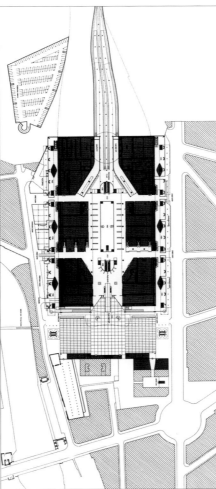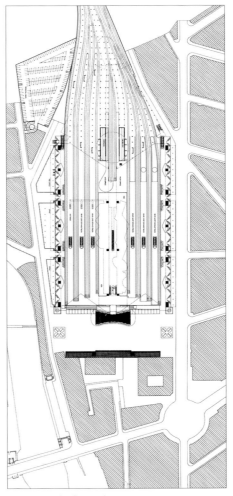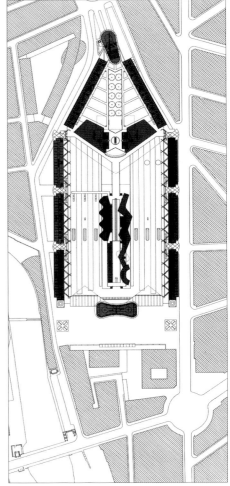

Bus station, basement level

FEVE station and concourse, ground level

RENFE station, first floor level

Second floor level

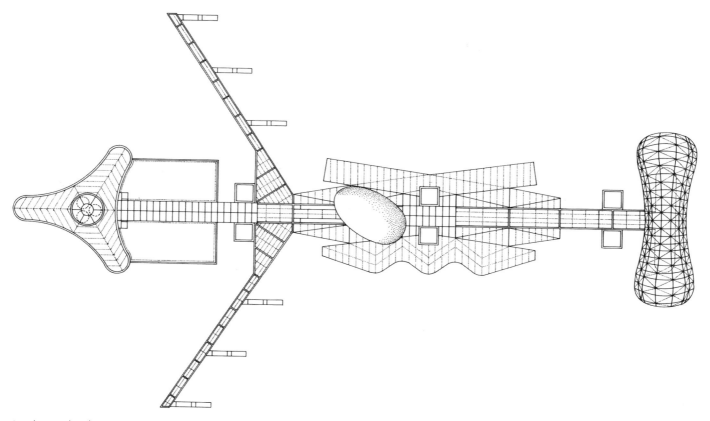

Central spine and circulation connections

Centreline longitudinal sectional model

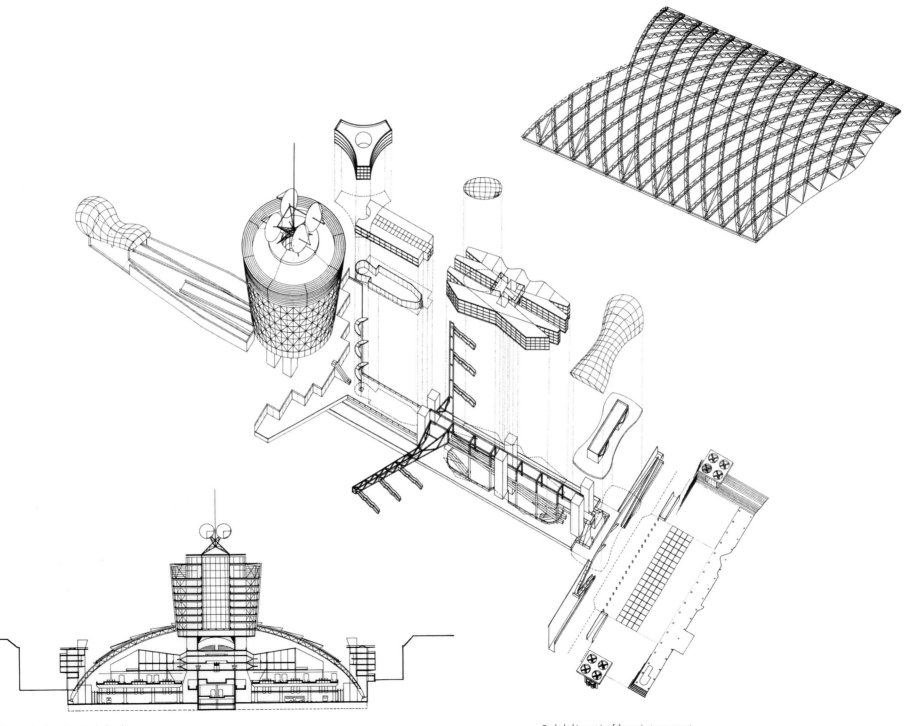

Cross-section through station hall and tower

Exploded isometric of the project components

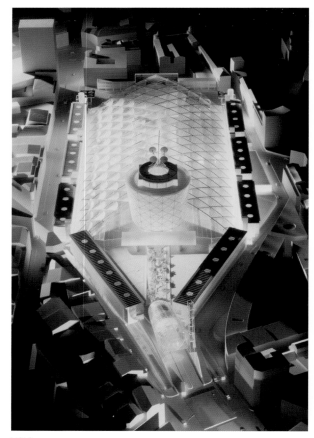

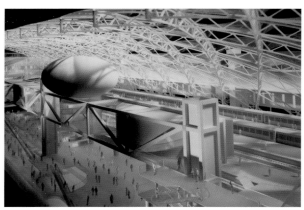

RENFE station interior

Vehicle access ramps

Plaza and street facades

Entrance plaza

Cross-sectional model

Pedestrian entrance facade to the plaza

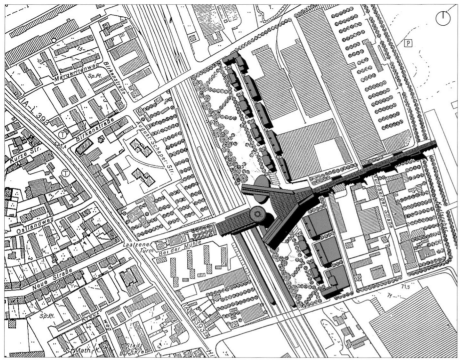

Context plan

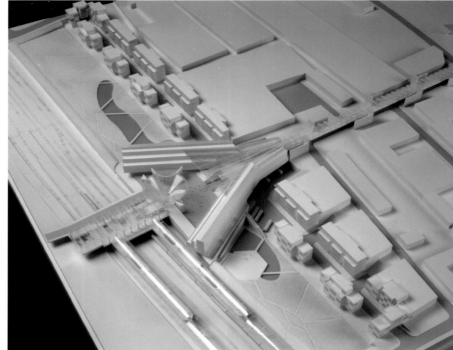

EXPO 2000 RAILWAY STATION
HANNOVER, GERMANY, 1995
Michael Wilford & Partners

The new railway station and raised triangular plaza containing bus and taxi drop-off with parking beneath, provides a dramatic and efficient gateway for visitors arriving at the Expo by train, bus or car. A new public park on either side of the station accommodates large residential 'villas', office buildings and small workshops.

The plaza, lined with retail offices, hotel and information kiosks, guides visitors via generous stairs and escalators to an elevated boulevard and travelator tube which passes between information and advertising screens shielding from view the non-descript hinterland between the station and exhibition site and providing an attractive weather protected connection to the Expo. In addition to its occasional intense transport activity, the plaza will provide a vibrant focus for the surrounding residential community.

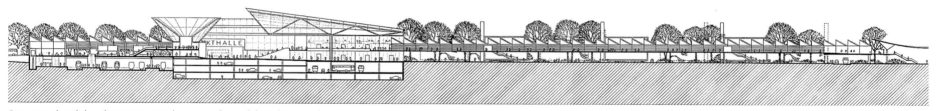

Cross-section through the railway station, triangular entrance plaza and elevated Expo travelator connection

Longitudinal section through the railway station and plaza facade

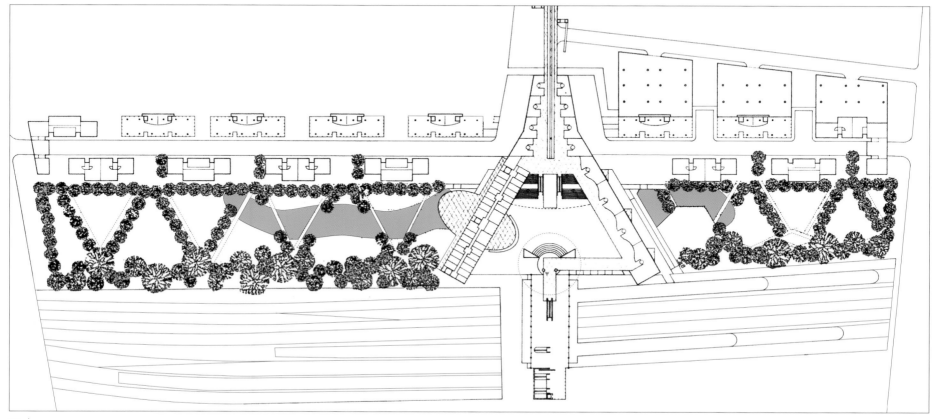

Site plan

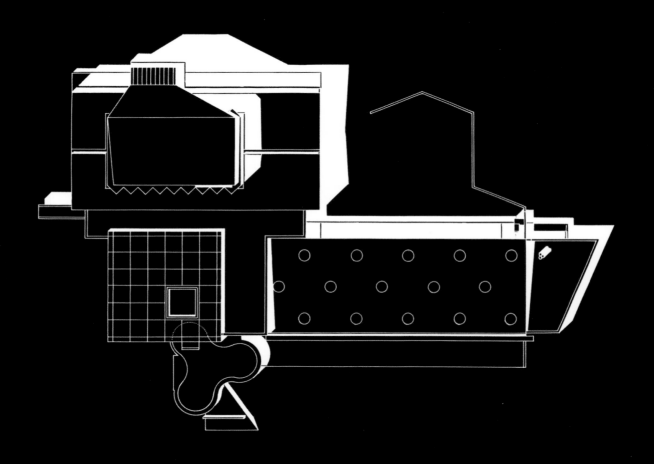

PRODUCTION + DISTRIBUTION

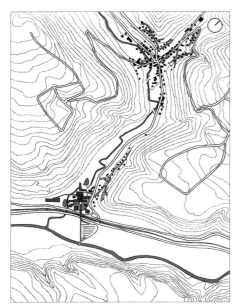

Context plan

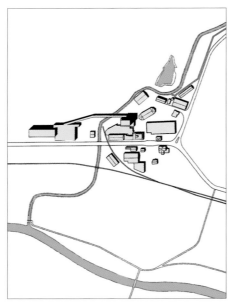

Pre-existing situation

STO AG HEADQUARTERS AND PRODUCTION PLANT MASTERPLAN
WEIZEN, GERMANY, 1992

Michael Wilford & Partners

The company's main production plant is located in the Black Forest adjacent to the German/Swiss border and situated on a plateau at the confluence of two river valleys. Historically the plant developed in a piecemeal manner and due to rapid expansion the company required larger and more efficient accommodation for production, research and administration. The masterplan integrates new and existing buildings into an arcadian campus and satisfies functional requirements within an ecologically responsible environment. The flexible plan allows phased construction of new buildings and reconstruction of the existing facilities, as and when required, without interrupting operations.

Re-routing into the valley the busy road which previously subdivided the plant, offered the opportunity to unify the separate areas and project the presence and identity of the company to passing motorists and train passengers through dramatic new buildings accommodating research, marketing and training facilities. A new semi-circular central garden situated across the line of the original road is the focus of the campus and an entrance court for many of the new buildings. Existing and new office and laboratory buildings provide a backdrop to the garden and form a scale transition to the larger production areas beyond.

A new truck route for material delivery and product despatch encircles the campus, defining a new lake and traffic free central core.

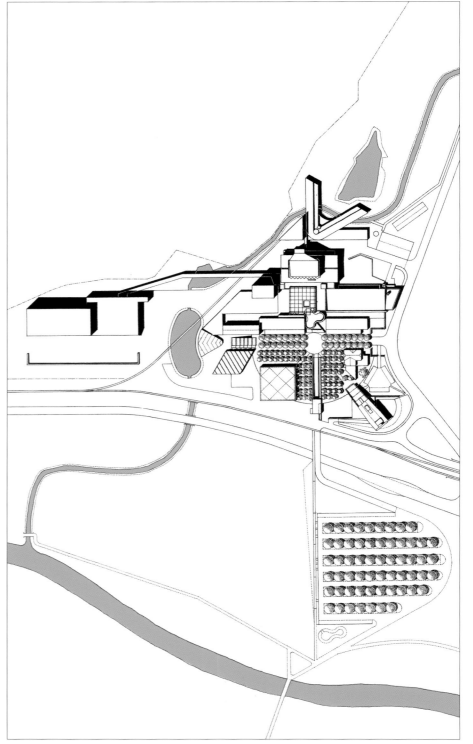

Development masterplan

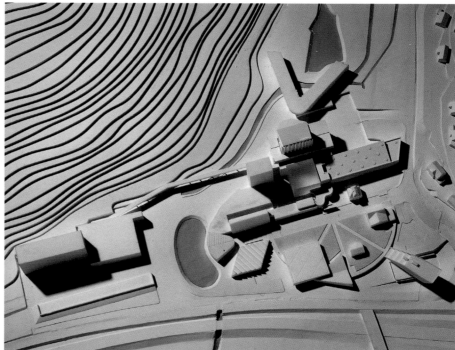

Masterplan model

Masterplan model

Pre-existing situation

Pre-existing situation

Site plan

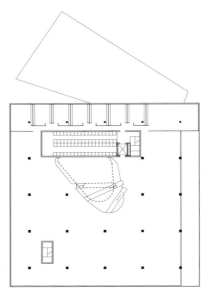

First floor plan

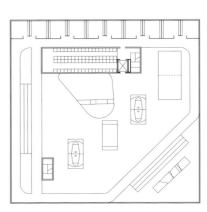

Roof plan

ADIDAS FACTORY OUTLET
HERZOGENAURACH, GERMANY, 2002
Wilford Schupp Architekten

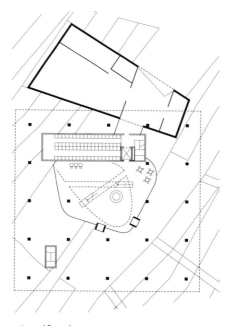

Ground floor plan

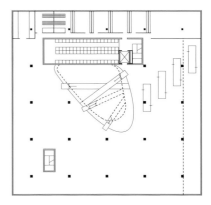

Second floor plan

The site is situated on a shallow hillside on the edge of the town, close to an autobahn. This competition design maximises the potential of the highly visible location and generous site area to highlight the company's presence and demonstrate its products both visually and experientially.

The building is positioned on the highest point with gymnasium, sales and demonstration areas, contained within a floating, translucent square building. Products are highly visible in a fully automated glazed storage tower.

Parking follows the site contours and leads directly up to the entry lobby beneath the pavilion. Visitors move between levels and are introduced to the activities within by escalators passing through a top-lit freeform atrium at the heart of the plan. Offices, shipping/receiving, toilets and other support spaces are accommodated along one edge of the pavilion. The pavilion roof also provides an outdoor garden and exercise area for product sampling and testing.

The new facility is intended to provide a unique, out-of-town shopping experience. Both the tower and pavilion will be illuminated at night, acting as a beacon and registering its presence in the landscape.

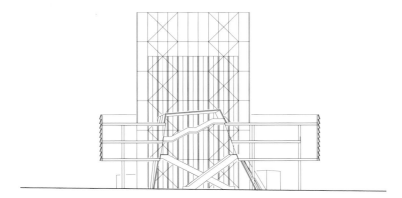

Section looking northwest

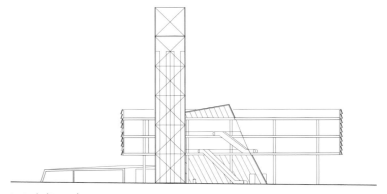

Section looking northeast

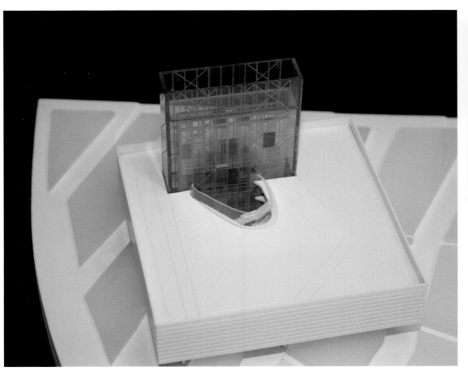

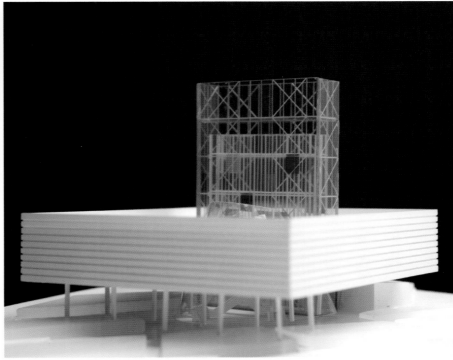

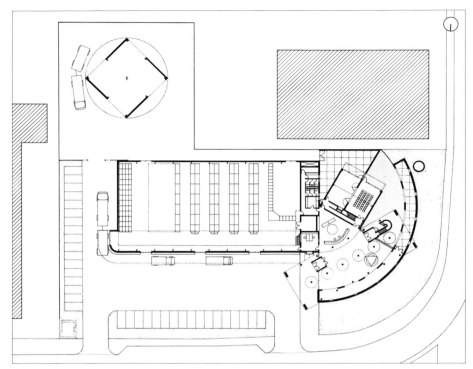

Ground floor warehouse, entrance hall and training pavilion plan

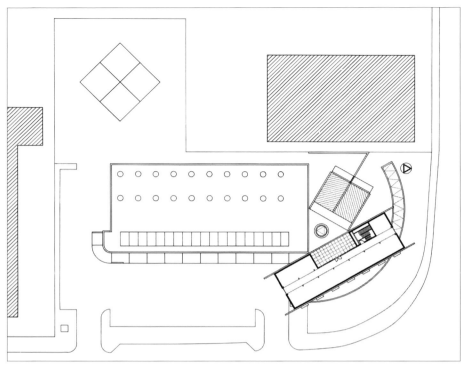

Second floor office and roof plan

STO AG REGIONAL DEPOT PROTOTYPE
HAMBURG, GERMANY, 1994–1995
Michael Wilford & Partners

This building is a prototype for a series of regional depots planned throughout Germany for local distribution of the company's products. Each will comprise four building elements— warehouse, offices for the regional sales force, an exhibition area and a customer training pavilion. Modular forms and envelopes have been designed for each of these elements which are capable of assembly in a variety of combinations to suit different site configurations.

The Hamburg Depot is located on a corner site in an industrial park on the city fringe. The warehouse is situated parallel to the primary street frontage with the offices set diagonally across the corner of the site and the training pavilion facing the entrance. A curved display wall beneath the offices encloses the exhibition area and a secluded garden. The tower sign registers the building in its largely featureless context.

External walls comprise prototype factory-made cladding panels developed for a wide range of applications in office, industrial and residential buildings. The external colour scheme represents Sto's corporate identity, with the offices, training building painted in primary colours to enhance their individuality and to communicate Sto's business interest in colour.

The design is an extrovert expression of each functional building element through contrasting architectural form and colour to provide a stimulating and attractive environment for customers and staff.

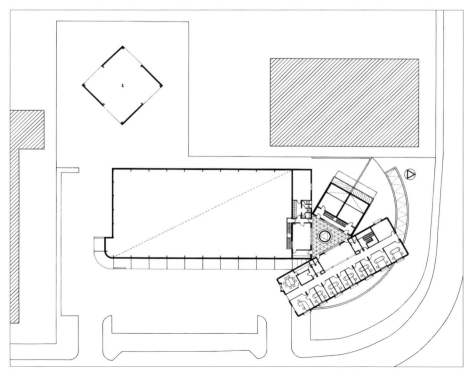

First floor office plan

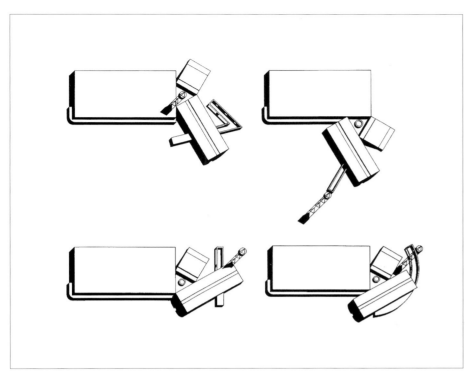

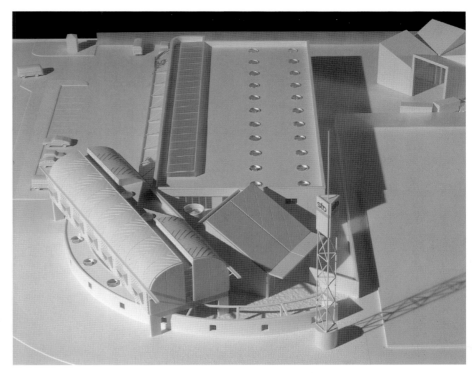

Elemental assembly combinations for different locations

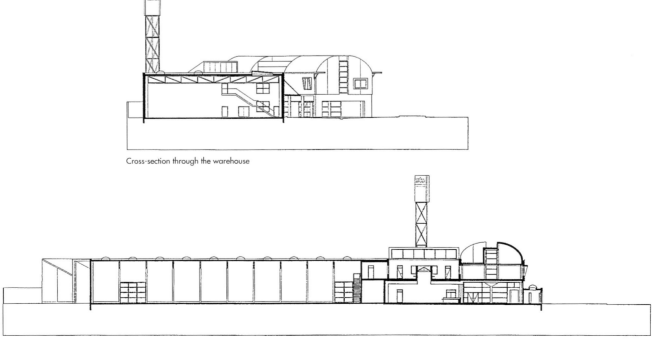

Cross-section through the warehouse

Longitudinal section through the warehouse, entrance hall and offices

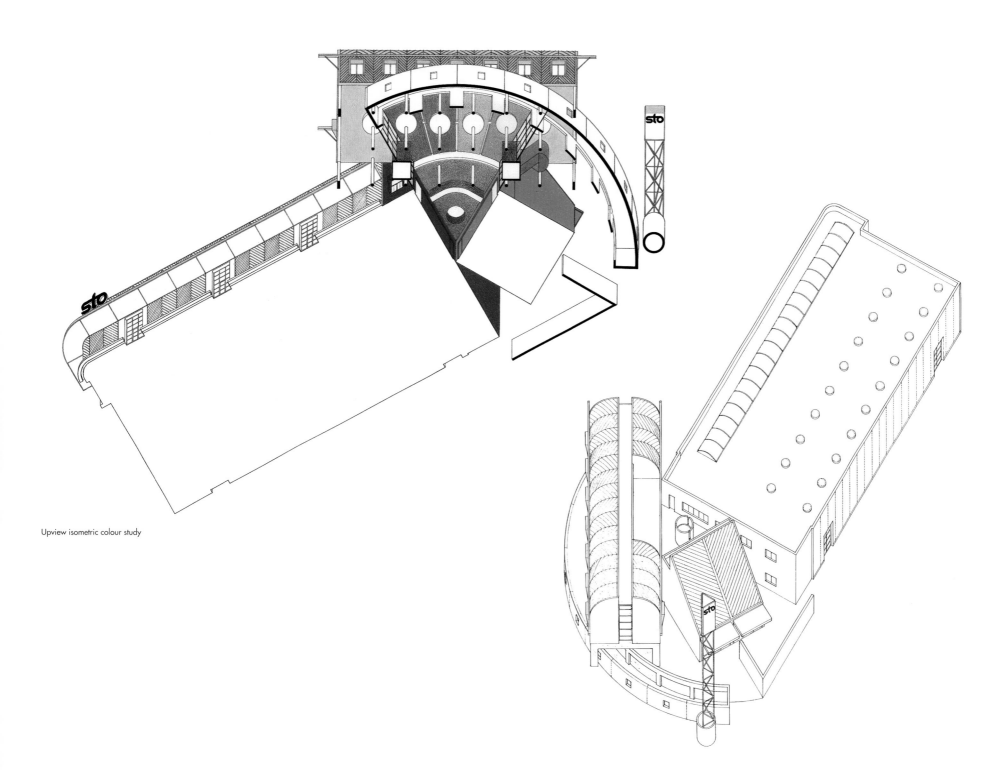

Upview isometric colour study

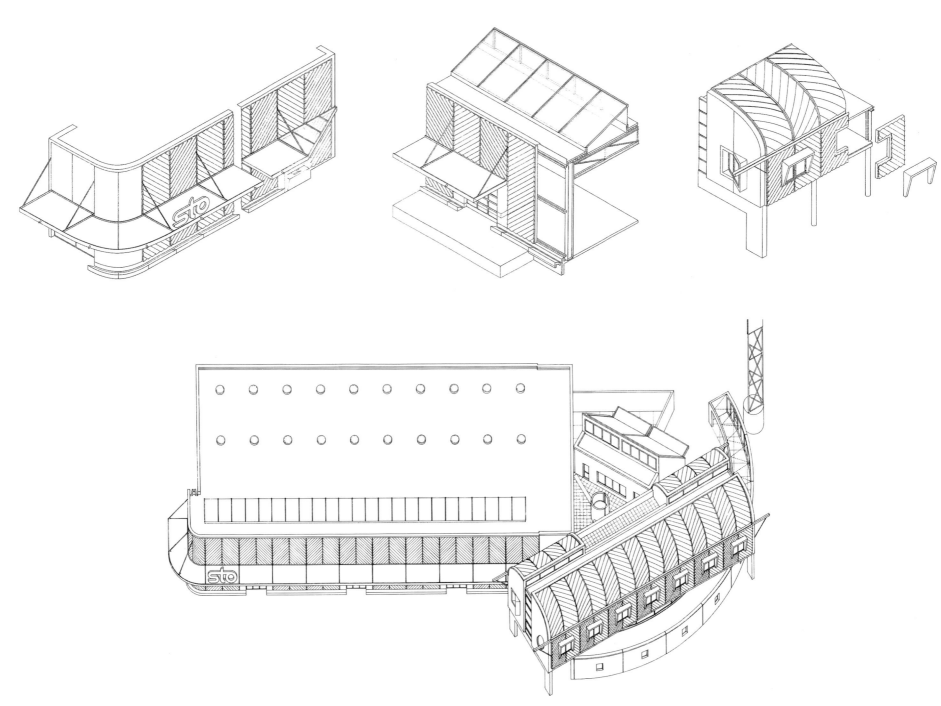

Panelised office and warehouse cladding system

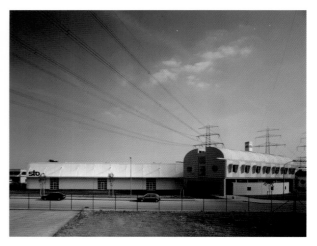

Entrance facade

Entrance hall and service counter

Entrance hall detail

Courtyard garden and external exhibition wall

Entrance hall detail

Training pavilion and office wing junction

Context plan

Site plan

B BRAUN AG CAMPUS ONE MASTERPLAN AND PRODUCTION BUILDING EXPANSION
PENANG, MALAYSIA, 2009–

Wilford Schupp Architekten in association with BYG Architects Penang

The Campus One Masterplan envisages replacement of existing structures by stacking new production areas in multi-layered buildings to increase capacity and maximise land utilisation. The masterplan envisages phased development of two fanning production wings responding to adjacent urban grids and joined at one end by a central canteen and administration tower. Each wing contains three production levels contiguous with those in the existing building.

The two wings enclose a central garden forming a social focus to the campus and are lined by covered promenades reminiscent of the traditional local 'five foot way', providing protection from the extreme climate. The tower registers the presence of the plant in the featureless industrial landscape in which it is situated when viewed from the adjacent highway and airport.

Expansion of the existing production building into the vacant corner of the campus is the first phase of the development. The addition of a day-lit multi-layered service spine containing circulation, offices and staff facilities along the garden face of both the extension and the existing building, ensures direct raw material and product circulation together with staff access to the combined building. The spine will integrate old and new buildings together into an efficient and harmonic organisation.

Relocation of the truck loading/unloading bays and warehouse to the end of the new building, confines commercial vehicle movement to the top corner of the campus and allows a traffic-free core. A central security checkpoint on the street frontage controls all vehicular and personnel access to the campus.

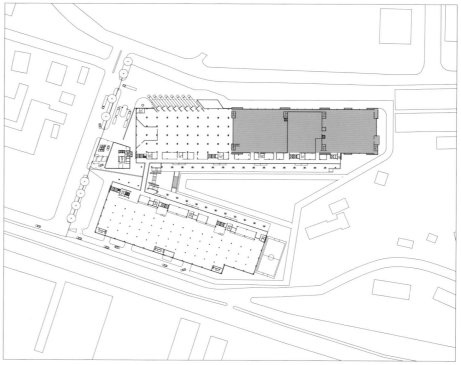

Groundfloor production areas, warehouse, pedestrian promenade and forklift circulation spine, central garden and office entrance

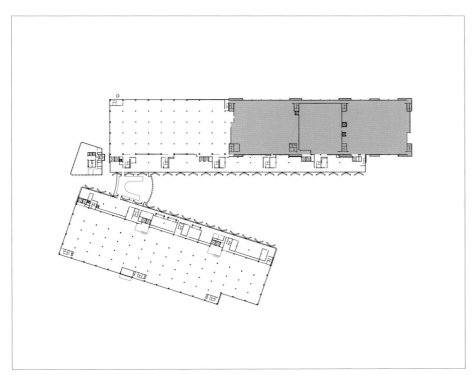

Second floor production areas, production office spines, administration office tower and canteen balcony

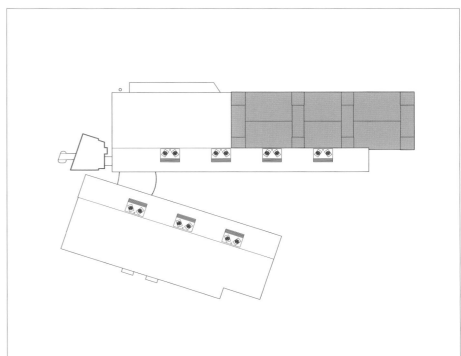

Roof plan

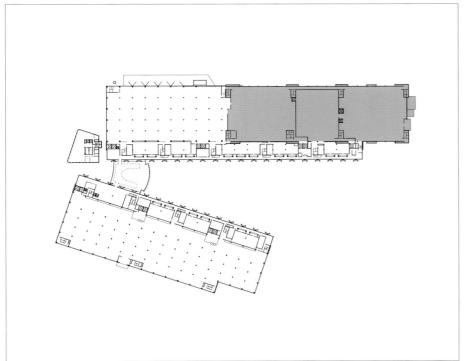

First floor production areas, staff changing facility in spines, canteen connection and administration office tower

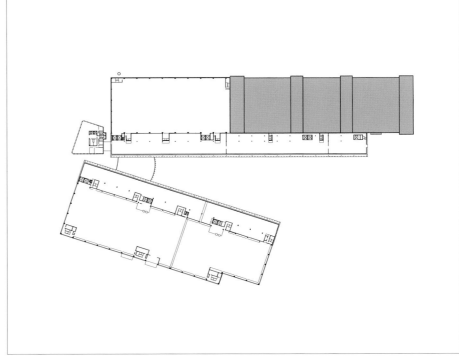

Third floor production areas, mechanical plant spines and administration office tower

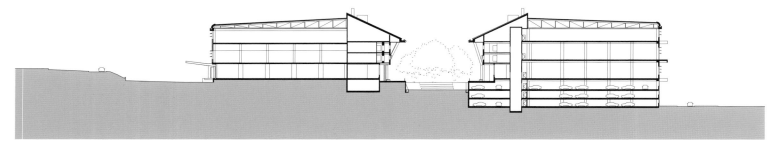

Cross-section through the production wings, spines and central garden

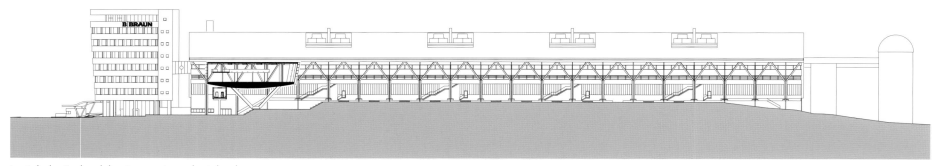

Longitudinal section through the entrance, canteen and central garden

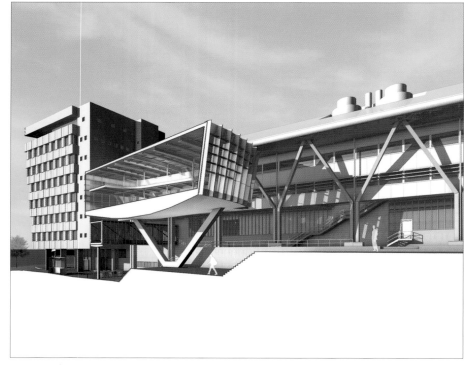

Section view of the canteen, spine and administration tower relationship

Canteen as focus of central garden and connection between the wings

Central garden and spine circulation

Loading dock

Spine circulation

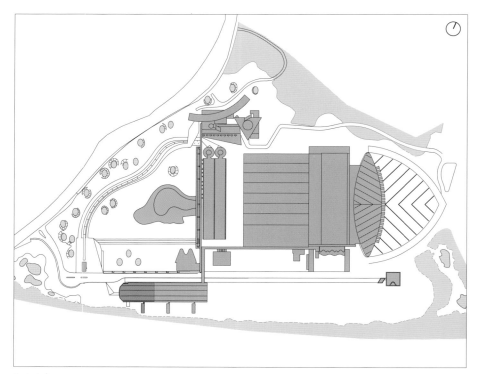

Context plan

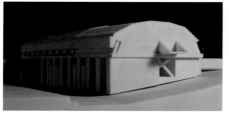

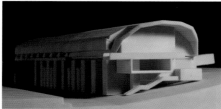

Early alternative concept models

B BRAUN VISITOR CENTRE AND PRODUCTION EXPANSION
MELSUNGEN, GERMANY, 2007–2009
Wilford Schupp Architekten

The building comprises the first phase of production expansion as envisaged in the original masterplan together with a new visitor reception and exhibition facility. It is the first building of the 'City of Industry' encountered on entering the campus and with its arrival plaza and visitor entrance completes the western end of the production 'bar'. The building is an exemplar of the B Braun corporate culture of social, and ecological responsibility.

Visitors enter directly from the plaza and are received in the ground floor entrance hall. A multi-level exhibition with interactive displays explaining the company's history, products and business philosophy unfolds as visitors rise up through the various levels, culminating in the visitor balcony overlooking the full length of the extended production hall explaining the processes involved. The balcony also provides views over the valley and the entire campus. Conference rooms are located at mid-point of the exhibition sequence and visitors return by lift to the entrance hall.

The sectional organisation of the extended production areas continues the principles established in the initial phase with a fair-faced concrete structure, metal cladding and glazing systems used in an unadulterated form both inside and outside the building. A projecting machine loading balcony cantilevered from the southwest corner of the production hall, allows direct machine installation and removal by mobile crane from an upper service road.

With its protective roof projection and company logo, the building establishes a welcoming and representative presence for staff and visitors.

West elevation

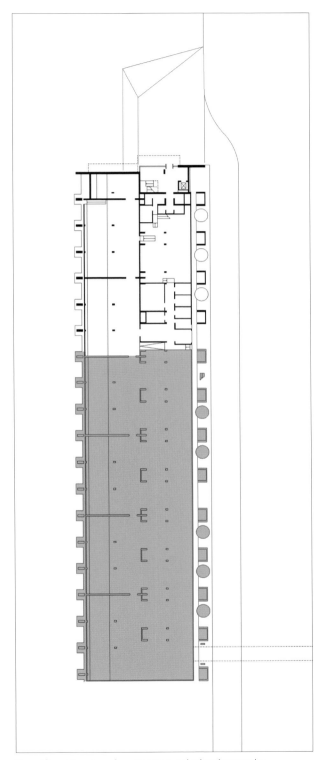

Ground floor visitor entry and reception areas, and technical support plan

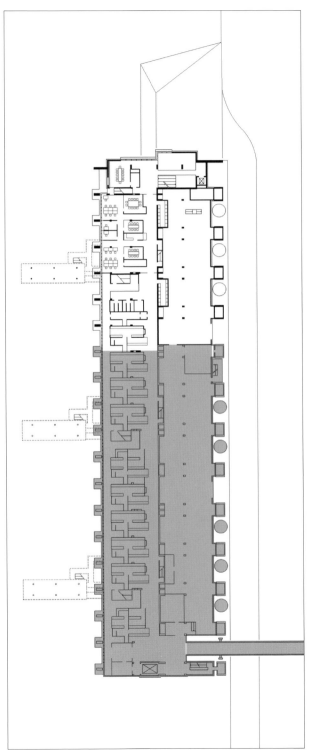

First floor exhibition, office and conference room plan

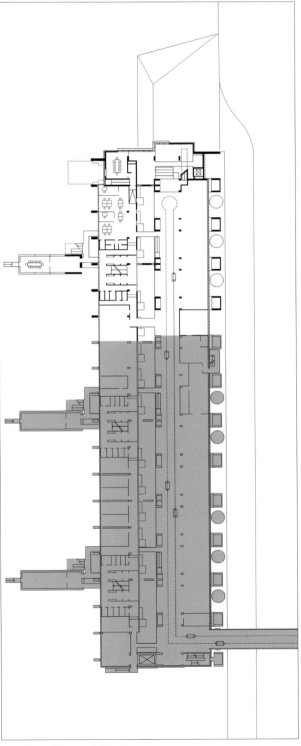

Second floor exhibition and offices plan

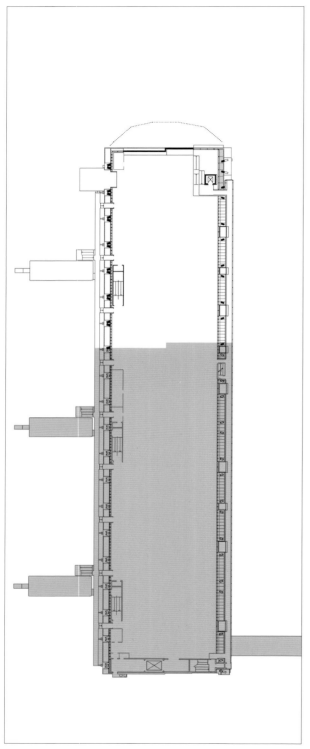

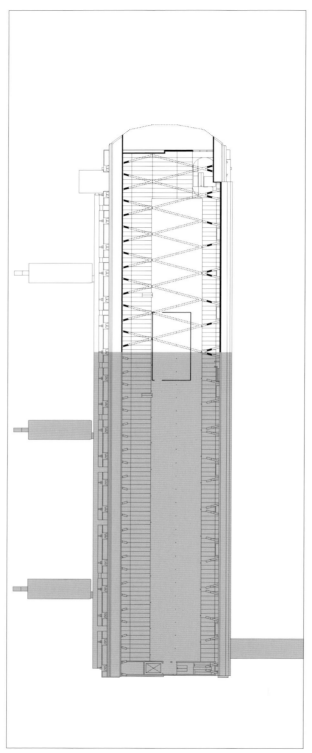

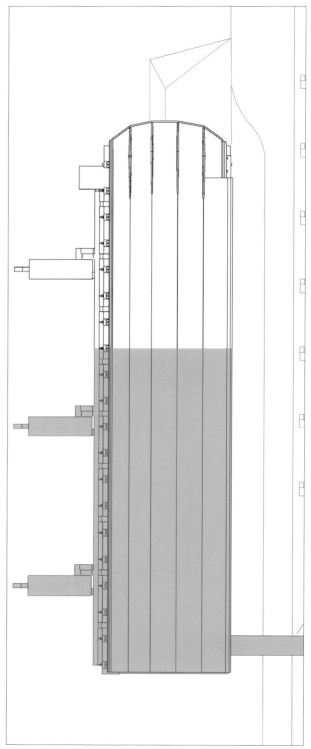

Extended production floor level and visitor observation balcony

Extended mechanical plant level

Extended roof plan

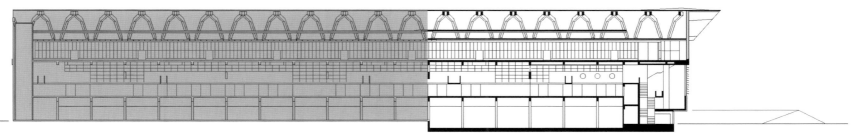

Longitudinal section through the production extension, visitor reception and exhibition

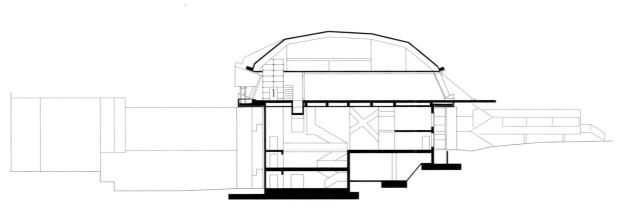

Cross-section through the exhibition and production extension

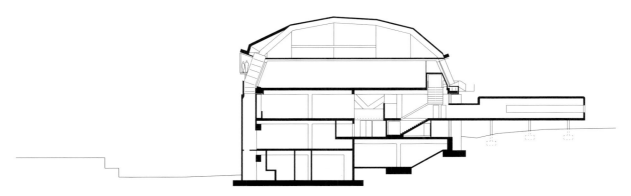

Cross-section through the production extension

Visitor entrance

Visitor balcony above the production level

Site entry and approach

Machine loading platform

Visitor balcony overlooking the production floor

Intermediate exhibition level

Access to the visitor balcony from exhibition

Office/exhibition connection

Upper exhibition levels

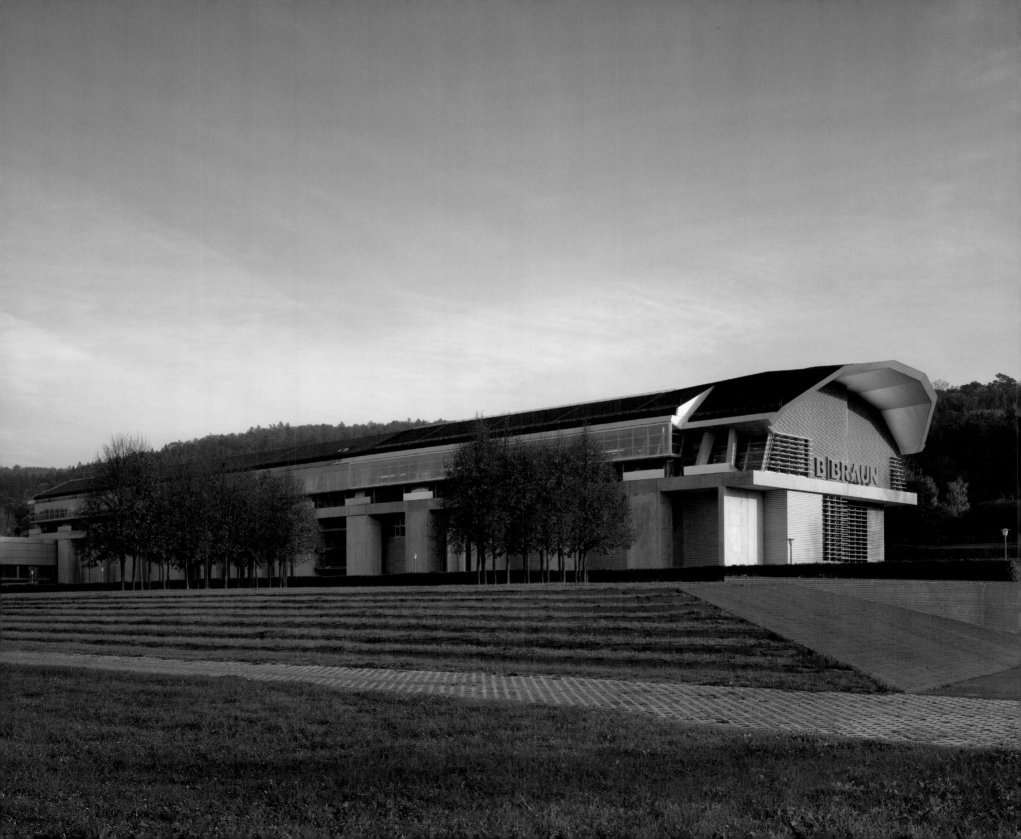

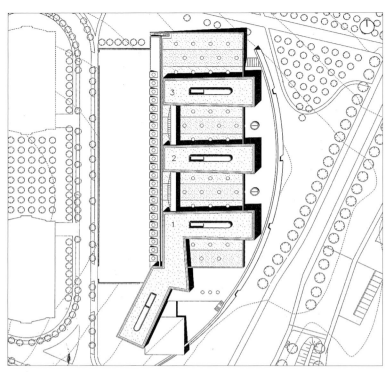

Site plan

KRYSTALTECH LYNX AG, EUROPEAN HEADQUARTERS, PRODUCTION AND DISTRIBUTION BUILDING
REUTLINGEN, GERMANY, 2000
Wilford Schupp Architekten (formerly Michael Wilford & Partners, London and Stuttgart)

For its new Headquarters the company required a differentiated and flexible development plan representative of its innovative philosophy and response to the special quality of the landscape in which it is situated. The powerful character of the building enhances the company's corporate identity and encourages employee pride and commitment to its activities.

It is situated in a new business park containing mixed building typologies at the urban/rural interface on the edge of the town and adjacent to the autobahn between Stuttgart and Tubingen. The site has views across the surrounding landscape towards Reutlingen and the Swabian Alps.

The different functions are clearly expressed by independent structures and the first phase of the building together with the prominent location of the entrance foyer, canteen and social areas, forms a gateway to the Headquarters. The production, warehouse and shipping/receiving areas are contained in a two level plinth building with a curved outer face and windows overlooking the autobahn and surrounding landscape. Flexible offices are accommodated in connected linear wings, spanning above the plinth and its roof gardens. The whole development is designed to allow construction in phases as and when required.

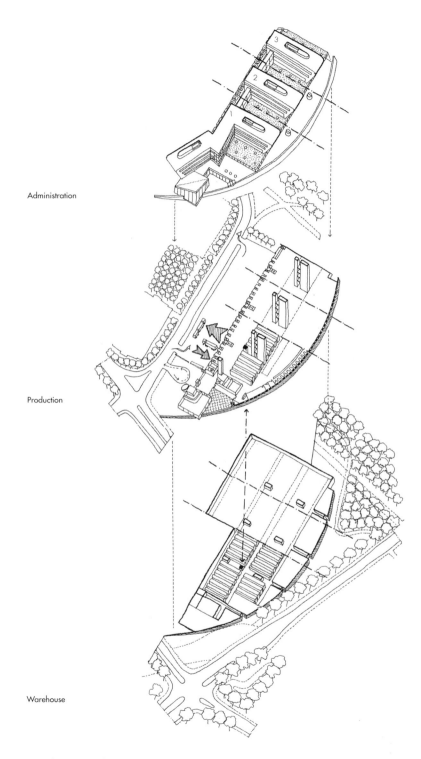

Administration

Production

Warehouse

Layered organisation diagram

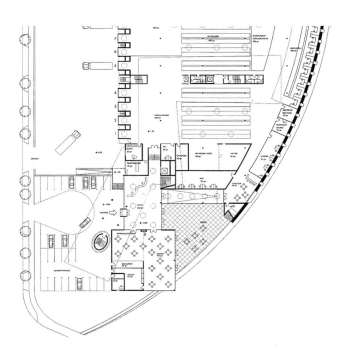

Production floor and administration entrance

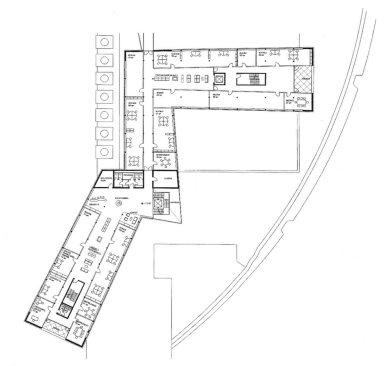

Office floor plan

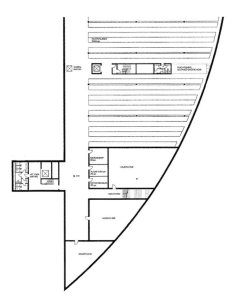

Lower warehouse level

Interior view of production

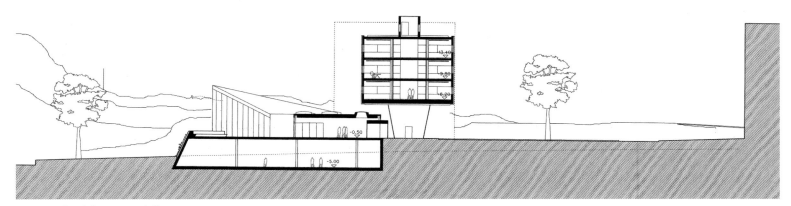

Cross-section through the entrance and office wing

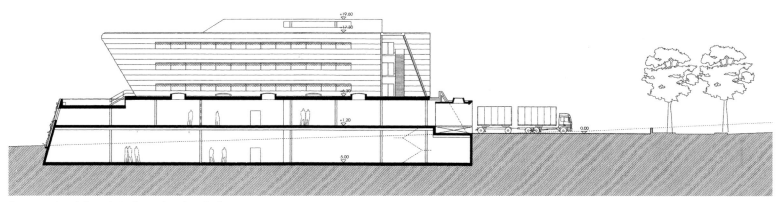

Cross-section through the production floor and warehouse levels

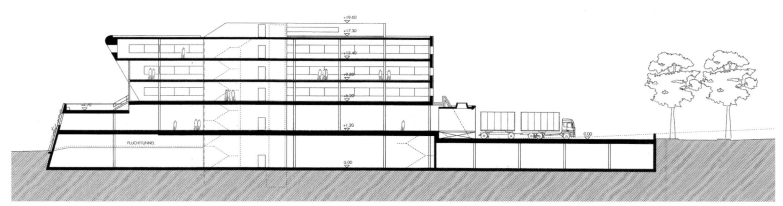

Longitudinal section through the second construction phase

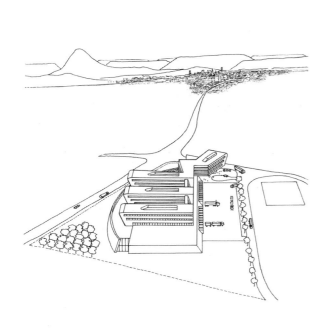

Relationship to the city of Reutlingen

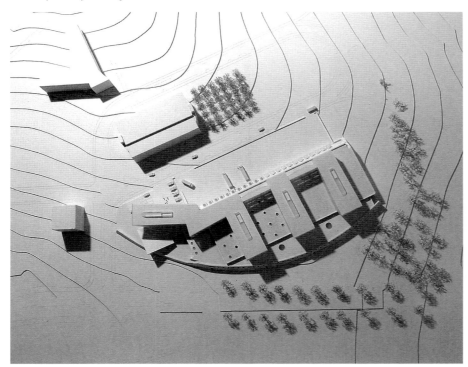

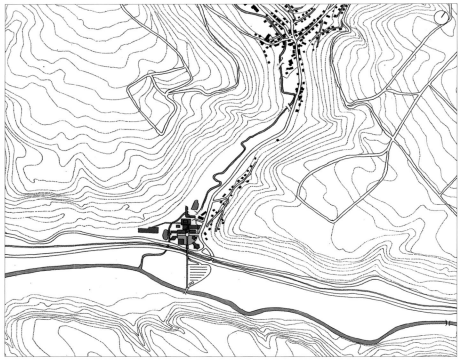

Context plan

STO AG PRODUCTION AND EXHIBITION BUILDINGS
WEIZEN, GERMANY, 1999–2003

Wilford Schupp Architekten (formerly Michael Wilford & Partners, London and Stuttgart)

The new production building comprises the second phase of the masterplan for the phased reconstruction of the Weizen plant. It combines two contrasting forms in a Z-shaped arrangement to cradle a future exhibition cube on the public face of the building and service yard at the rear. The forms express different production systems—vertical, gravity-fed material storage, mixing, packaging and loading in the tower and horizontal 'just-in-time' special products in the linear bar. Offices, testing laboratories and staff facilities for both production systems line two sides of the future exhibition cube.

The upper section of the tower forms a landmark in the valley containing a cluster of raw material storage silos and clad in vertical folded metal panels. Production levels in the base of the tower have temporary end facades, demountable to facilitate expansion and equipment replacement. The saw-toothed profile of the north facade comprises a series of transparent horizontal planes to allow maximum daylight penetration into the deep production levels. Its lowest plane folds out to form a continuous canopy for loading finished products.

Both sections of the tower are connected to the service yard by a latticed structure containing the battery of tubes which deliver raw materials to the top of each of the silos from bulk tanker trucks parked under the large canopy at its base.

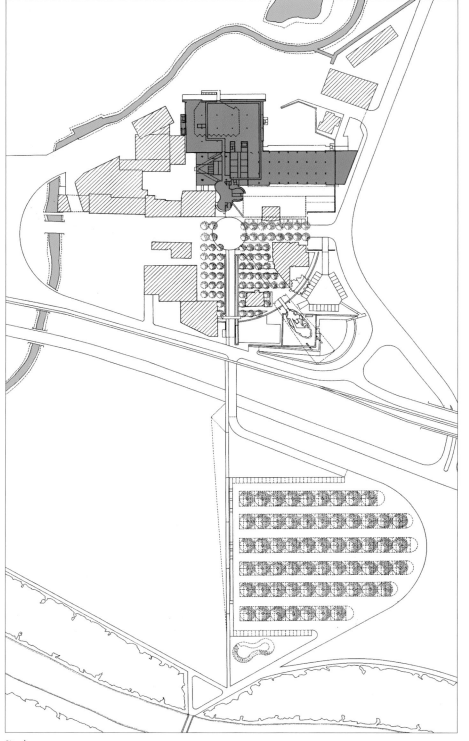

Site plan

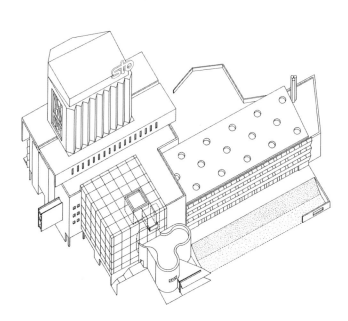

Isometric view from the south

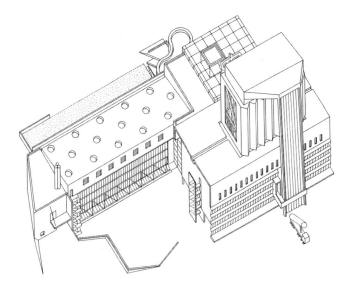

Isometric view from the north

Model of entrance trefoil, exhibition cube and vertical production tower

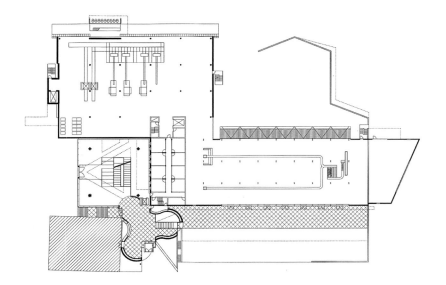

Ground floor entry, exhibition and production level

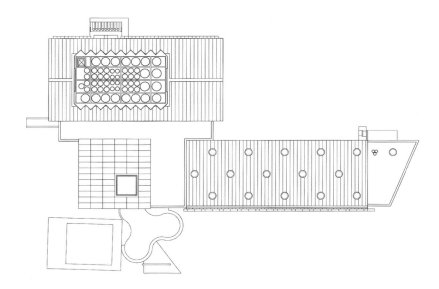

Silo tower and roof

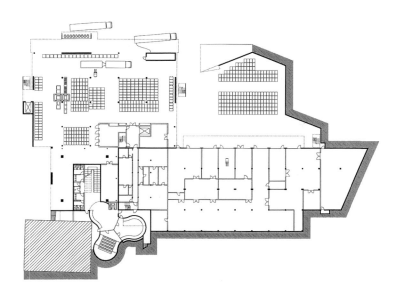

Basement storage and workshop floor

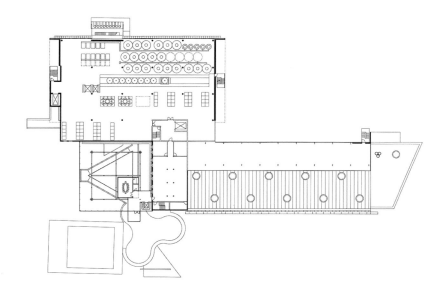

Upper production floor

Northeast elevation

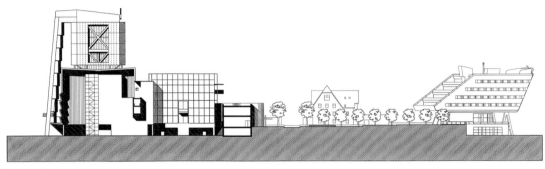

Southwest elevation

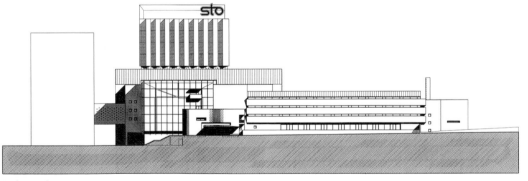

South entry elevation

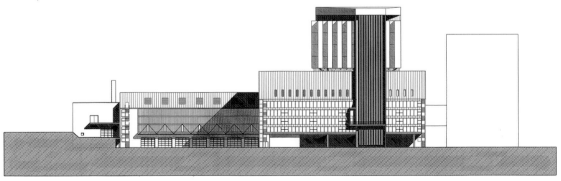

North service yard elevation

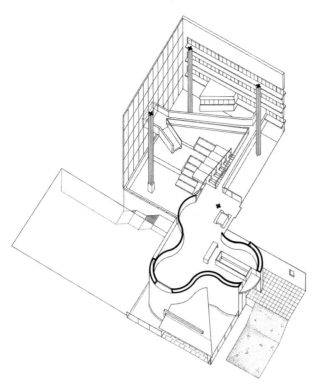

Bird's-eye isometric view of entrance trefoil and exhibition cube

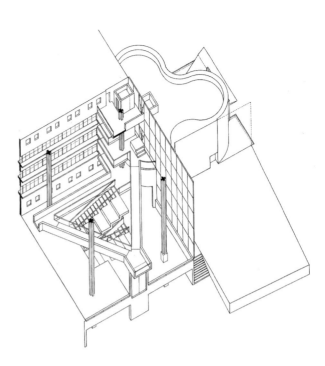

Bird's-eye isometric view of exhibition cube

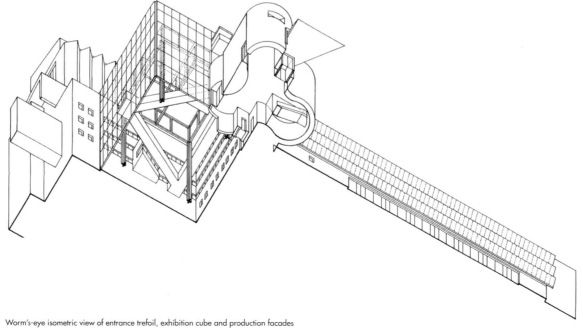

Worm's-eye isometric view of entrance trefoil, exhibition cube and production facades

Site of the future entrance trefoil and exhibition cube

Detail of the horizontal production building service facade

Detail of the silo filling structure

Vertical production tower and silo filling structure

Horizontal production

Horizontal production

Vertical production

Base of the material silos in vertical production

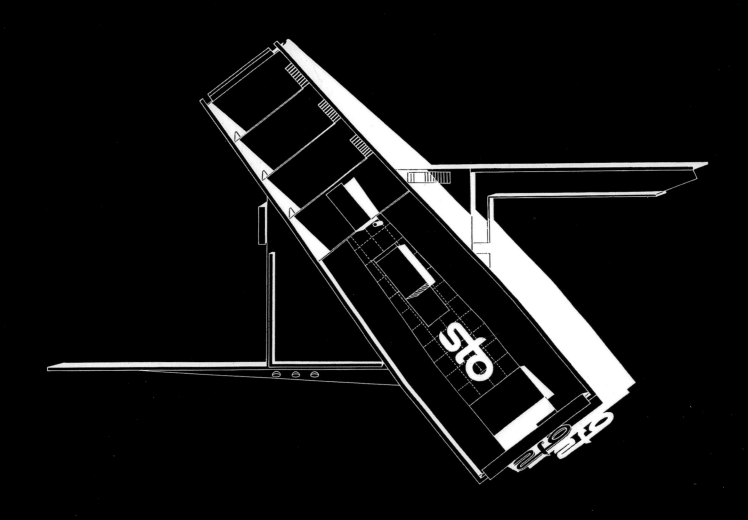

ADMINISTRATION

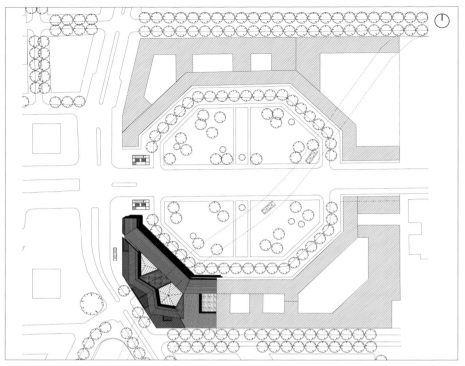

Site plan

LEIPZIGERPLATZ OFFICE, APARTMENT AND RETAIL DEVELOPMENT
BERLIN, GERMANY, 2001

Wilford Schupp Architekten (formerly Michael Wilford & Partners, London and Stuttgart)

This competition submission for the restoration of Leipzigerplatz and its hinterland to its early twentieth century pre-eminence seeks to establish variety and individuality within a strong overall identity and an expression of appropriate civic scale and materiality.

Linear buildings define the edges of the site with connecting structures enclosing two inner courtyards. The inner Leipzigerplatz frontage is emphasised with a taller dominant element as required by the city's urban development guidelines. The lower scale of the outer segmental building establishes a precedent for future adjacent buildings. The facades express the pedestrian routes, entrances and other geometric penetrations within the massing.

Within the total project, shops, offices and apartments are organised into five building volumes, each of which addresses either Leipzigerplatz or Stresemannstrasse with colonnades containing lobbies and shop fronts. Offices are situated on the intermediate levels with entrances and vertical circulation individually articulated to provide identifiable addresses within the colonnades at street level. The inner courtyards and connecting arcades are also lined with shops to encourage public circulation through the block. They also accommodate more private entrances to the apartments on the upper levels of the project and access to the underground parking garage which extends under the whole development.

The stone clad facades reflect the ordering principles of the massing and articulation of the project with colours further expressing the constituent parts.

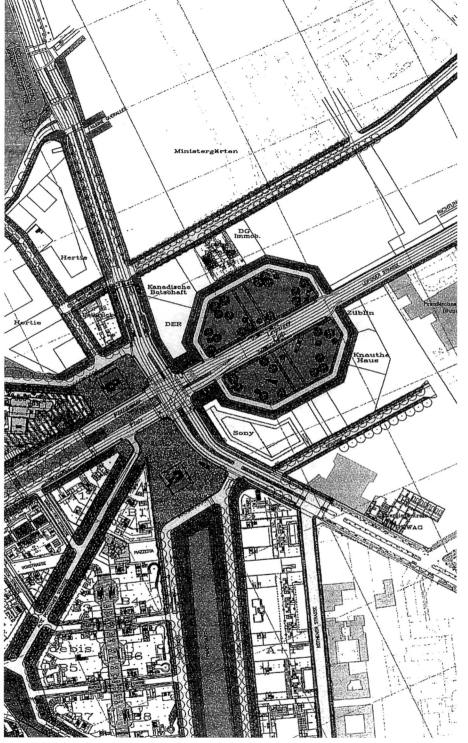

Context plan

First floor

Sixth floor

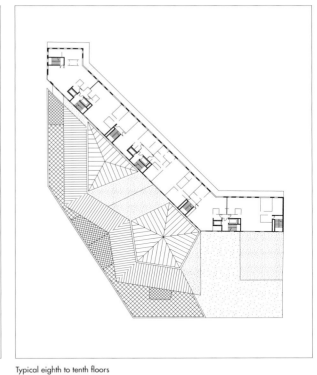

Typical eighth to tenth floors

Ground floor

Typical second to fifth floors

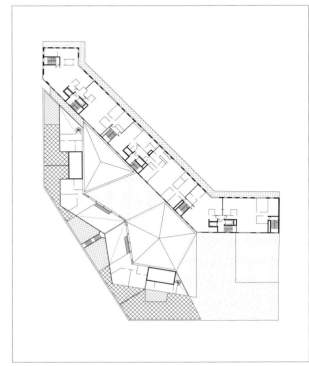

Seventh floor

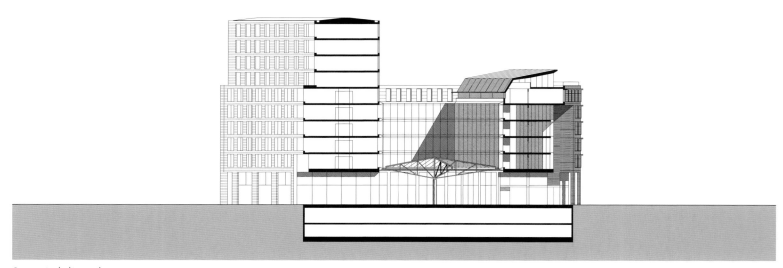

Cross-section looking south

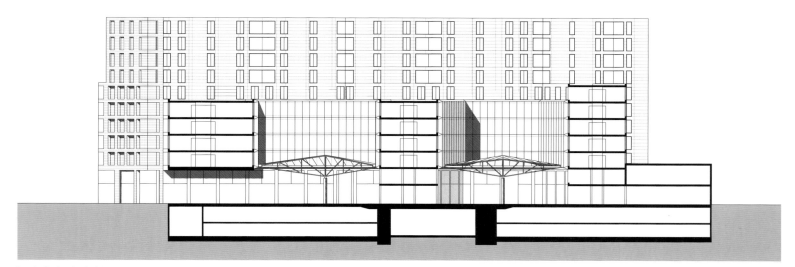

Longitudinal section looking east

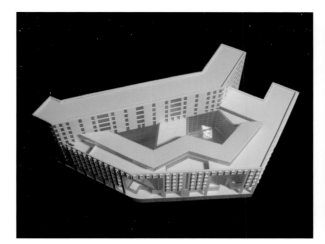
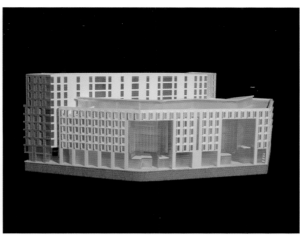
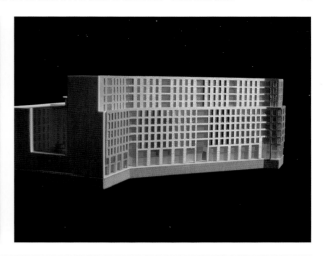

Perspective view from Leipzigerplatz

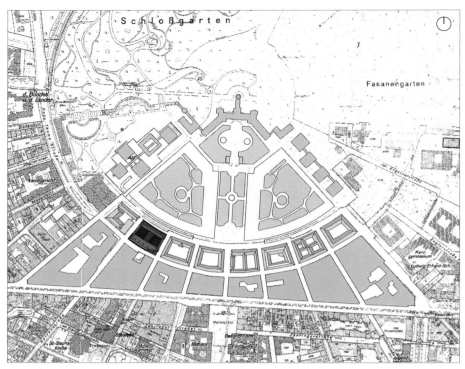

Context plan

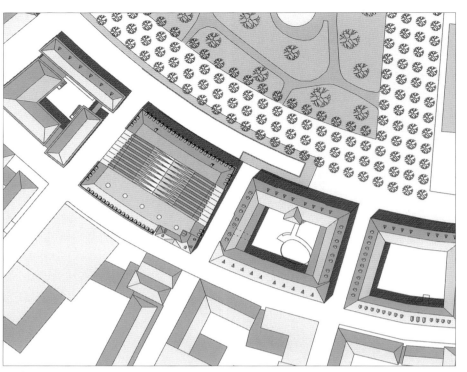

Site plan

LANDESBANK OFFICE BUILDING
KARLSRUHE, GERMANY, 2004
Wilford Schupp Architekten

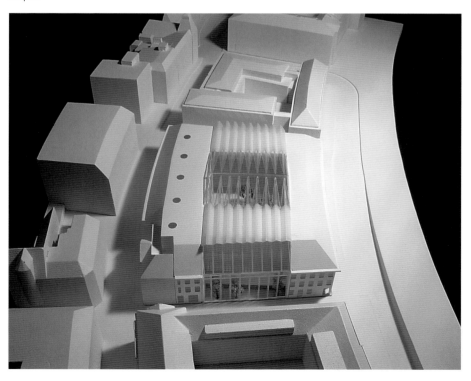

This competition submission inserts a modern, environmentally responsible office building into an urban block in the strategic civic ring fronting the castle and park and forming the inner edge of the unique radiating plan at the centre of Karlsruhe. An historic building on the southeast corner of the site had to be functionally engaged and integrated into the new fabric.

In our proposal the office plan forms the core of the building in a pure geometry to satisfy the rational brief. The internal organisation is characterised by a central longitudinal zone extending across the full width of the plan and enclosed by two parallel office wings. A central courtyard and two flanking wintergardens are spatially connected at ground floor level to provide an enfilade of rooms accommodating the foyer, cafeteria and conference hall, allowing these activities to have views of the exterior through the wintergardens which also form environmental buffers and reconcile the orthogonal core with the tapered shape of the site.

The curved site geometry is accentuated on the front and rear facades by a series of stepped planes. The central zone is further emphasised by a continuous ribbon of glazing across the longitudinal section unifying the facades and roofs into a singular three-dimensional composition.

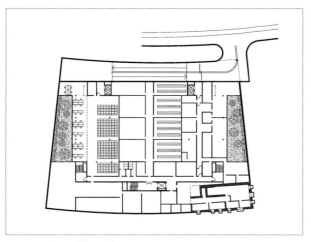

Basement archive and library plan

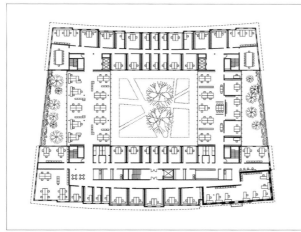

First floor plan

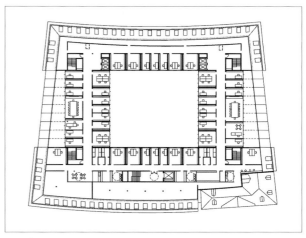

Fourth floor plan

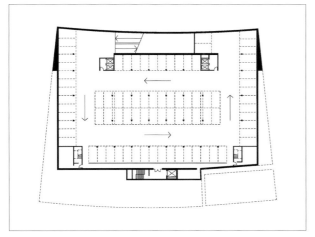

Second basement parking plan

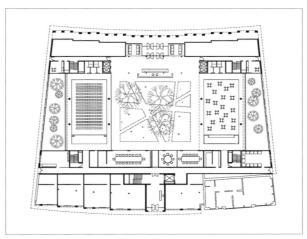

Ground floor plan of conference, canteen, central courtyard and wintergardens

Second and third floor plans

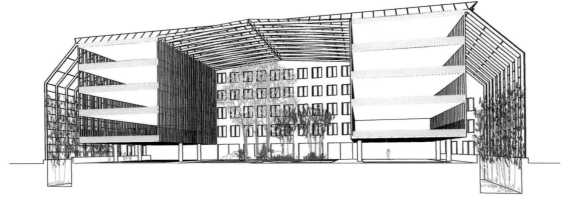

Sectional perspective through the central courtyard and wintergardens

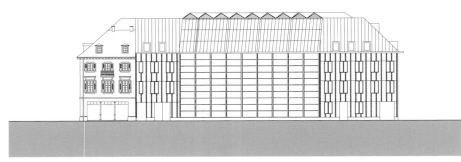

East facade

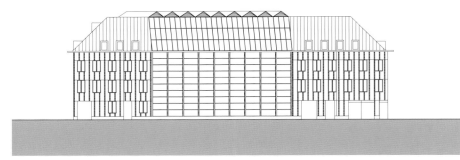

West facade

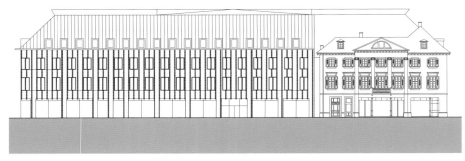

South facade

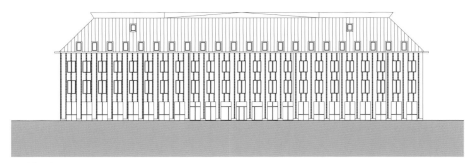

North facade

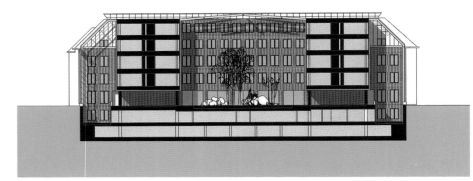

Longitudinal section through the central courtyard and wintergardens

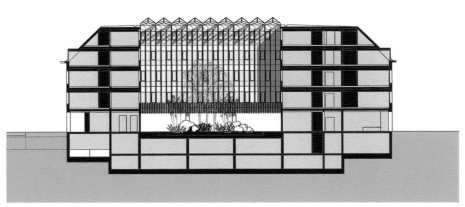

Cross-section through central courtyard

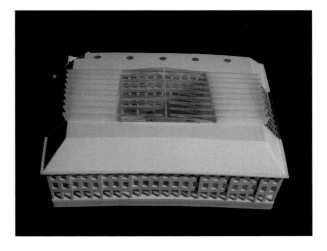

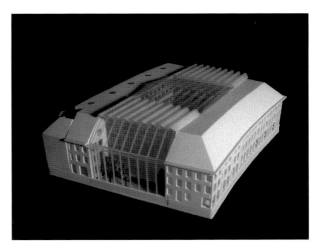

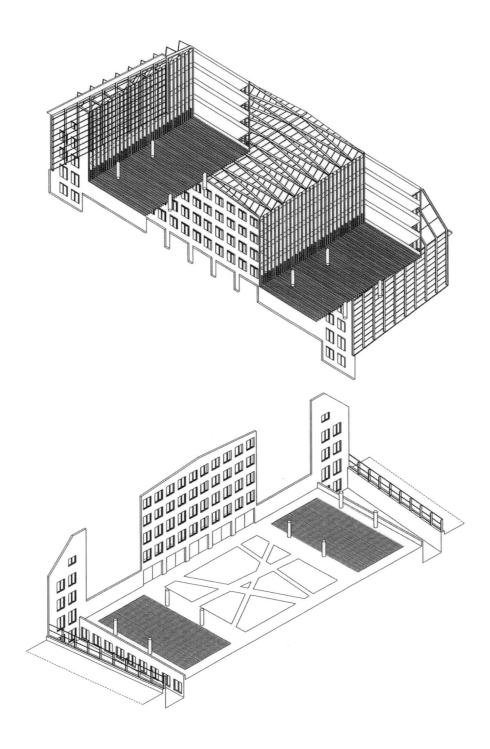

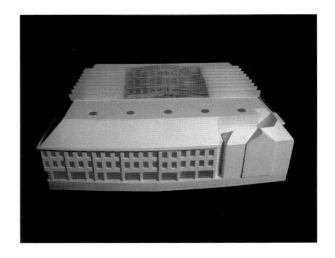

Cut-away isometric views of internal facades, central courtyard and wintergardens

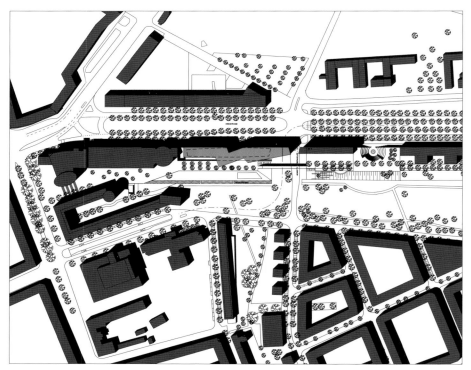

Context plan

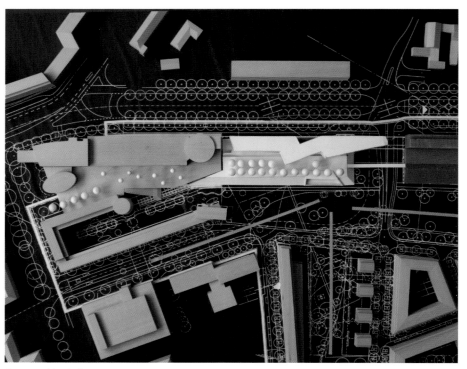

Concept model and influences

LBBW REGIONAL HEADQUARTERS
KARLSRUHE, GERMANY, 2004–2007
Wilford Schupp Architekten

The linear site for this seven-storey building is adjacent to a significant urban grid shift and forms part of a masterplan for the regeneration of disused railway lands to the east of the city centre. A new landscaped park forms the heart of the masterplan together with an elevated promenade along its northern edge to protect it against traffic noise from a new boulevard. The masterplan also required new buildings along this boundary of the park to be accessed both from the boulevard and promenade.

The primary street entrance, marked by the red canopy, is cut into the plinth which forms the base of the building as well as the street facade of the elevated promenade in the park beyond. A special lift and stair within the multi-level entrance hall connect the street and promenade entrances and provide access to the basement car park. Vertical circulation cores situated at the main entrance and at two secondary entrances along the street facade, provide access to all levels. Ground floor seminar rooms overlook the park entrance and the canteen cuts through the promenade slope to provide spectacular views into the park.

The intermediate linear office levels connect the plinth to the stepped office block above which cantilevers beyond the base to form a gateway to the park. The staggered form of the upper section responds to the adjacent intersection of urban grids and articulates possible future subdivision of the building into three separate units.

Aerial view of completed building

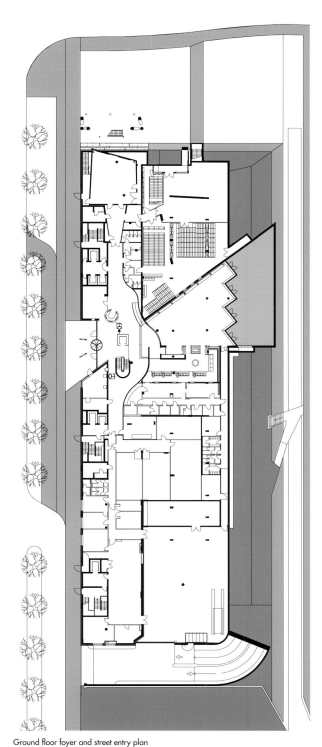

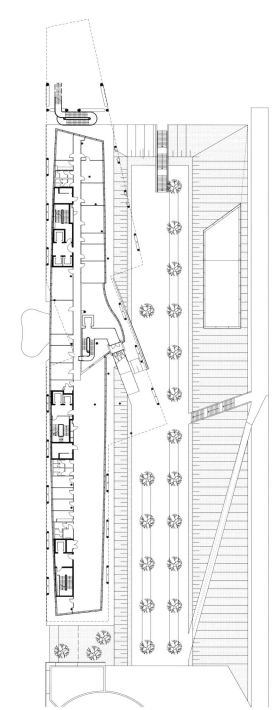

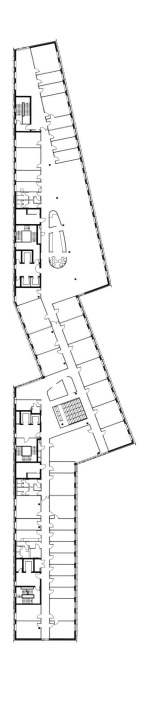

Ground floor foyer and street entry plan

First and second floor offices and promenade entry plan

Typical third to sixth floor office plan

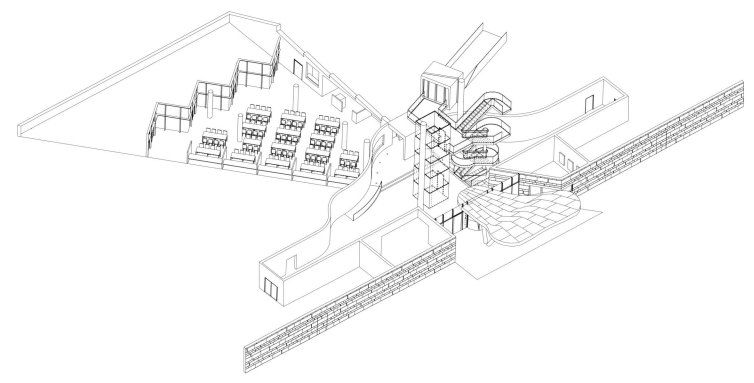

Isometric view of the entry and vertical circulation sequence linking through to the canteen and terrace in the park

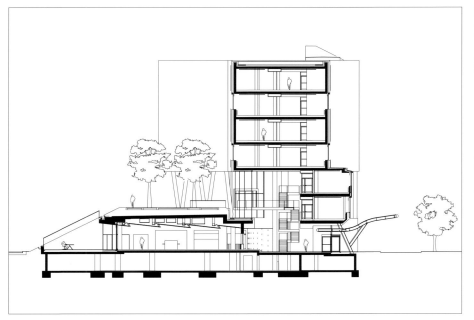

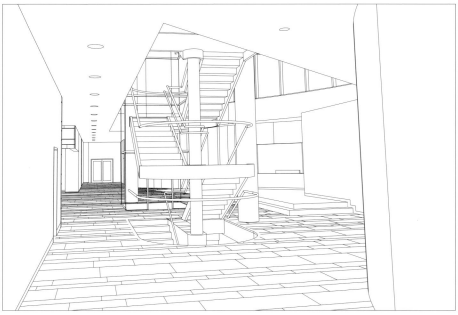

Cross-section

Entry foyer

Street frontage

View into the canteen from the entry foyer

Sub-divisible ground floor conference room

Ground floor entry foyer and connection to the upper promenade entrance

Park facade

Street entry canopy

Promenade facade

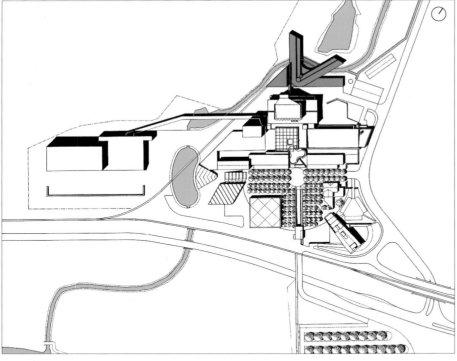

Context plan

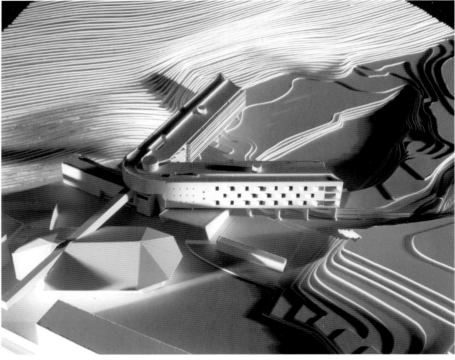

Massing model from the east

STO AG OFFICE AND TRAINING BUILDING A/B
WEIZEN, GERMANY, 1994
Michael Wilford & Partners

This project, containing offices, staff training facilities and meeting rooms, was designed as the first building to be constructed under the masterplan for redevelopment of the headquarters and manufacturing plant. It comprises two primary elements: a pair of spreading office wings which embrace the existing lake and a cluster of free-form ground-level training spaces situated beneath the junction of the wings.

The three office floors are elevated on zig-zag columns, allowing the undulating landscape and meandering river to flow beneath the building. Individual office spaces are ranged along either side of a central corridor in each wing and are connected by a flexible meeting room and central reception area. Saw-toothed glazing to the meeting rooms provides diagonal valley views.

Training spaces define the factory truck yard and screen it from the valley. A cafe opens onto a riverside terrace with views across the lake, framed by the office wings above. The lift shaft pins both elements of the building together and a bridge over the truck yard connects the building to the main entrance of the headquarters as an extension of the major north–south pedestrian axis.

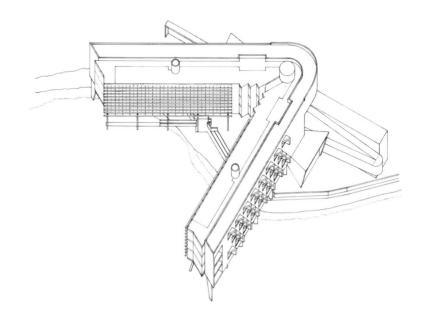

Bird's-eye axonometric from the northwest

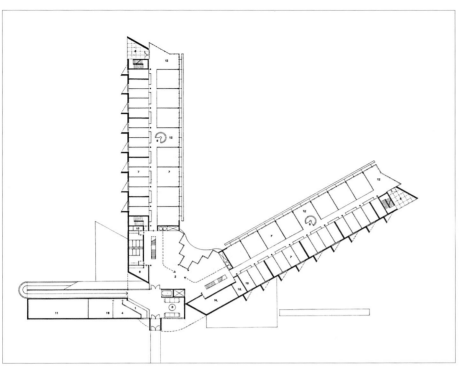

First floor office and conference room plan

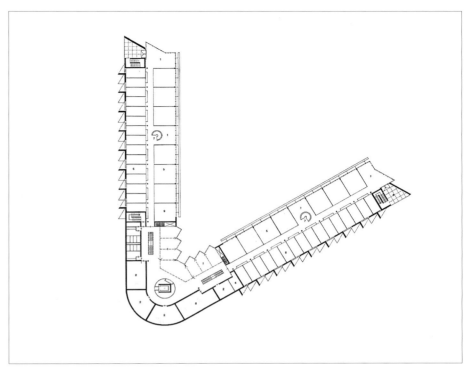

Third floor office and meeting room plan

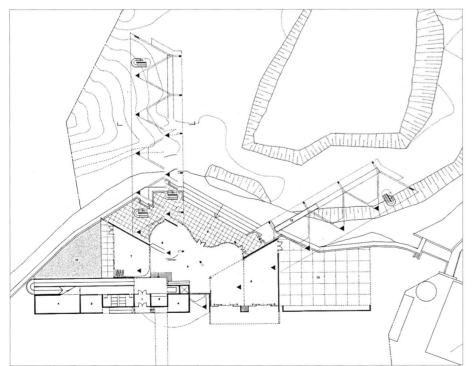

Ground floor plan with canteen and communal facilities

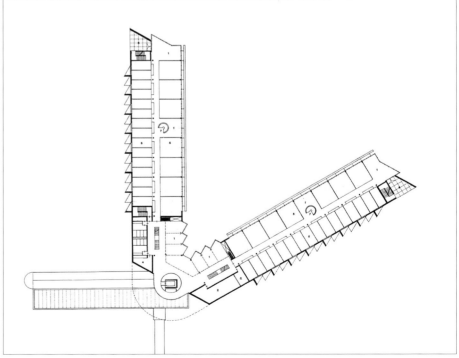

Second floor office and meeting room plan

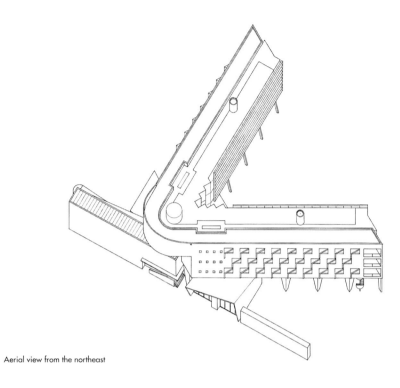

Aerial view from the northeast

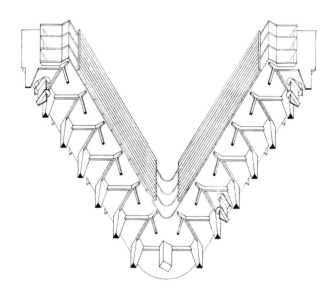

Worm's-eye view beneath the wings

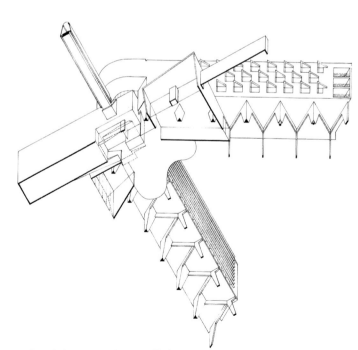

Worm's-eye view beneath the entrance and communal facilities

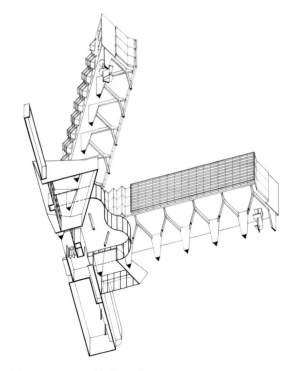

Worm's-eye view beneath the entrance, communal facilities and wings

South elevation

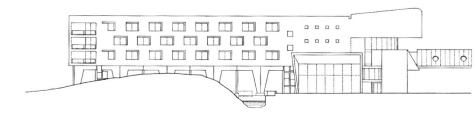

West elevation

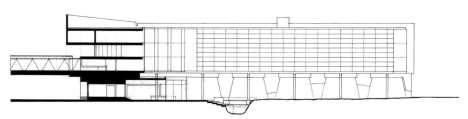

Cross-section through the entrance and communal facilities

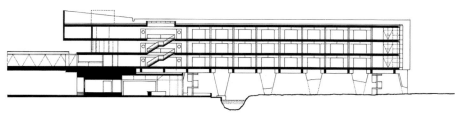

Longitudinal section through the west wing

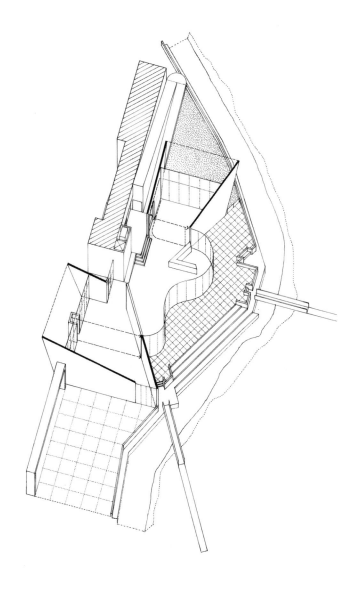

Bird's-eye view of the canteen

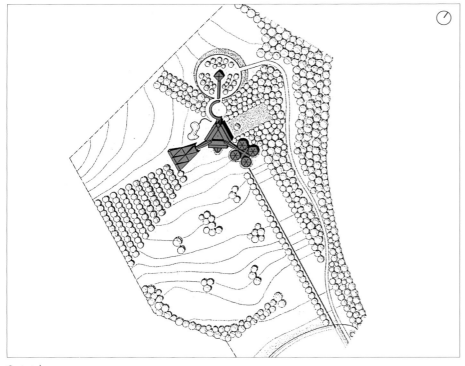

Context plan

RARE LIMITED,
RESEARCH AND DEVELOPMENT CENTRE
TWYCROSS, ENGLAND, 1995
Michael Wilford & Partners

Concept model

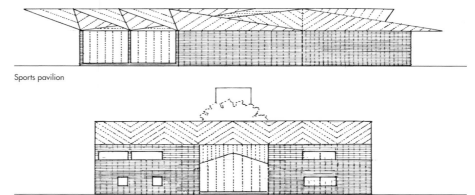

Sports pavilion

Entrance and administration core

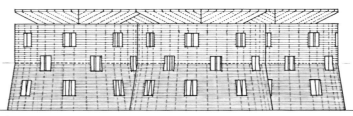

Development cluster

Rare Limited, a computer and software development company, responsible for some of the best-selling computer games, believe the key to their success is their unique working environment in the heart of the English countryside. They planned to double their staff and relocate to a new headquarters in landscaped grounds close to their present location.

The tripartite plan is centred upon a triangular cloistered building containing administration, restaurant and other shared elements of the brief, to form the central meeting and security point for staff and visitors. The restaurant forms the social hub of the campus with dramatic views into and across the surrounding landscape. The main entrance, cluster of circular development studios and the tapered sports building are each linked to a corner of the cloister. The building mass is kept as low as possible to minimise its visual impact with each function individually expressed and capable of independent construction.

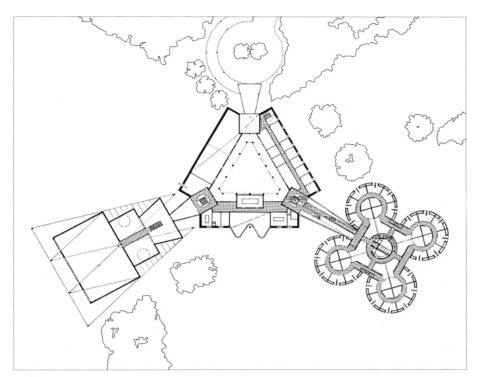

First floor plan

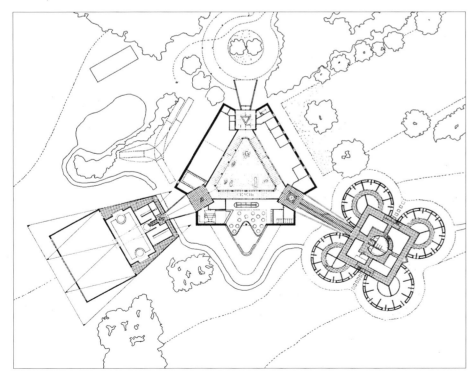

Ground floor plan

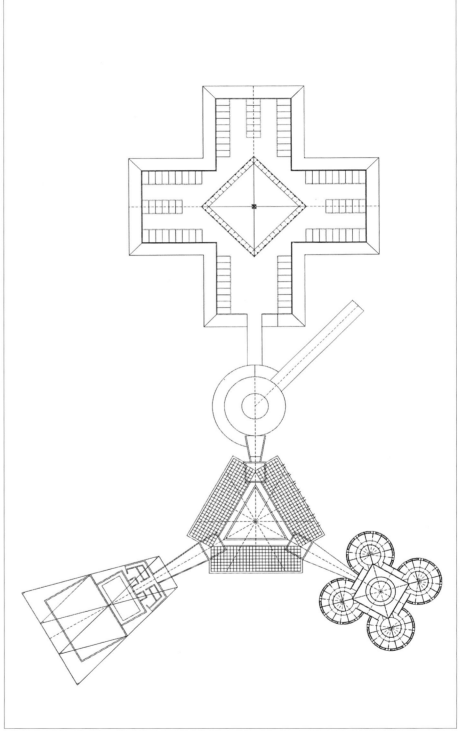

Roof and parking plan

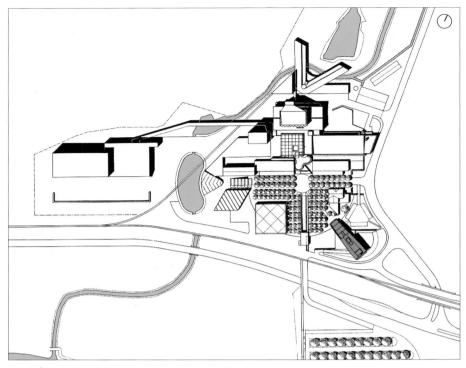

Context plan

STO AG COMMUNICATIONS BUILDING K
WEIZEN, GERMANY, 1995–1997
Wilford Schupp Architekten (formerly Michael Wilford & Partners, London and Stuttgart)

This is the first new building to be realised in accordance with our Headquarters Masterplan. The upper section of the building registers its presence in the valley, highly visible to passing motorists and faces towards the primary approach to the campus to form an entrance gateway.

The building comprises three layered elements; linear marketing offices, an oval entrance pavilion and a square training base. It nestles between existing structures and the sloping site contour allows visitors and staff to enter by footbridge directly from the raised central garden which forms the heart of the campus. The office wing glides above the lower two elements and minimises obstruction of views of the valley from the central garden.

The four office levels, with spectacular views along the valley, are arranged in a tapered plan enclosing a central lift, stair and service core. Each floor has a slipped relationship with the one below, providing a dynamic silhouette and stepped balconies to reconcile the scale difference between the new and existing buildings. The oval entrance and exhibition pavilion is connected by lift and stairs to the offices above and training facilities below. For outdoor social functions, the exhibition area opens on to a large terrace above the training facilities. Screen walls extend into the landscape from opposite corners to exhibit the company's products.

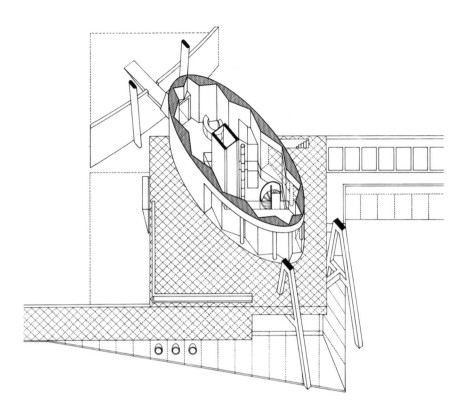

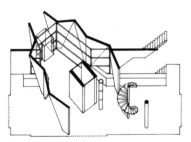

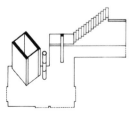

Cut-away axonometric downview of the entry levels

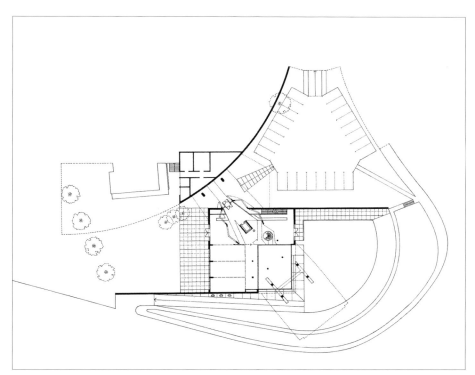

Theoretical training level with lower entrance and courtyards

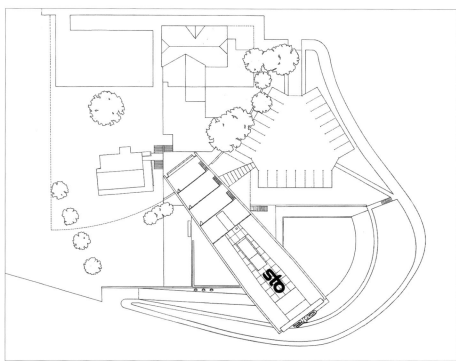

Roof plan

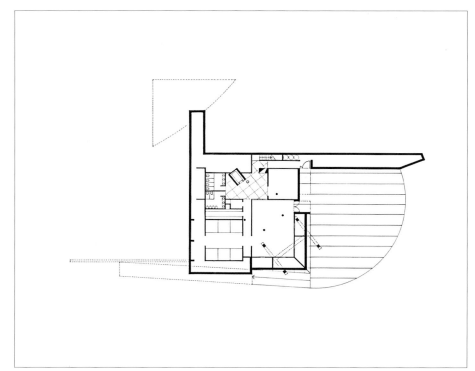

Lower practical training level and yard

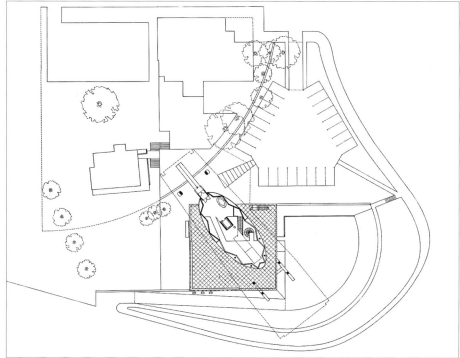

Ground floor entry pavilion and terrace level plan

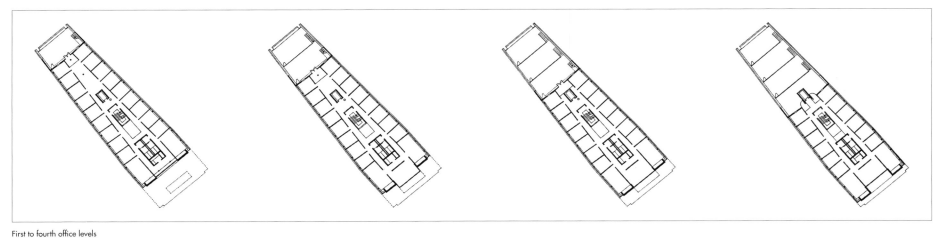

First to fourth office levels

Southeast elevation

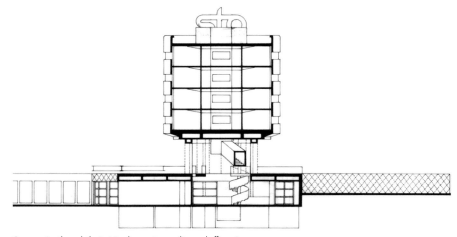

Cross-section through the training base entry pavilion and office wing

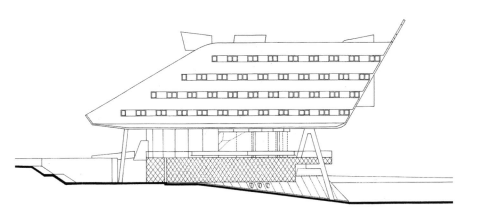

Southwest elevation

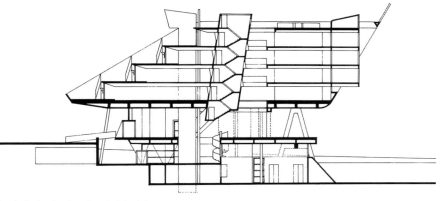

Longitudinal section through vertical circulation

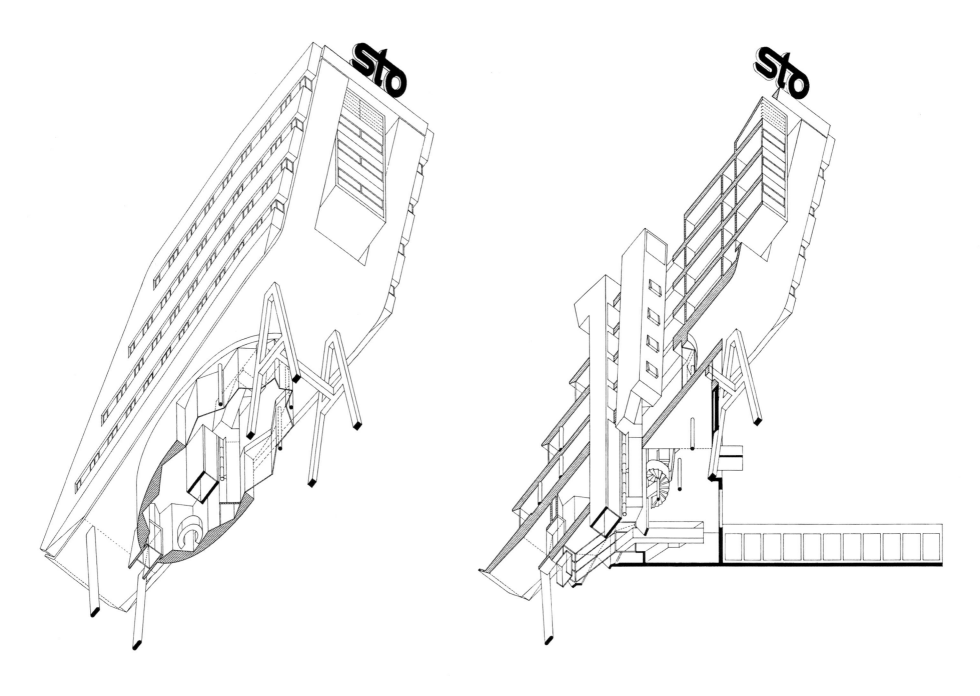

Worm's-eye axonometric of the entrance pavilion and office wing

Worm's-eye cut-away axonometric of the office wing and circulation cores

View on approach from the southwest

View on approach from the north

View of the entrance to campus

Office conference room stack

Terrace detail

Upper and lower entrances

Entrance pavilion and office balconies

Stair tower and office circulation balconies

Product exhibition wall

Practical training workshop

Entry pavilion interior views

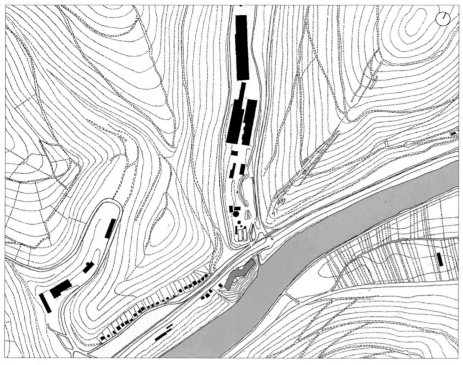

Context plan

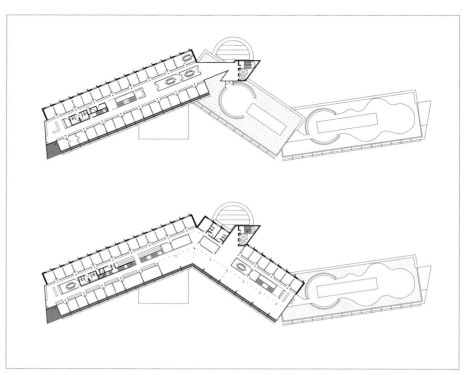

Typical upper level office plans

DGF STOESS AG HEADQUARTERS
EBERBACH, GERMANY, 2000

Wilford Schupp Architekten (formerly Michael Wilford & Partners, London and Stuttgart)

The linear site is situated on a plateau alongside a busy road and railway line at the junction between the River Neckar meadow and a narrow tributary valley in which the company's production facilities are located.

The new headquarters building, responding to the linear site, comprises three overlapping office wings in a relaxed weaving formation above the entrance hall, canteen, conference and exhibition spaces. In order to avoid the appearance of a dividing wall between the road and river, the building ascends in height from the entrance to a floating climax supported on piloti, evoking images of waterside architecture.

The outer side of the offices overlooks the river meadow and the enclosing hills beyond through fully glazed walls with service zones and more enclosed fenestration on the inner side to protect the interior from traffic noise. Each wing relates to department sizes and is flexibly planned with cascading staircases connecting all levels to the entrance, public areas and outdoor terraces at ground level. Office roof gardens integrate the building into the valley landscape and its elevated form minimises disturbance of the local micro climate.

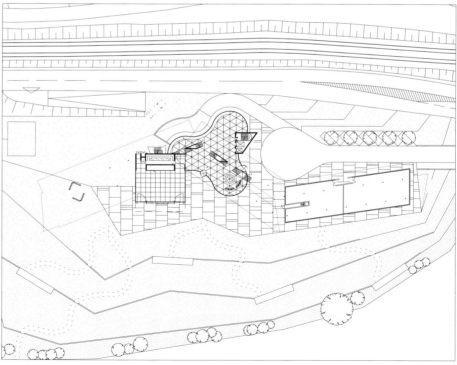

Site and ground floor plan

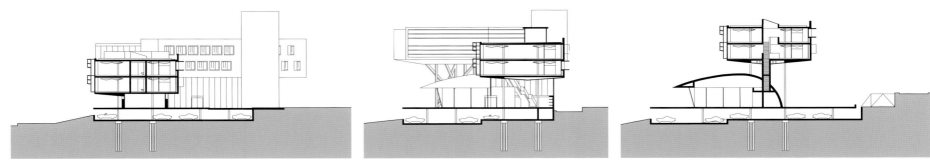

Cross-section through the lower office wing

Cross-section through the entrance hall

Cross-section through the meeting room

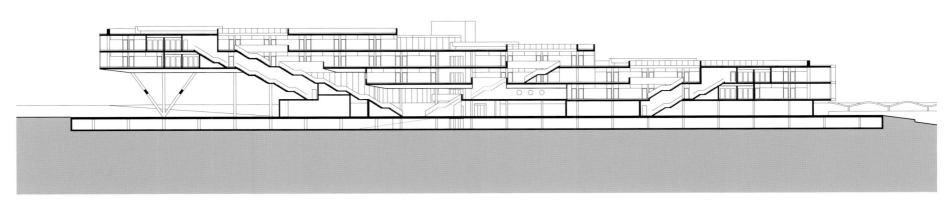

Longitudinal section through the office stair connections

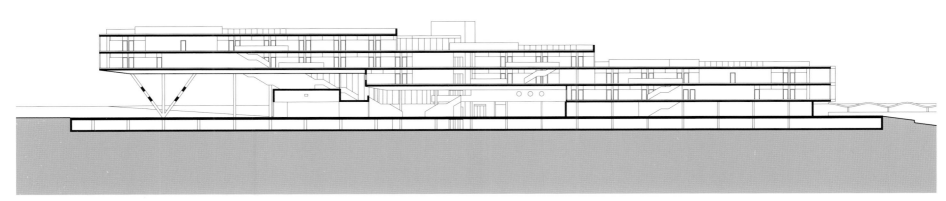

Longitudinal section through the office levels

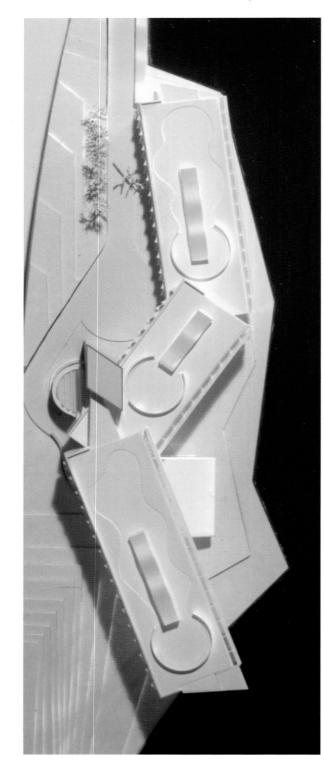

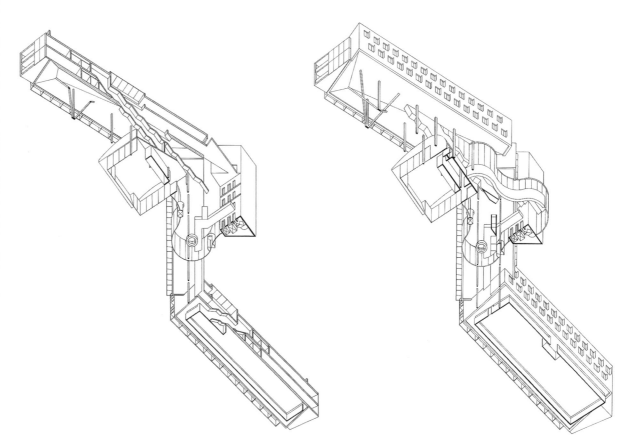

Worm's-eye cut-away axonometric of the office wings and stairs

Worm's-eye axonometric of the communal facilities beneath office wings

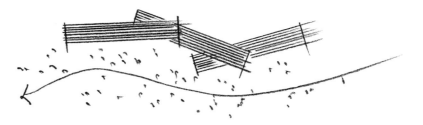

Concept sketch

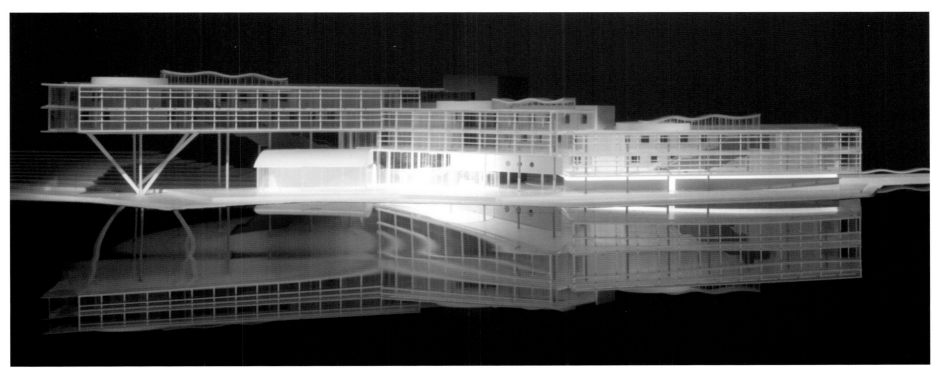

Model view from the river

Model view from the road and railway

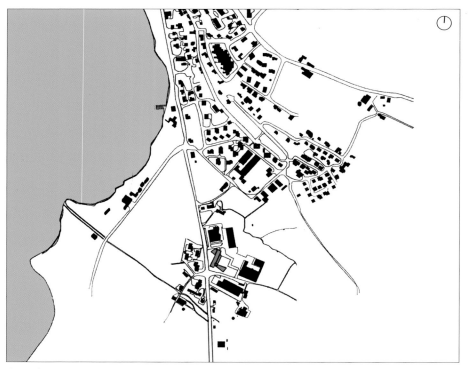

Context plan

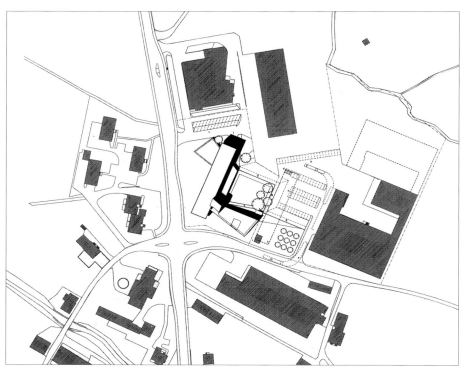

Site plan

B BRAUN AG SWISS HEADQUARTERS
SEMPACH, SWITZERLAND, 2000
Wilford Schupp Architekten (formerly Michael Wilford & Partners, London and Stuttgart)

The site is located in the low density industrial fringe of Sempach overlooking a major approach road to the town. The design consists of three primary elements; a Z-shaped base containing entrance hall, exhibition and conference facilities, an elevated office wing and a central garden cloister. The composition is arranged to emphasise both extroversion—proudly announcing the presence and identity of the company to the community and passing traffic and introversion—creating a quiet secluded oasis for staff and visitors within the nondescript industrial landscape.

The base is of monolithic brick construction, contrasting with the glazed office wing hovering above enjoying panoramic alpine views. The office building accommodates flexible planning with open work places, lounges and coffee bars to stimulate communication between employees. The brick, glass and metal cladding materials express the hygiene and technology of the company's products and symbolise consistency, solidity and ease of maintenance.

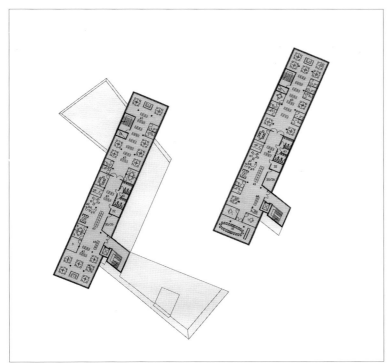

Upper office wing plans

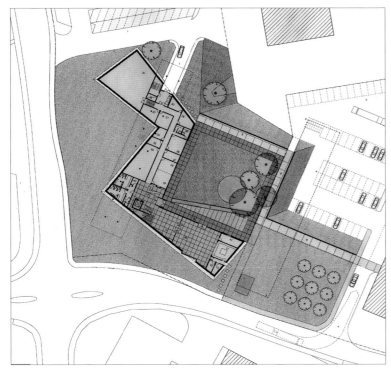

Ground floor plan of the entrance, conference and exhibition spaces

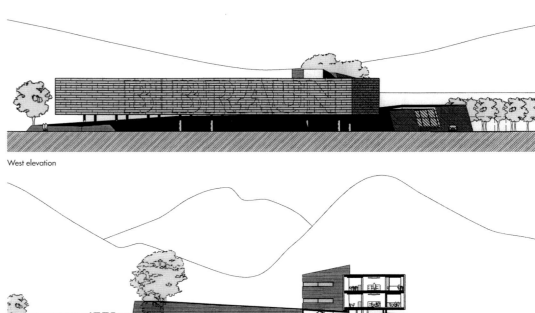

West elevation

Cross-section from the north

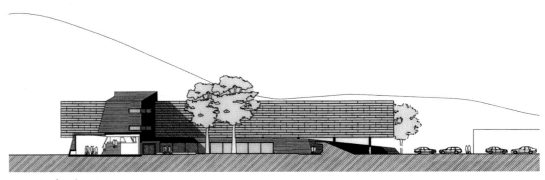

Cross-section from the east

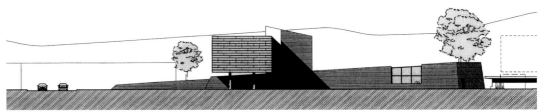

South elevation

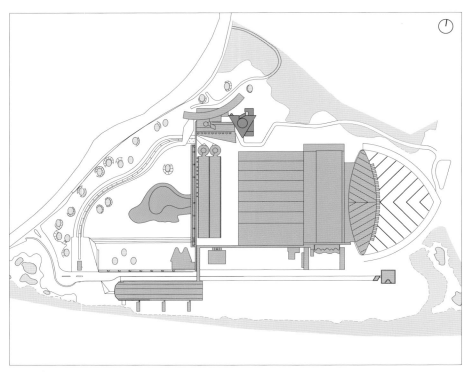

Context plan

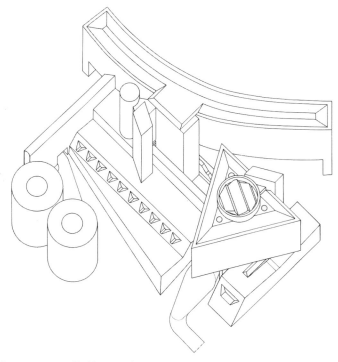

Combined bird's-eye axonometric of building A1 and A2

B BRAUN AG ADMINISTRATION BUILDING A2
MELSUNGEN, GERMANY, 1999–2002

Wilford Schupp Architekten (formerly Michael Wilford & Partners, London and Stuttgart)

The new building is an extension to the B Braun Headquarters and 'City of Industry', situated on the southern edge of Melsungen, the first stage of which was completed in 1992. The triangular building continues the masterplan strategy of articulating each building in the landscape in order to avoid the monotony of a large monolithic industrial complex.

It nestles adjacent to the first administration building and its vertical organisation contrasts with the horizontality of the initial building. Its elevated massing maintains the visual link between the open landscape and production buildings and its prismatic form provides a clear and distinct identity.

The building comprises three distinct formal elements, in a layered six level composition around a central roof-lit court. Three triangular office levels levitate above a circular plant room, resting on a two-level rectangular office base.

Circulation routes surrounding the court on the upper office levels and provide efficient staff movement with visual connections between floors. An open shaft containing two glass lifts and double interlocking staircases connect all levels.

The new building shares the entrance foyer of the first administration building, connected to it by a steel bridge and exhibition gallery. The internal office organisation accommodates new flexible working arrangements and supports the company policy of openness and transparency in personal communications.

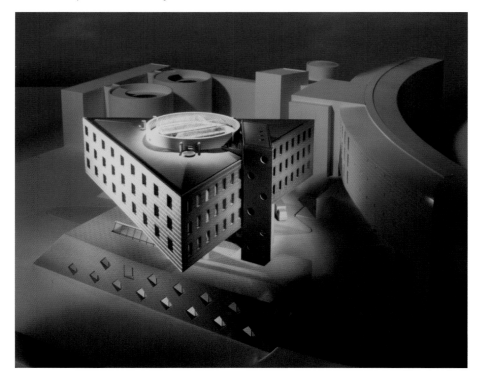

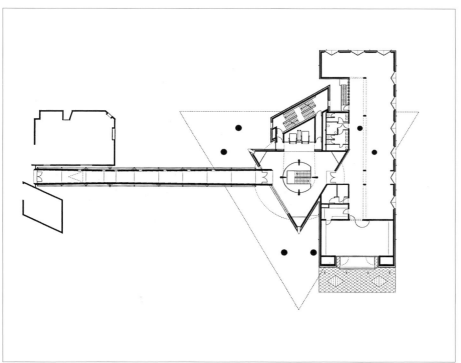

First floor office and upper entry level plan

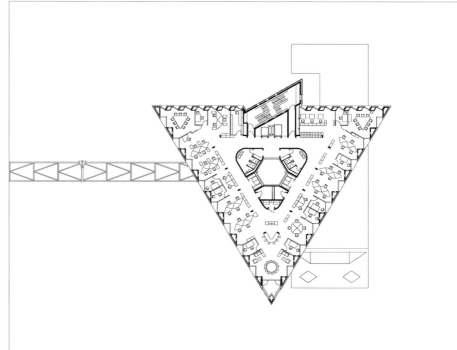

Third, fourth and fifth office floor plans

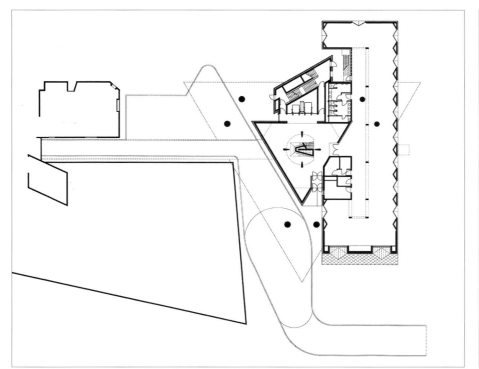

Ground floor office and lower entry level plan

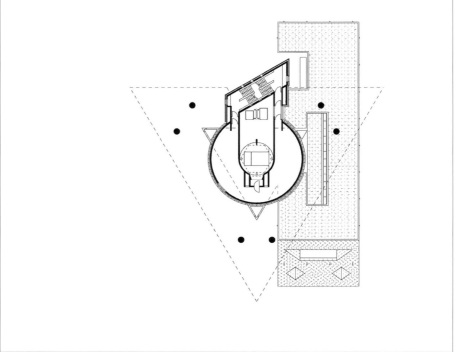

Second floor mechanical plant level

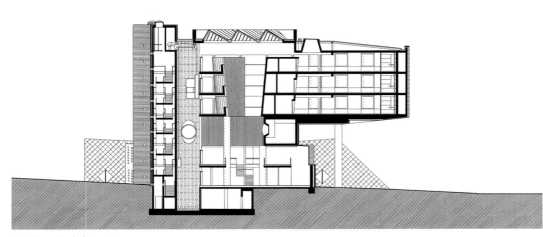

Centreline section looking east

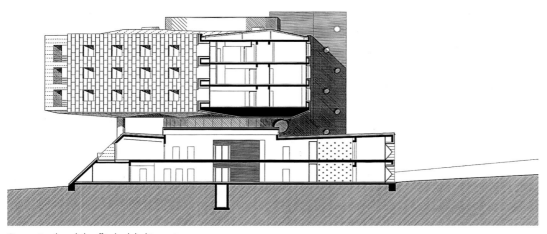

Cross-section through the office levels looking west

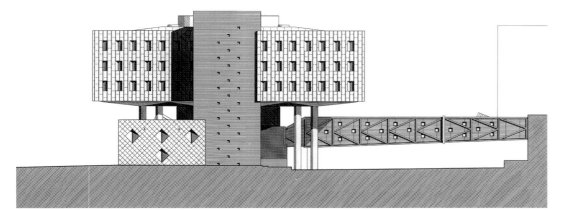

North elevation

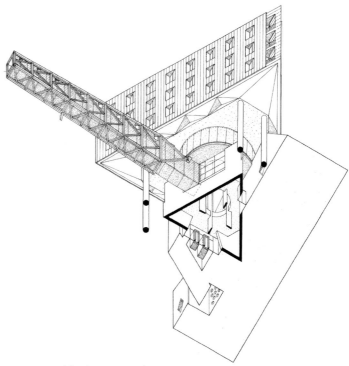

Worm's-eye axonometric

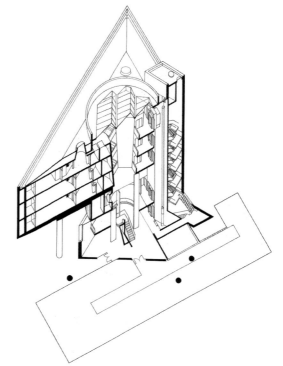

Sectional centreline isometric

Stair tower, offices and entrance bridge intersection

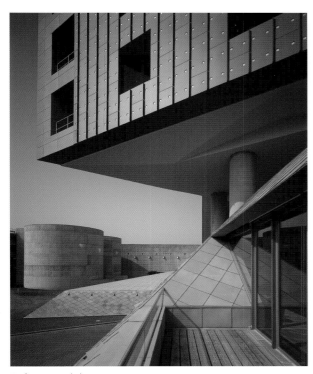

Conference room balcony

Lower entrance and foyer

Entrance bridge and exhibits looking west

Entrance bridge looking east

Views of the glazed elevators and entrance lobby

View up through the central court to the rooflight

Typical office social centre

Fifth floor service pod and rooflight

Lower entrance lobby

Typical open office and enclosed private cockpit layouts

Study booths around the central court

Typical cockpits and conference room

Typical corner conference room

RESIDENTIAL

Context plan

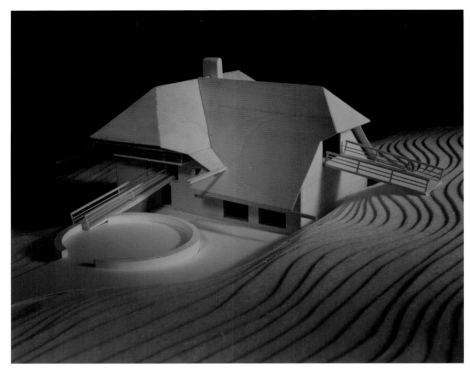

STOTMEISTER HOUSE
BALZHAUSEN, GERMANY, 1990–1992
Michael Wilford Architects

A traditional farmhouse on a steep sloping site in a small village of a dozen houses, high up in the Black Forest was purchased for a new family home. The four-storey building originally provided accommodation for the farmer's family, his animals and hay storage and was in poor condition, requiring major restoration.

The Stotmeister family required modern accommodation with close visual contact to the village and surrounding forest. The old hayloft which extended over the entire footprint of the original building, accommodates the new communal living areas—lounge, snug, dining area and kitchen—on the upper level. The gable walls of the T-shaped roof are fully glazed to introduce maximum daylight and allow views out into the surrounding landscape. Projecting gable roofs protect full width balconies with ramp and stair connections to adjacent gardens. The principal entry is at the living level, reached by an inclined bridge from the drop-off circle.

The kitchen is contained within the semi-circular form which cuts through the inclined roof line to provide the volume required and register its presence on the exterior of the building. Bedrooms are situated on the intermediate level with staff quarters and garaging at ground level.

The basic envelope of the farmhouse has been restored to its original condition using traditional materials and construction techniques. Major insertions into its volume use pure abstract figures to accommodate the modern facilities and efficiently collage new over old.

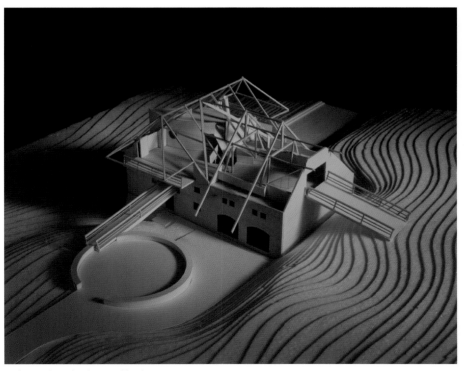

Roof removed revealing the second floor living areas

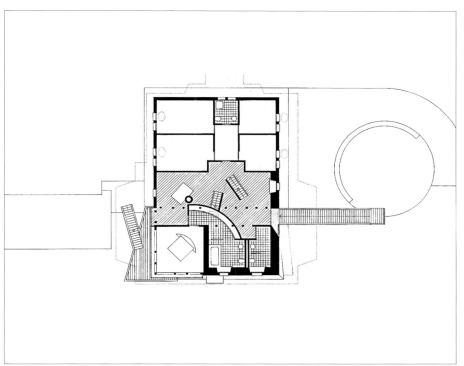

First floor entry and bedroom level

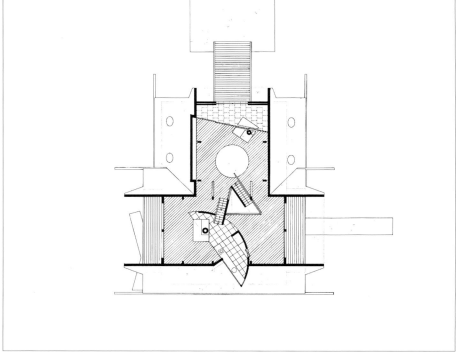

Third floor office mezzanine

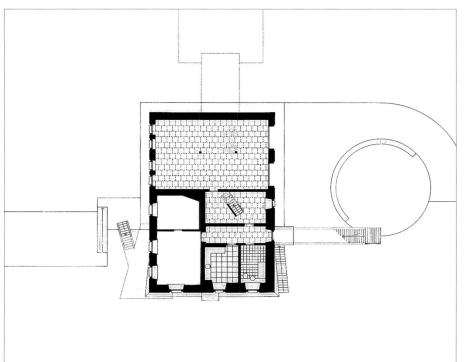

Ground floor garage and staff accommodation

Second floor living, kitchen and dining areas

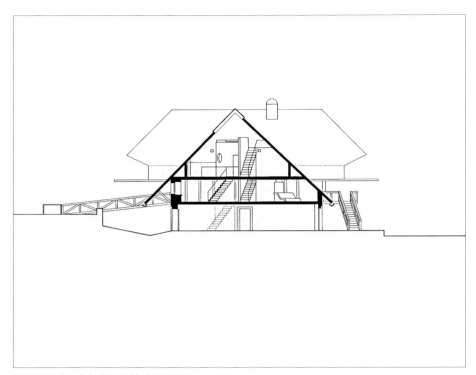

Cross-section through the living and bedroom wing

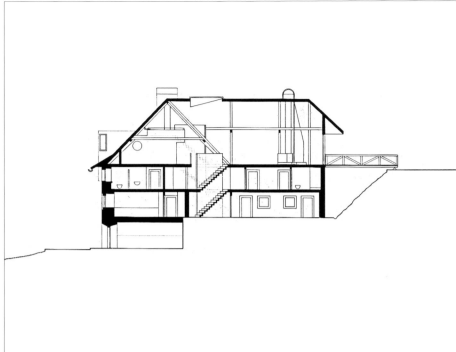

Longitudinal section

Roof removed revealing the second floor living areas

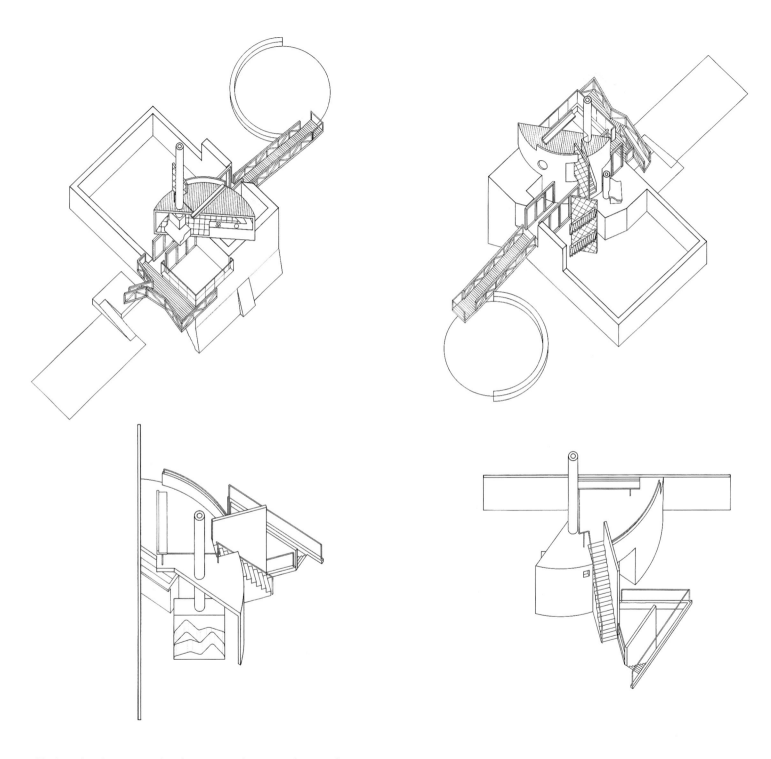

Axonometric downviews of the abstract formal interventions and circulation system into the pre-existing historic envelope

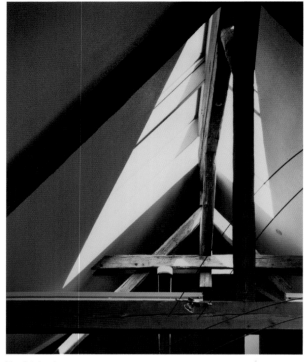

New interior views

New roof construction

Original interior view

Kitchen projection

View from the northwest

View from the northeast

View from the south

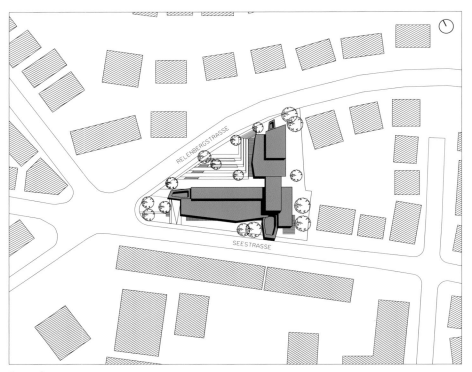

Context plan

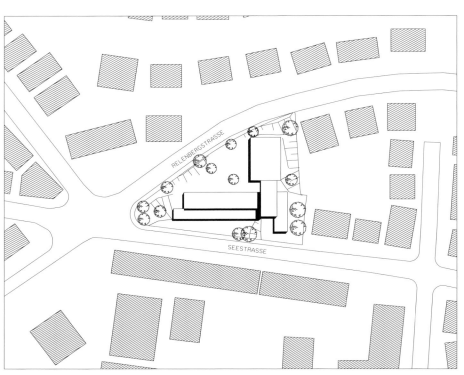

Context plan before conversion

RESIDENTIAL CONVERSION
STUTTGART, GERMANY, 2004–2007
Wilford Schupp Architekten

The building is located on a hillside overlooking the centre of Stuttgart in a transitional zone in the urban fabric where university buildings intersect with private houses in a residential district.

A research building used by the Max Planck Institute became redundant and we were commissioned to convert it into 23 high quality apartments. The building was stripped back to its structural frame, extended where necessary and re-fenestrated.

New internal planning divides the building into three separate vertical elements, each with their own entrance and vertical circulation in order to reduce the apparent scale of the project to apartment owners. Each entrance is connected to the street by its own canopy and unique colour schemes extend throughout the circulation areas to further enhance the individuality of each apartment. Large windows, balconies with minimal railing and roof terraces provide spectacular unobstructed views across the city and surrounding hills.

Aerial view of the original building

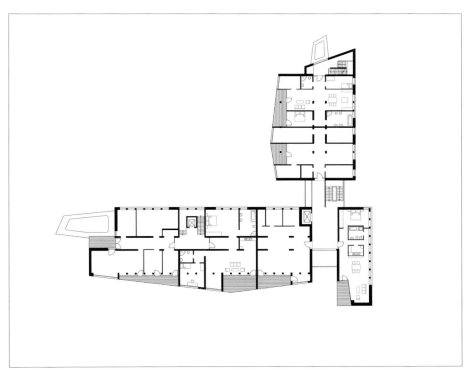

First and second floors

Fourth floor

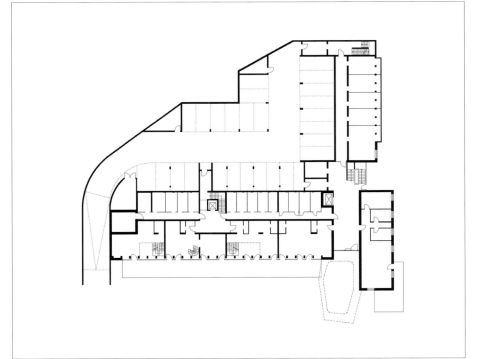

Ground floor and parking garage

Third floor

South facade and primary entrance

South facade

Junction of the north and west facades

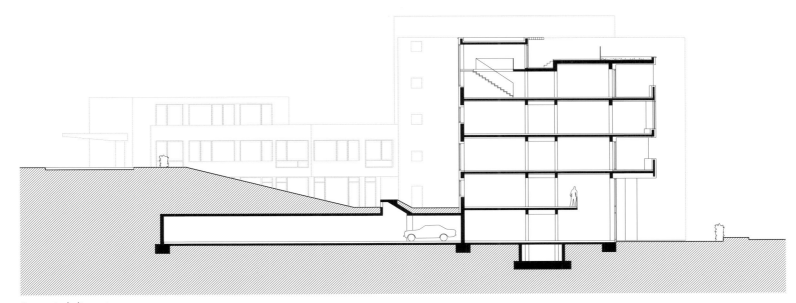

Cross-section looking east

North facade and communal garden

Junction of the north and west facades

Primary street entrance and canopy

Typical wall murals in the common circulation areas

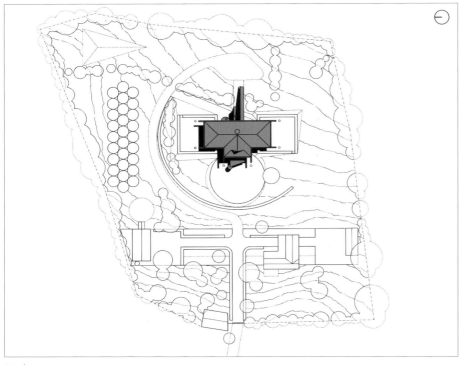

Site plan

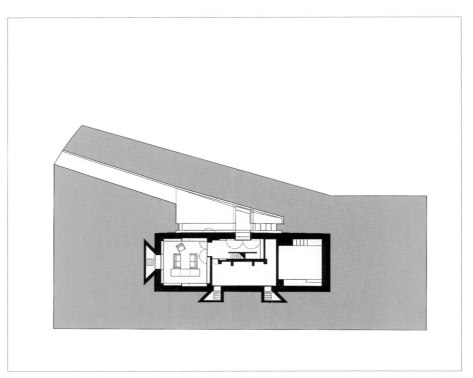

Sub-basement service level and access ramp

WILFORD HOUSE
SUSSEX, ENGLAND, 1997–2000
Michael Wilford & Partners

Situated in the Ashdown Forest and area of Outstanding Natural Beauty, the site enjoys panoramic views across a wooded valley to heathland beyond. The four-storey house, based on a traditional linear Wealden hall type is set into the sloping terrain with the master bedroom, living and kitchen/dining spaces contained in three square volumes on the first floor to maximise views and overlook the surrounding landscaped gardens.

The section is organised to allow entry to both the ground and first floor levels by ramped bridges to a central entrance hall which displaces the central living room and balcony from within the linear building form out over the lower terrace and circular lawn.

Guest rooms with plunge pool are situated on the ground floor with utility areas in the basement. A mezzanine office balcony is accommodated in the roof space above a snug around the living room fireplace. A stainless steel clad trefoil form containing the master bathroom and guest shower, together with a warped cube containing the kitchen food store, clip on to the entrance elevation as extensions of their respective spaces. They also contrast modern sculptural elements with the traditional Douglas Fir timber and sandstone materials used for the basic pavilion of the house.

View from the northwest

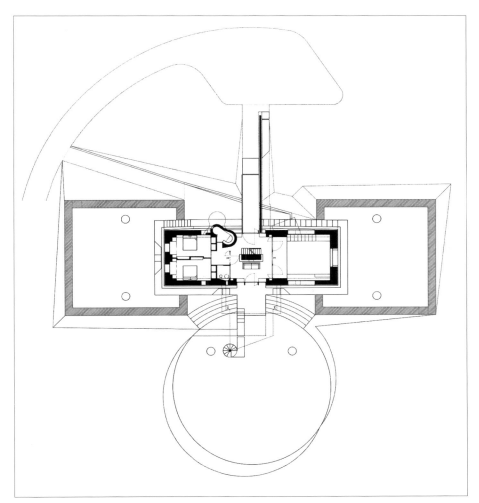

Ground floor entrance, guest bedrooms and plunge pool

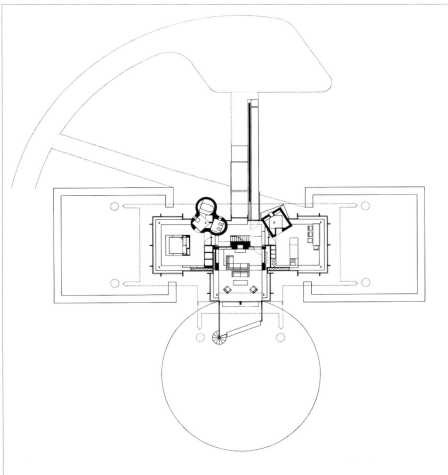

First floor, master bedroom, living and kitchen/dining rooms

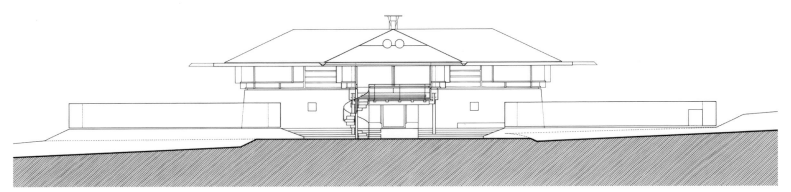

West elevation

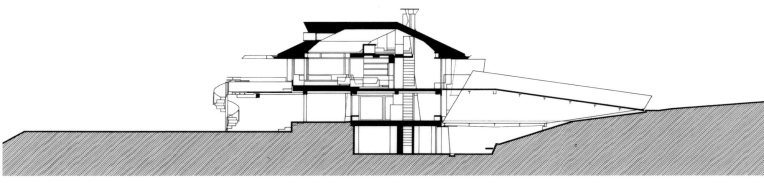

Cross-section looking north

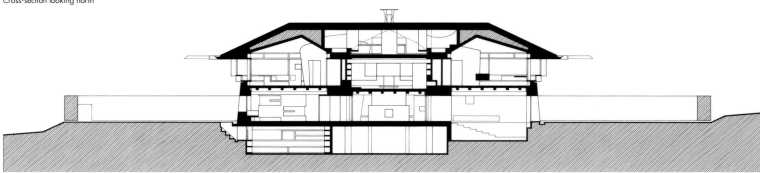

Longitudinal section looking east

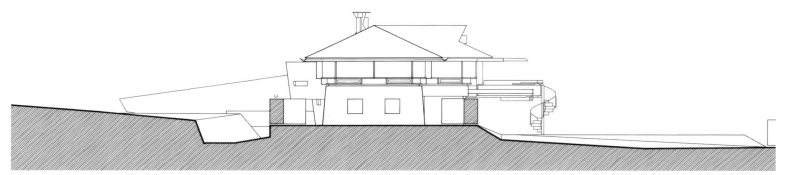

North elevation

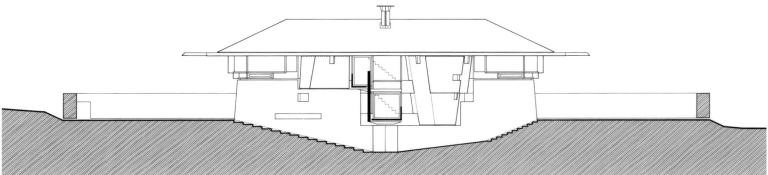

East elevation

South elevation

Entrance bridges

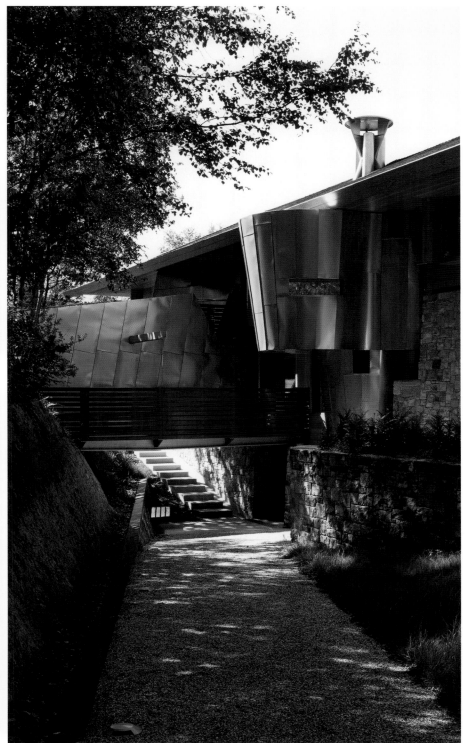

Bathroom trefoil, entrance bridge and basement access ramp

Living room snug

Kitchen

Master bathroom

Living room

Master bedroom

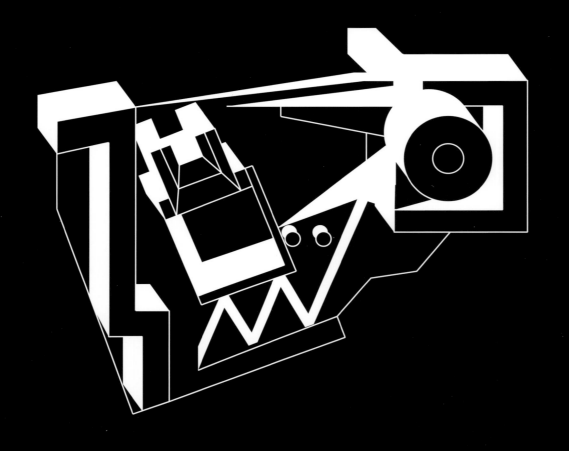

INSTITUTIONS

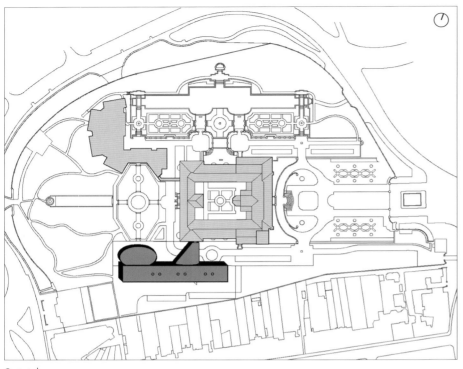

Context plan

Model of the Peace Palace and library/academy

PEACE PALACE LIBRARY AND ACADEMY
THE HAGUE, THE NETHERLANDS, 2003–2007
Wilford Schupp Architekten

The new building has its own unique personality whilst respectful of the Peace Palace in scale, material and colour. It accommodates a major expansion of the Palace Library and facilities for the Hague Academy of International Law and International Court of Justice. Each activity is given its own identity through three formal elements—triangular reading room, elliptical conference room and linear office building.

The three-storey foyer for registration, reception, informal discussion and relaxation connects the library and academy to the central entrance beneath the reading room with extensive views over the entrance court and west garden. Visual connections with the upper levels of the academy and reading room encourage a sense of community amongst users and visitors. Offices are accommodated on the upper floor bridging the foyer.

The academy hall, terminating the west garden axis, is a flexible space to accommodate various conference configurations for 150 delegates and 100 observers. The room can also accommodate lectures and audio visual presentations for an audience of 320. Its glazed north facade allows extensive views and direct access into the garden.

The Library entrance is reached by stair and lift from the foyer below and opens directly to the reference desk and catalogue area. The reading room for 120 readers, with peripheral reading tables, central book stacks, and upper reading balcony, also functions as a connector to the original corner reading room and secondary entrance in the Peace Palace. Its stepped section reconciles different floor levels between the two buildings.

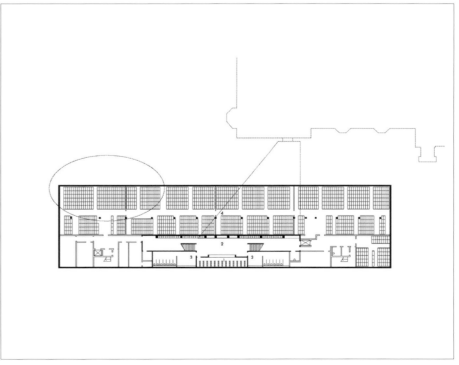

Basement book storage

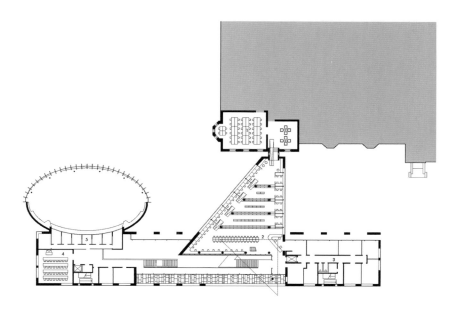

First floor library and academy seminar spaces

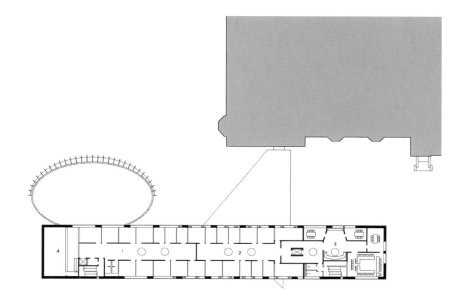

Third floor offices

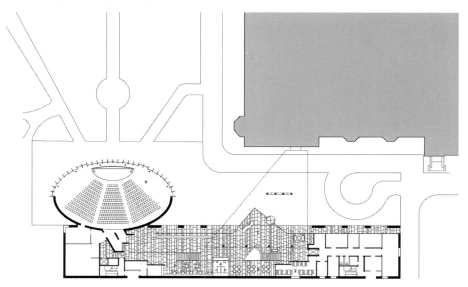

Ground floor entrance foyer and academy conference hall

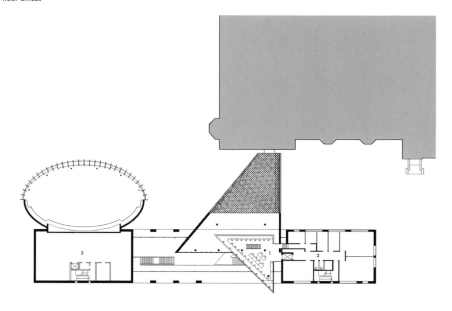

Second floor library mezzanine and offices

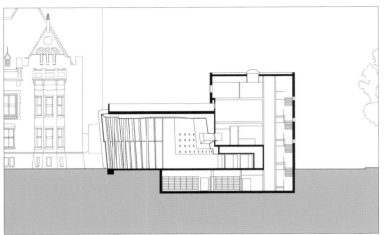

Cross-section through the academy conference hall

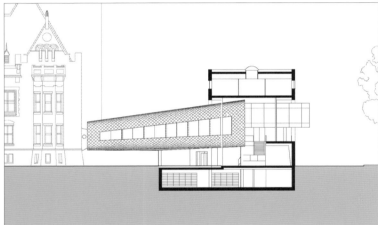

Cross-section through the entrance foyer

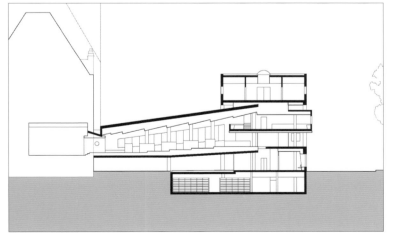

Cross-section through the library

Library entrance stair

Entrance foyer looking east

Entrance foyer looking west

Library looking south

Library looking north

Library/Peace Palace connection

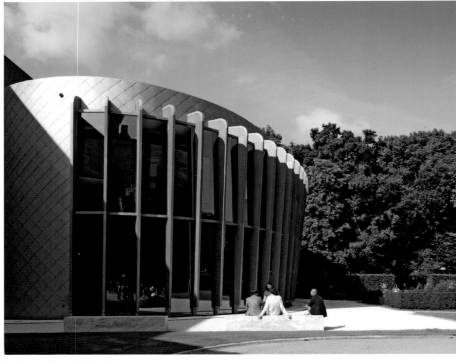

Academy conference hall exterior

Academy conferences in session

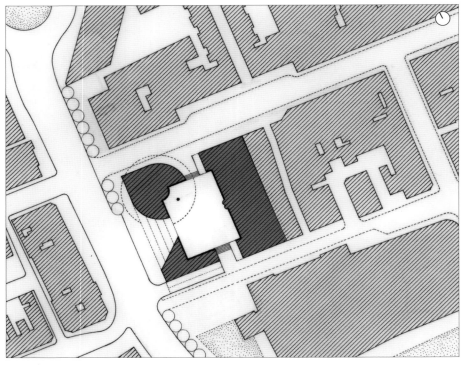

Context plan

Sketch of City Reference Library

NATIONAL LITERATURE CENTRE AND CITY LIBRARY
SWANSEA, WALES, 1994
Michael Wilford & Partners

Ty Llen is located on a boulevard at the western edge of the town centre, as a significant public building and cultural nucleus of the city. An enclosed public square linking two major streets provides an outdoor communal space to relax and meet friends. Entrances to Ty Llen and the City Library face each other across the square, stimulating day and night activity. In fine weather people can move outdoors and further enliven the space.

Ty Llen defines three sides of the square and its top-lit exhibition galleries at first floor level extend across the boulevard frontage, with the striking form of its rotunda providing a memorable presence and encouraging cross-fertilisation of ideas amongst writers. Within the City Library the main entrance, exhibition areas and children's library at ground floor level are linked by a grand stair to the music, drama and lending libraries on the first floor above. They share a central reading room overlooking the square. The stair continues up to the spacious roof-lit, Reference Library on the second floor. A translucent wall faces the square, expressing the book stack as a literary 'treasure house'. Reading rooms enjoy views across the square and city skyline.

The base and flanking walls of Ty Llen are faced with Welsh slate and the drum and gallery roof-lights, clad in green pre-patinated copper.

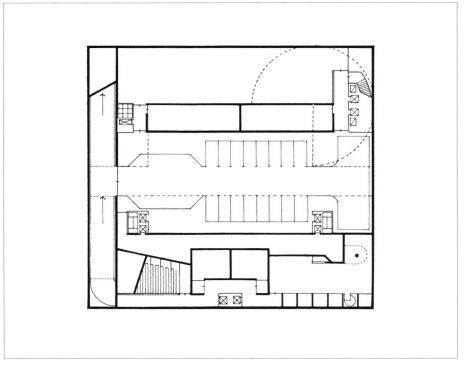

Basement car parking and storage

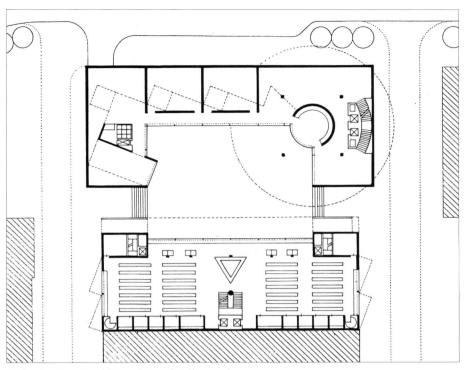

First floor literature centre exhibition galleries and city library reading room

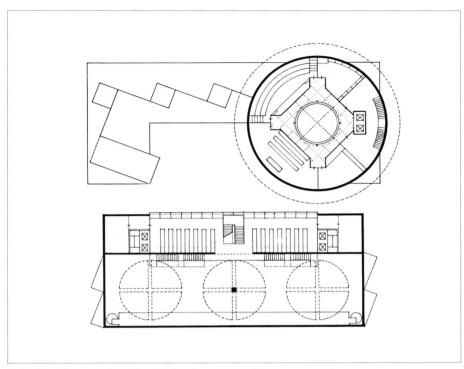

Third and fourth floors, city reference library book stack, mezzanines and literature centre recital rooms

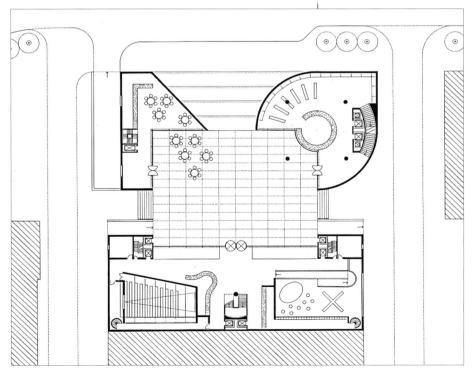

Ground level public square, entrances, cafeteria and lecture theatre

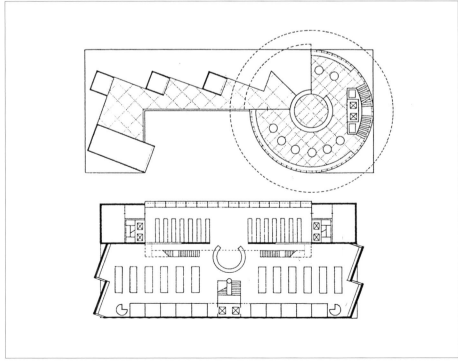

Second floor, city reference library and Literature centre lounge

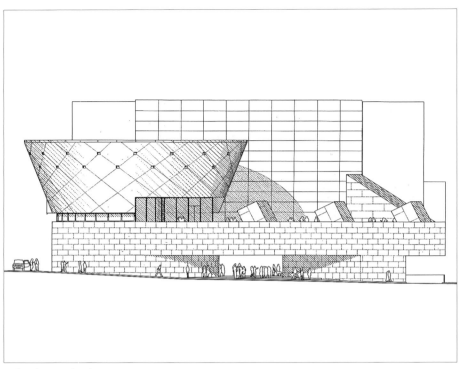

Boulevard entrance facade

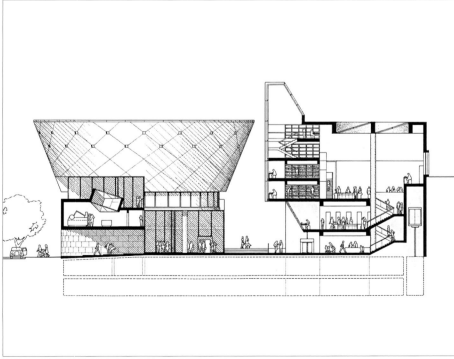

Cross-section through the square looking north

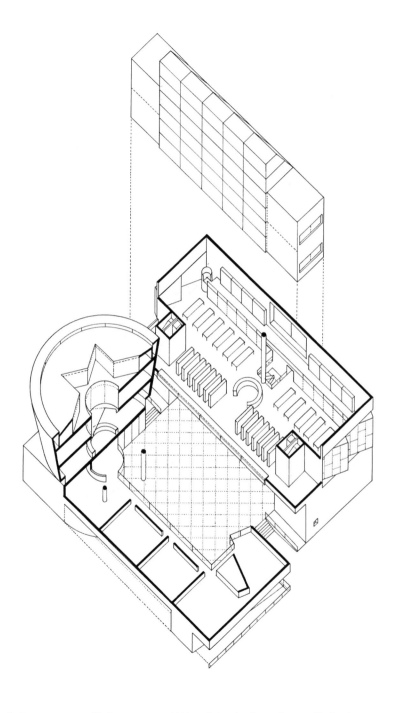

Cut-away bird's-eye axonometric of the literature centre exhibition galleries, city reference library and bookstack

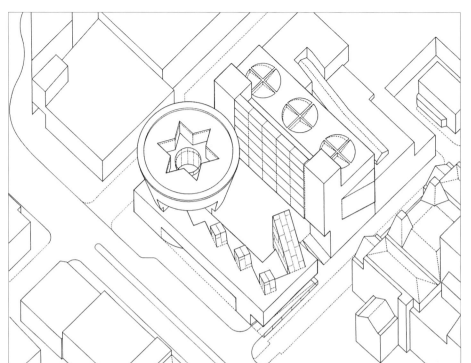

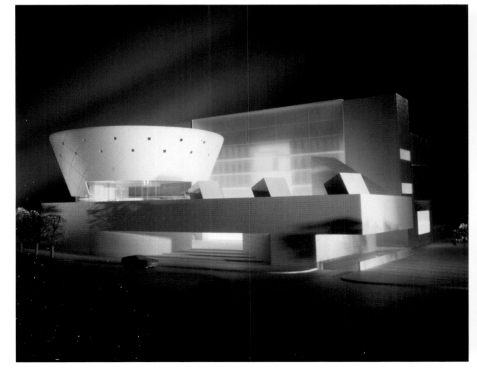

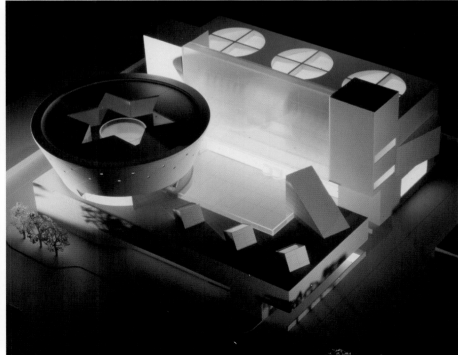

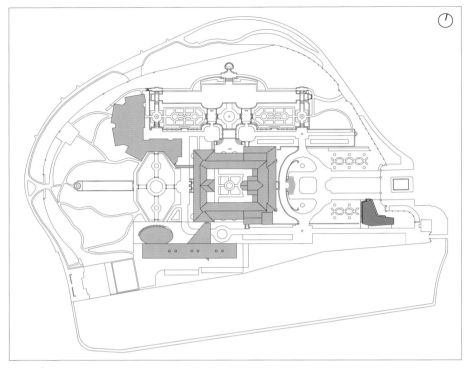

Context plan

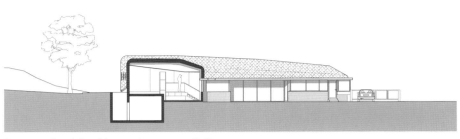

Cross-section through the exhibition and entry courtyard looking west

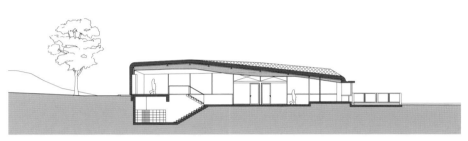

Longitudinal section through the entrance and security areas

PEACE PALACE VISITOR CENTRE
THE HAGUE, THE NETHERLANDS, 2008–2011
Wilford Schupp Architekten

The new discreet building serves two primary functions—control of access in and out of the Carnegie Plein by vehicles and pedestrians and an introduction to visitors of the history and current activities of the Peace Palace.

The L-shaped form responds to the constricted site by echoing the boundary wall of the Carnegie Plein. The entrance court accommodates parallel entry and exits for judges/ VIPs and visitors. Separate security lines are also provided inside the building and a projecting booth controls truck and car access.

A visitor exhibition sequence telling the story of the Peace Palace rises by a shallow ramp around a central display from the Entrance Hall to an observation level providing unobstructed views to the Peace Palace and gardens. Visitors return to the entrance level and souvenir shop via a short stair and can either pass through security for a tour of the Palace or exit the building.

The height of the Visitor Centre rises gracefully to the south and west from the adjacent boundary wall, opening views to the Palace from the interior. Its mass is screened by the boundary wall and when viewed from outside the Carnegie Plein avoids intrusion into the classic view of the Palace from the city. Together with the Academy Hall and Library, the Visitor Centre forms a trilogy of new architectural forms on the Carnegie Plein that respect the historic monumental quality and materiality of the Palace but also have their own contemporary personality.

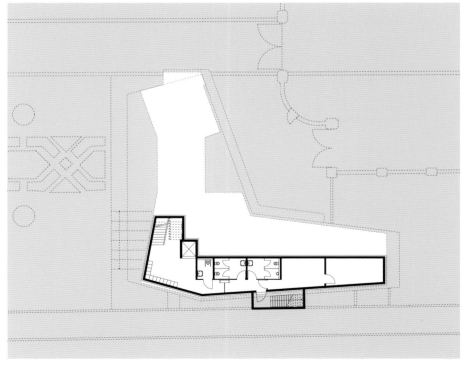

Basement locker, washroom and service plan

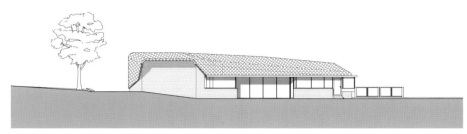

East elevation

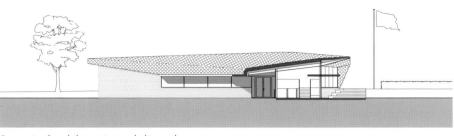

Cross-section through the security area, looking south

West elevation

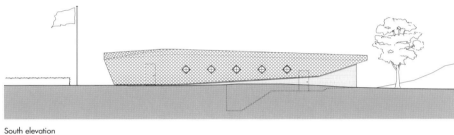

South elevation

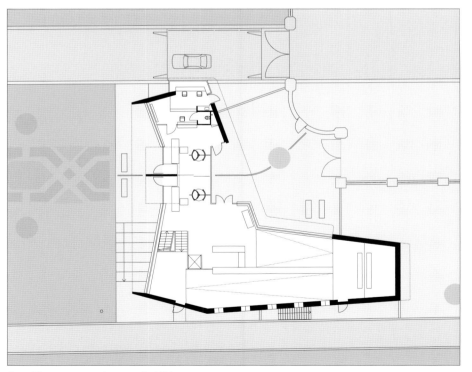

Ground floor entrance, security area and exhibition

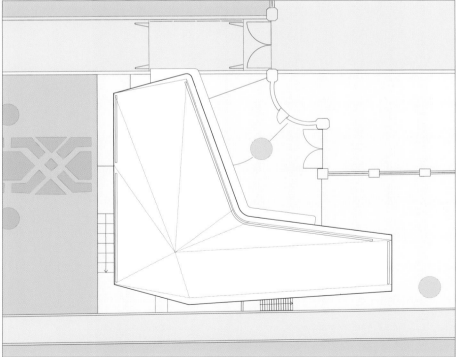

Roof plan

South and west facades

Separate security entrance and exits for staff and visitors

Aerial view from the Peace Palace

Vehicle security check enclosure

North and west facades

West facade

Entrance courtyard

View of the exhibition ramp from the enquiry desk

View of the exhibition from observation area

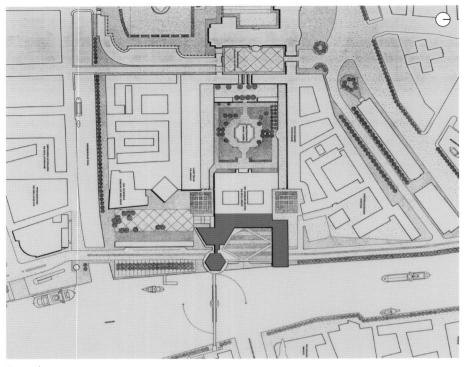

Context plan

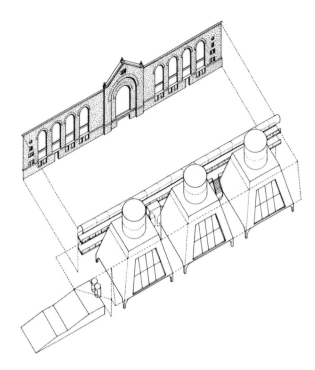

Original 1906 facade restored. New entrance, information concourse and reading rooms

ROYAL LIBRARY EXTENSION
COPENHAGEN, DENMARK, 1993
Michael Wilford & Partners

The 1965 office extension built immediately against the east facade of the original 1906 Library forms a barrier to the extension and we proposed its removal to allow appropriate connections and to restore the 1906 facade to its former stature.

The new extension responds to the form and scale of adjacent buildings and is integrated with the existing Library to form a single functional entity. An elevated entrance facing a new public plaza is located at the interface between new and existing buildings, signalled by a wide stair and projecting canopy. The circular pavilion housing the Society for Danish Language and Literature, together with the raised garden, provides a formal and spatial focus to the composition with panoramic views over the Havnelop River.

An Information Hall extends across the width of the new building as a tall conservatory at the 'piano nobile' level. It links the plaza entrance and Reference Library combining with the main axis of the existing Library to form a T-shaped public circulation armature. The conservatory, with the facade of the original building as a backdrop and overlooking the garden accommodates three elevated pyramids housing special libraries. The information desk, situated at the centre of the T, is the functional heart of the Library.

Each reading room has an individual memorable form and is connected directly to the book-stack reservoir on the lower levels of the building. The Reference Library containing multi-level reading balconies contributes to the enclosure of the garden and demonstrates the outward-looking nature of the new accommodation.

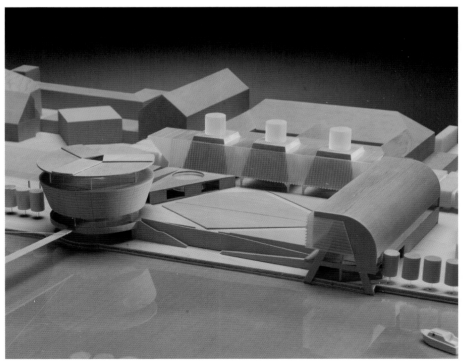

Model view of the elevated garden enclosed by the circular Danish Literature Pavilion, information concourse and reference library

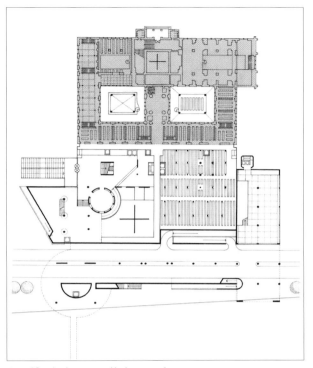

Ground floor book storage and highway tunnel

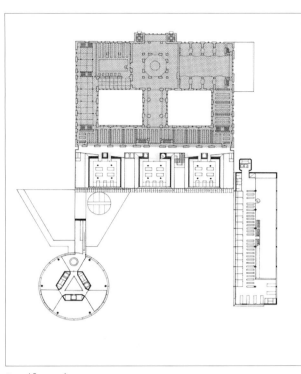

Second floor reading rooms

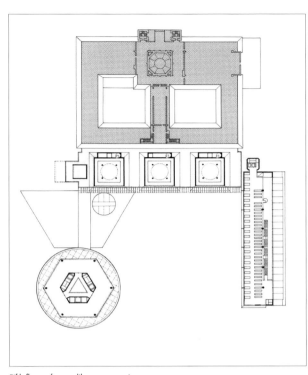

Fifth floor reference library mezzanine

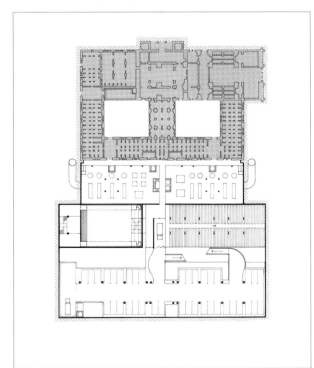

Basement parking and book storage

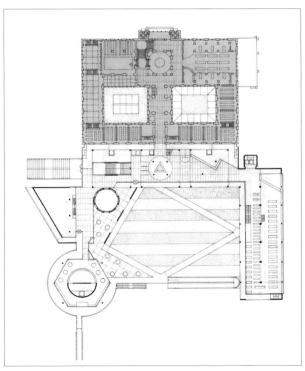

First floor elevated entrance, information concourse and garden

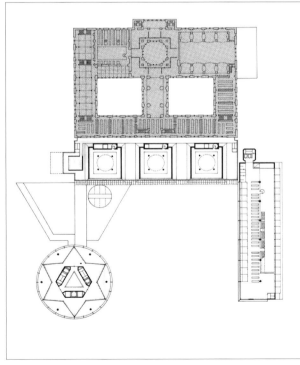

Third and fourth floor reading room mezzanines

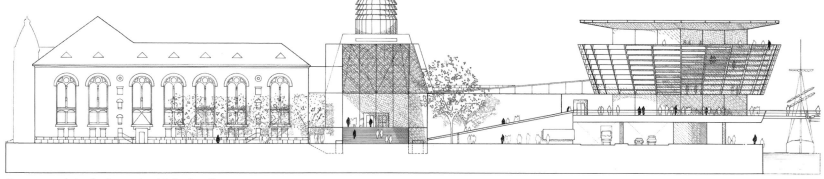

New entrance at the interface between the original and new library

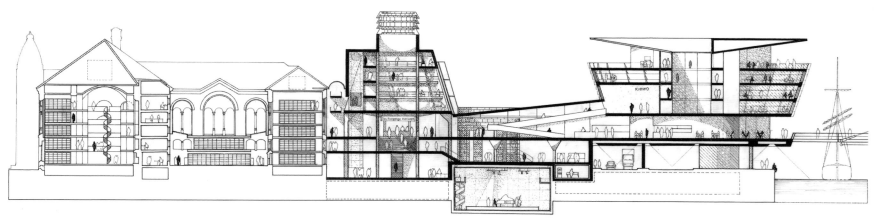

Cross-section through the original library, information concourse and the Danish Literature Centre

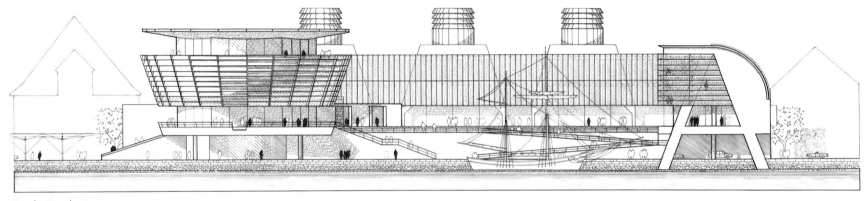

Havnelop River elevation

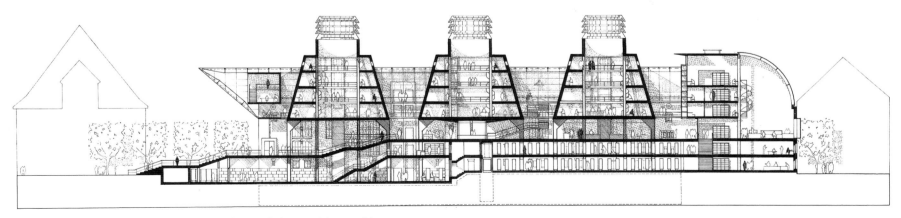

Longitudinal section through the information concourse and reading rooms looking towards the original library

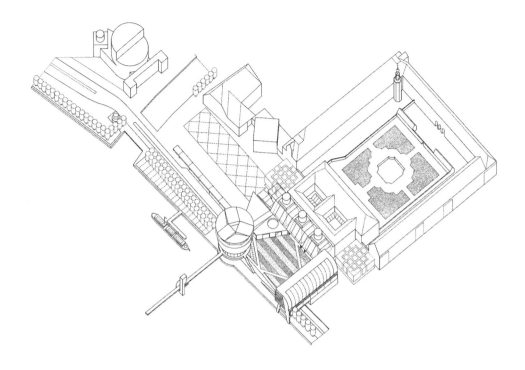

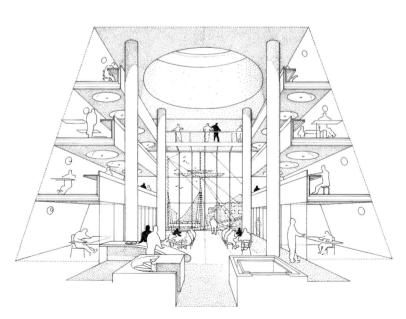

Interior sketch of a typical reading room pyramid

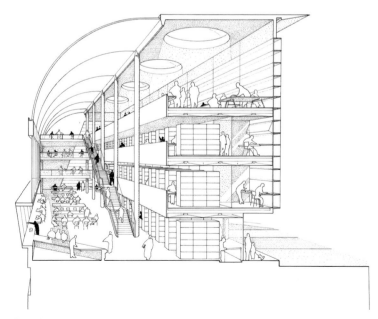

Interior sketch of the reference library

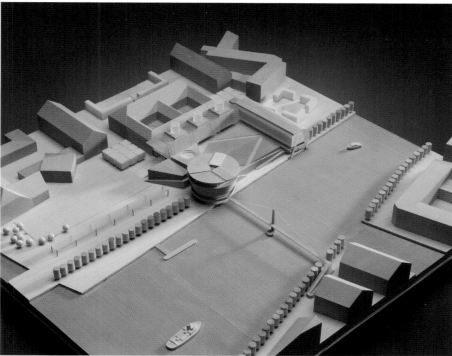

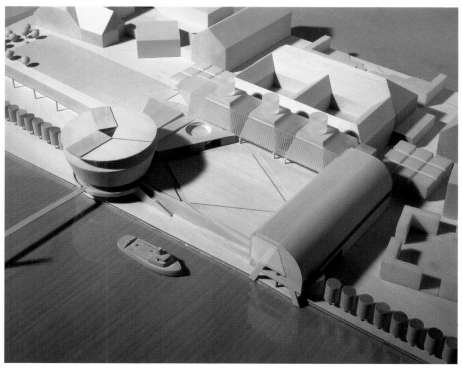

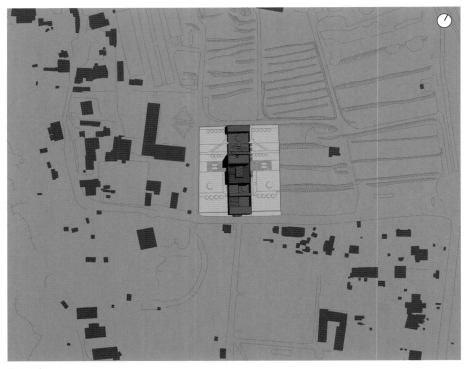

Context plan

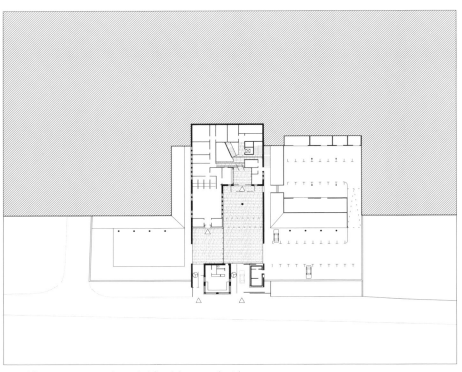

Ground floor entry courts, consulate to the left and chancery to the right

BRITISH EMBASSY
TBILISI, GEORGIA, 2006–2010
Wilford Schupp Architekten

The Embassy is situated on a hillside, south of Tbilisi with commanding views across the city. The cascading building and sequence of courts connect the Embassy entrance on the lower frontage with the Ambassador's Residence at the top of the site. Stepped gardens on each flank of the building mirror the former vineyard terraces and settle the building into the surrounding landscape.

Visitors and staff enter the Embassy through the lower portal and after passing through a further security check in the entrance hall, ascend a diagonal stair into the central atrium on the 'piano nobile' level above. The Consulate and Visa Hall occupy the remainder of the ground floor.

The roof-lit atrium, accommodating receptions and exhibitions, forms the social focus of the Embassy and brings daylight into the centre of the building. Sliding glazed doors allow the adjacent conference room and staff cafeteria to become extensions of the atrium for larger-scale events and both spaces open out onto terraces on either side of the building to allow activities to extend into the gardens in fine weather. Offices surround upper levels of the atrium.

The Ambassador's Residence is situated above the Embassy and entered through its own portal and entrance court. The official reception room opens onto a roof terrace overlooking the city.

The Embassy is faced externally with a local basalt stone with the Residence enveloped in a metal lattice similar to the ornamental screens enclosing the extensive external balconies in traditional Georgian houses.

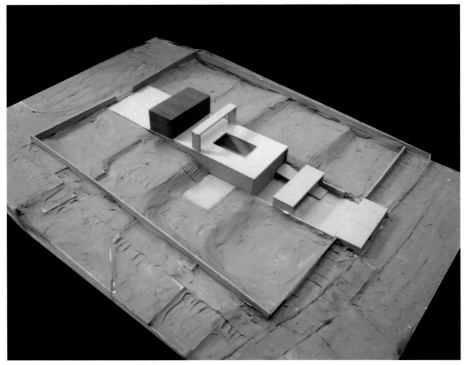

Early concept model

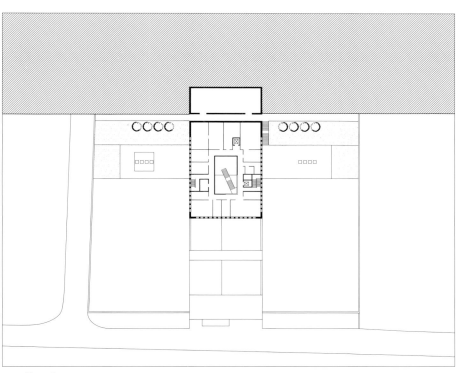

Second floor offices

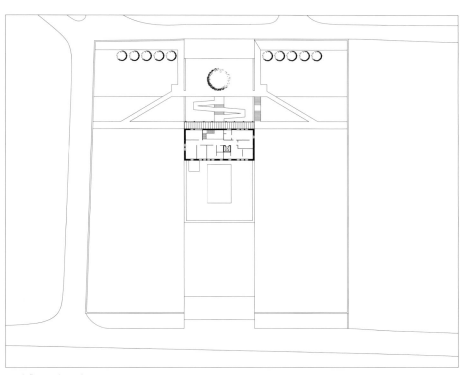

Fourth floor, ambassador's apartment

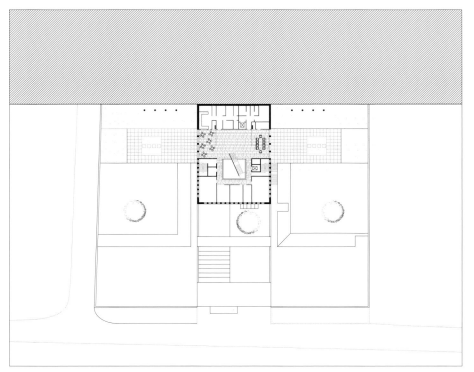

First floor atrium with cafeteria and conference room

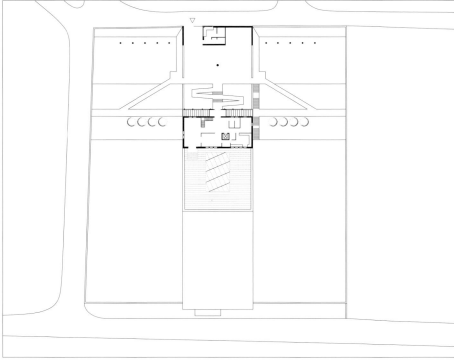

Third floor, ambassador's residence reception rooms

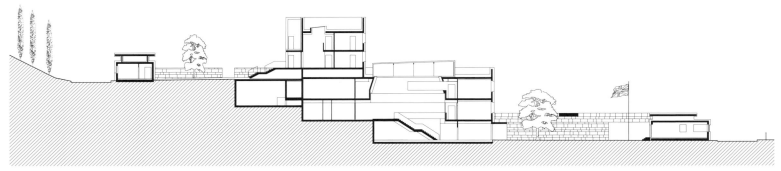

Centreline longitudinal section looking northeast

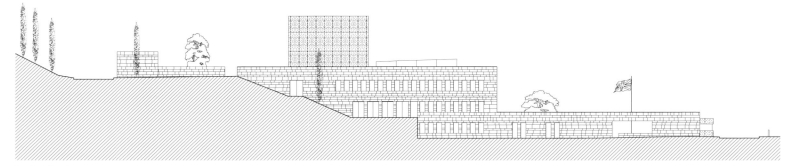

Southeast facade

Chancery entrance court

Ambassador's residence entrance

Lattice detail

Metal lattice enclosure to the ambassador's residence above basal clad embassy

Atrium and entrance stair

Lattice detail

Atrium rooflight

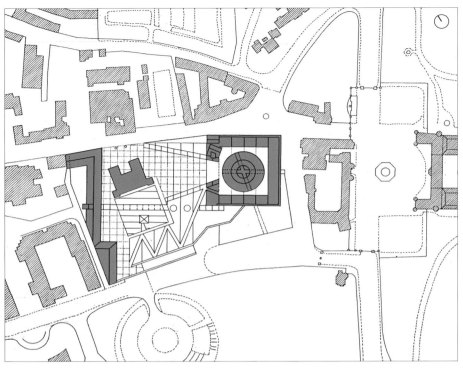

Context plan

SCOTTISH PARLIAMENT
EDINBURGH, SCOTLAND, 1998
Michael Wilford & Partners

The design is open and welcoming to the public. To satisfy security requirements its layered organisation provides separate zones for Scottish Members of Parliament and their constituents with defined intervening spaces for consultation between them. The Parliament has three primary entrances strongly marked in its organisation and its massing provides a powerful termination to the Royal Mile at Holyrood as a counterpoint to the Castle at its opposite higher end.

A wide ramp, as a continuation of the Royal Mile leads directly into a large public plaza situated on the roof of the main body of the building and providing the principal public approach and entrance to the building. SMPs enter from the Royal Mile at the northeast corner of the building and the ceremonial entrance overlooks the dramatic profile of King Arthur's Seat across a reflecting pool.

The public viewing gallery and press facilities are located on the upper levels, surrounding and overlooking the Debating Chamber. Queensberry House, an historic structure to be retained together with the staggered linear mass along the western boundary, accommodate SMPs' private offices linked by committee and conference room clusters to the main floor of the Debating Chamber.

The principal facade of Queensberry House addresses a private cloister for SMP deliberation and relaxation. Extensive terraces and gardens extend from the plaza over the building, providing routes into the public areas of the building. The Parliament is registered on the city skyline by the slender Piper's Tower together with the illuminated lantern above the Debating Chamber.

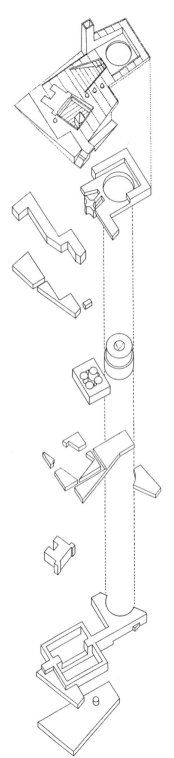

Exploded diagram of the constituent elements of the project

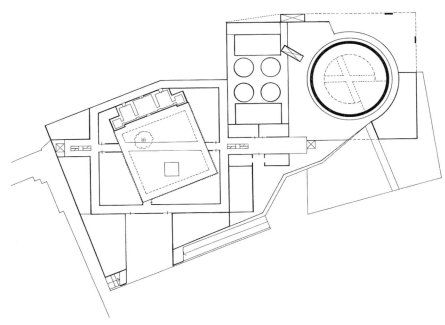

First floor SMP support spaces

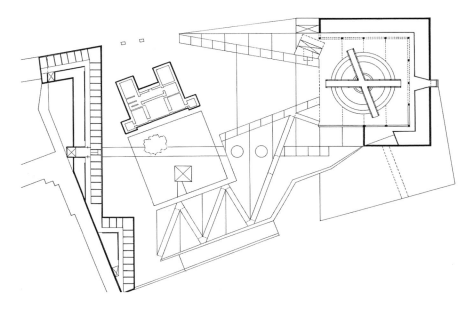

SMP consulting rooms around the debating chamber and third and fourth floor offices

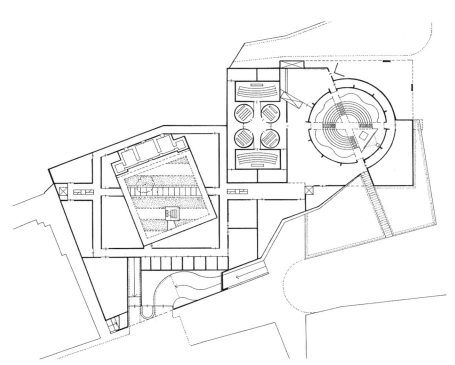

Ground level plan with the debating chamber, committee rooms and SMP's cloister garden

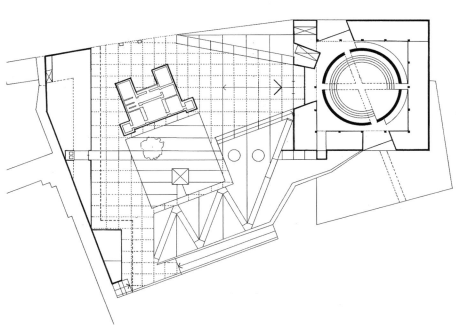

Second floor public plaza, roof garden and entrance to the public and press levels of the debating chamber

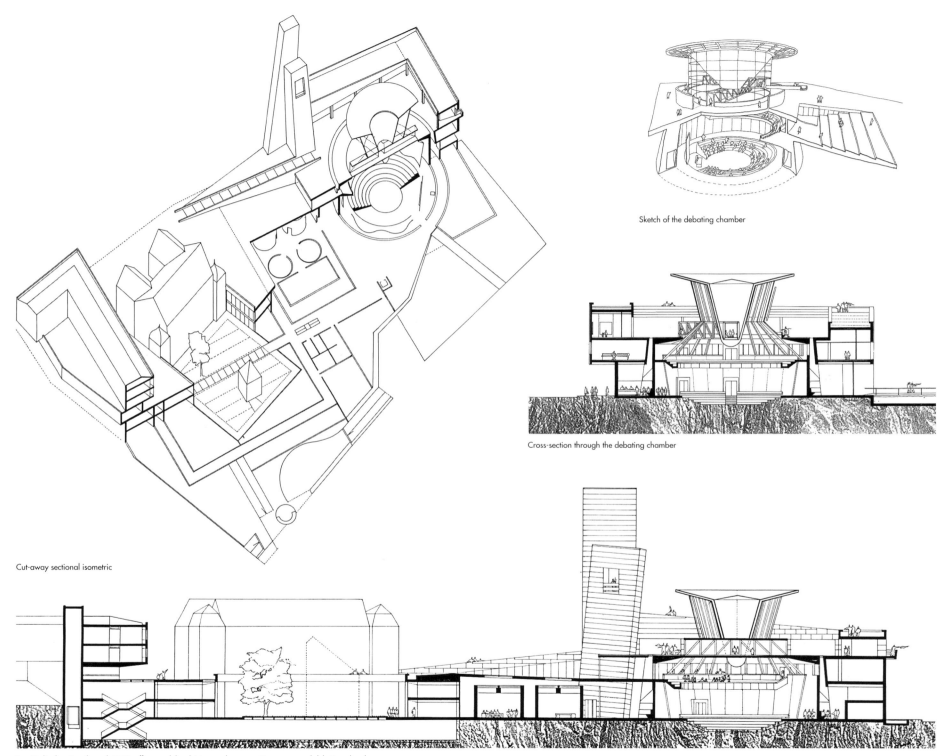

Sketch of the debating chamber

Cross-section through the debating chamber

Cut-away sectional isometric

Longitudinal section through SMP's offices and the cloister garden, committee rooms and debating chamber

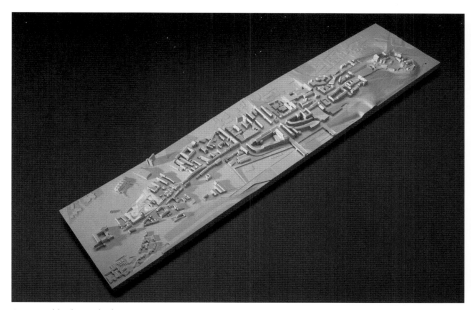

Context model—The Royal Mile

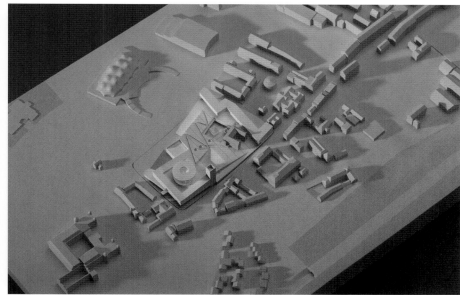

Context model—Holyrood

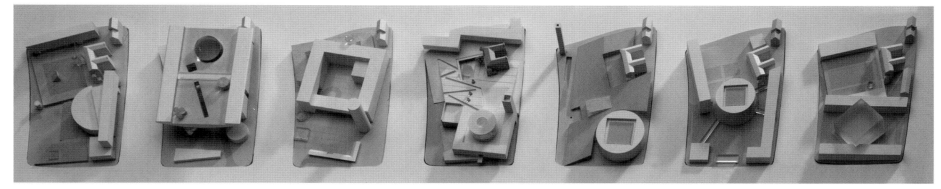

Alternative early concept models

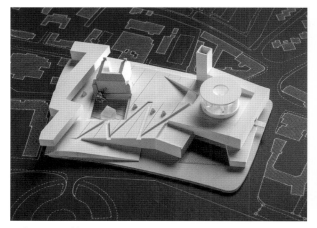

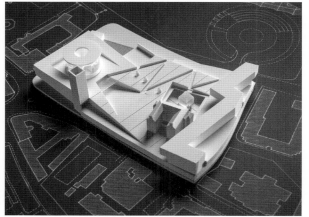

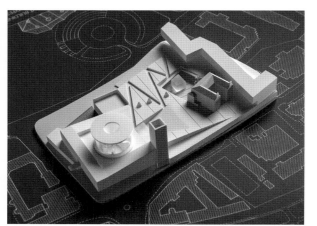

Final massing model

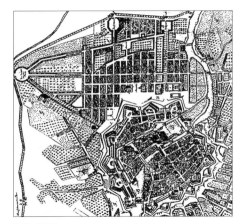

Berlin, 1737

Wilhelmstrasse and Pariserplatz, 1800

Wilhelmstrasse and Pariserplatz, 1936

Wilhelmstrasse and Pariserplatz, 1988

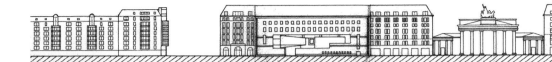

Context elevation to Wilhelmstrasse and the Brandenburg Gate

BRITISH EMBASSY
BERLIN, GERMANY, 1994–2000

Wilford Schupp Architekten (formerly Michael Wilford & Partners, London and Stuttgart)

The Embassy reoccupies its pre-war location on Wilhelmstrasse and the generous site allowed the incorporation of open spaces within the building, similar to the courtyards of the palais which previously lined the street, allowing daylight and natural ventilation into the heart of the Embassy.

A single vehicle and pedestrian entrance gate for visitors and staff leads directly to the entrance court providing an elegant approach and set-down within the building. The court is a transition in ambience between the city and Embassy interior. An oak tree at its centre provides an immediate association with Britain.

Visitors are escorted up the grand staircase to the roof-lit Wintergarden on the 'piano nobile' level which forms the focus and heart of the Embassy. A circular conference room and formal dining room are arranged around the Wintergarden to enable them to be used either individually or together for receptions, banquets and exhibitions. An Information Centre on all aspects of the UK is situated above the entrance gate and is the culmination of a pedestrian promenade around the public spaces of the building.

Office circulation balconies encircle upper levels of the Wintergarden, offering visitors glimpses of the routine activities in the building above and staff views of special events on the 'piano nobile' below.

The street facade expresses the layered internal organisation of the building comprising base, ceremonial level and offices. An abstract collage of coloured forms, hinting at the special spaces within, is revealed through a large opening in the facade. These mark the entrance and register the special character of the Embassy in relation to the neutrality of adjacent buildings. The Embassy is intended to convey a modern dignified presence whilst respecting Berlin's traditional building massing, articulation and materials.

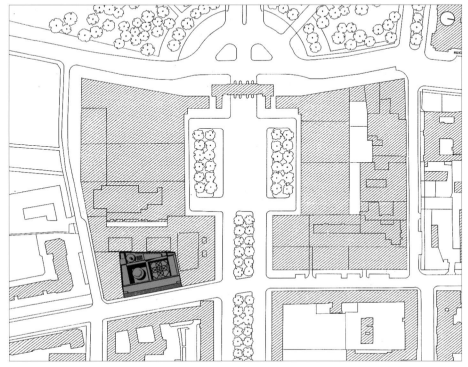

Context plan

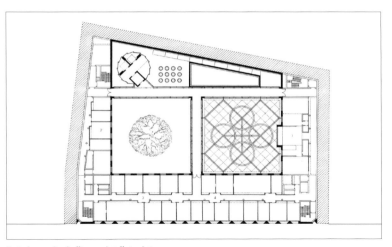

Typical upper level offices and staff circulation

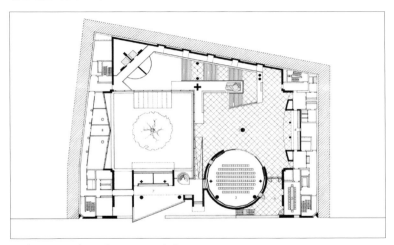

First floor wintergarden, conference room and information centre

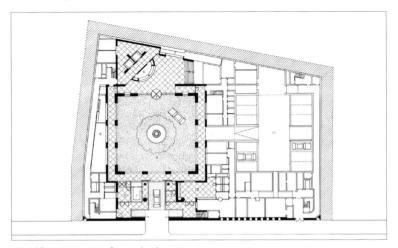

Ground floor entrance court, foyer and parking garage

Cross-section through the grand staircase and entrance court looking north

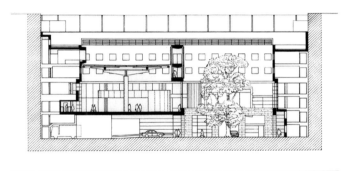

Longitudinal section through the wintergarden and entrance court looking east

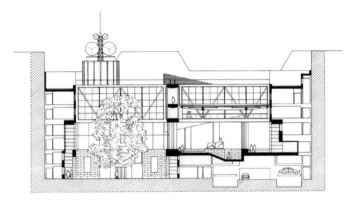

Longitudinal section looking west

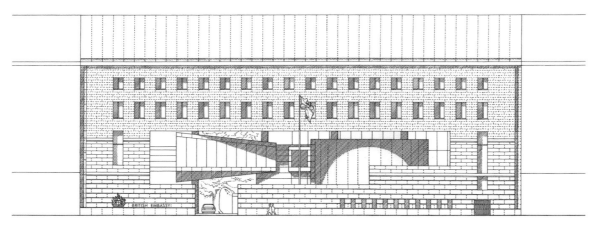

Wilhelmstrasse facade

Competition model

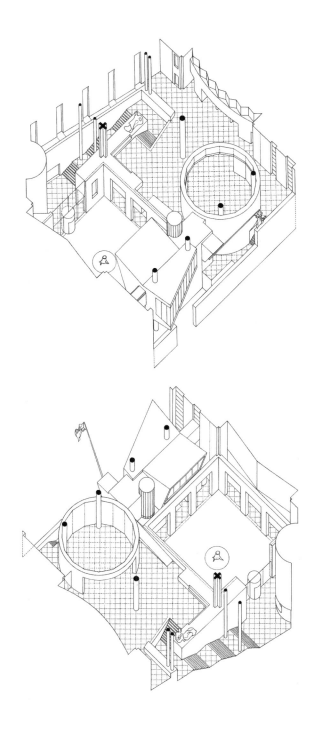

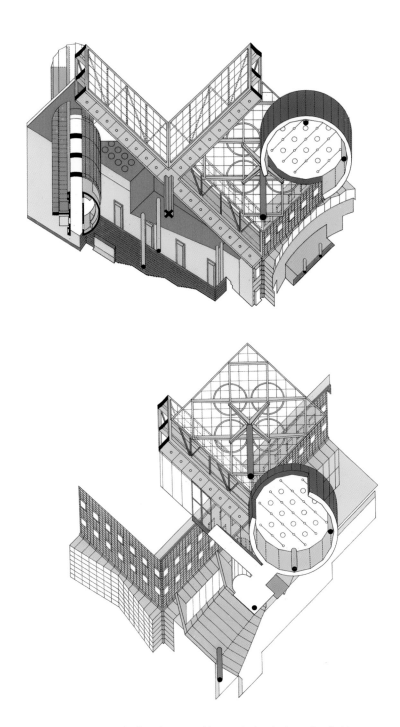

Bird's-eye axonometric views of the public promenade into and around ground and first floors

Worm's-eye axonometric views of staff circulation around the upper levels and colour studies of public spaces

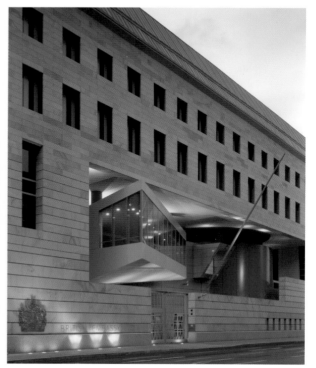

Wilhelmstrasse facade

Entrance court

Information centre

Entrance gate

Reception desk and grand stair to the wintergarden

Wintergarden servery and staff cafeteria

Staff circulation around the upper levels of wintergarden

Grand stair and wintergarden

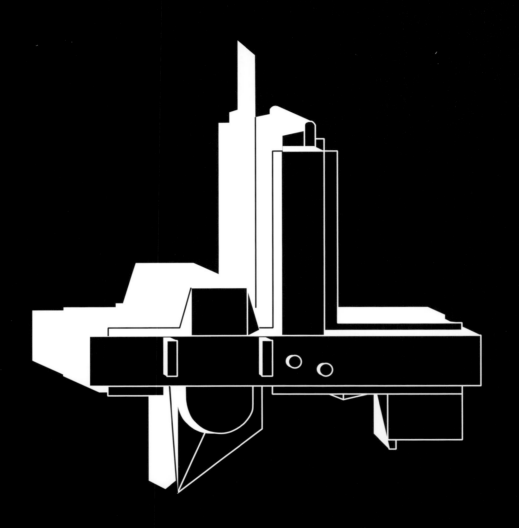

EDUCATION

Context plan

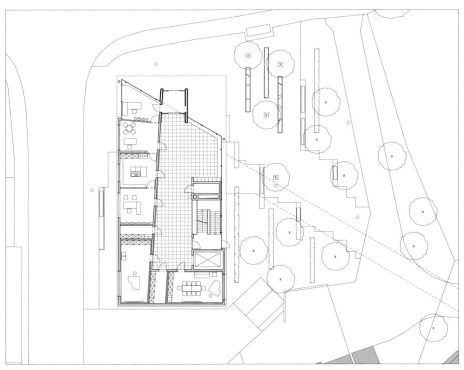

Ground floor plan with entrance and garden

MUSIC SCHOOL ADDITION
TROSSINGEN, GERMANY, 2003–2007
Wilford Schupp Architekten

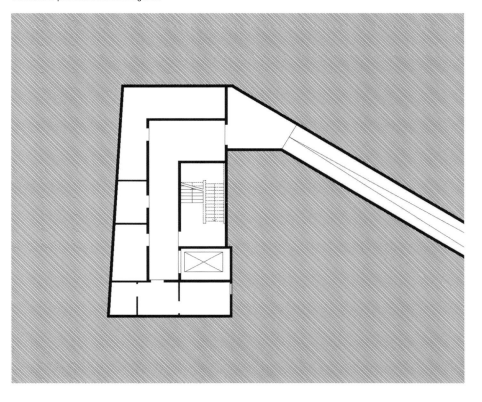

Located in a new public garden and respecting the scale of its surroundings in the centre of the music town of Trossingen, this modest building provides additional rehearsal rooms and offices for Orchestral Music, Ancient Music, Rhythm and Events Departments of the existing Music School. It is a compact, three-storey stand-alone building with an underground connection to the main building.

The entrance is marked by a coloured metal portal and to express their public functions, the front facade of the foyer and events office within it is fully glazed and set at an angle to the main street frontage. This gestures towards the interior of the building and allows a visual connection with the existing Music School complex beyond.

Passers-by can glimpse activities inside the building through the large picture windows to the studios of the Rhythm Department and circulation corridors on the upper floors. Contrasting colours are used to provide individual identities for the studios, rehearsal rooms, stairs and circulation corridors.

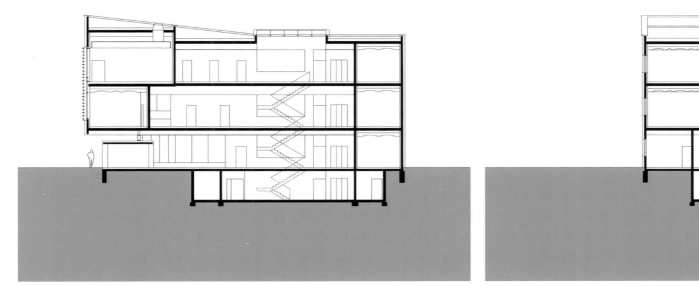

Longitudinal section through the circulation spine

Cross-section through the staircase

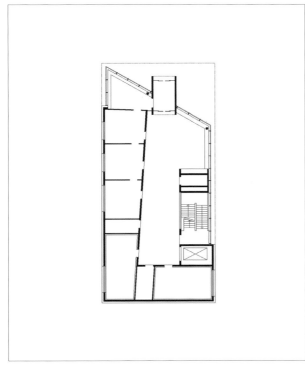

Ground floor plan

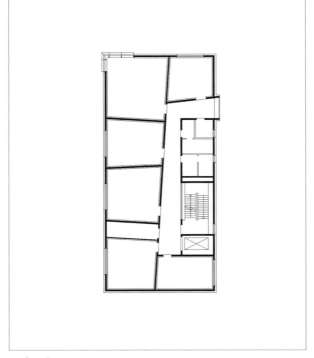

First floor plan

Second floor plan

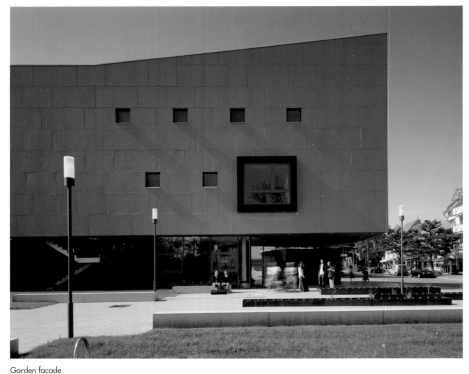

Garden facade

Entrance facade

Circulation spaces

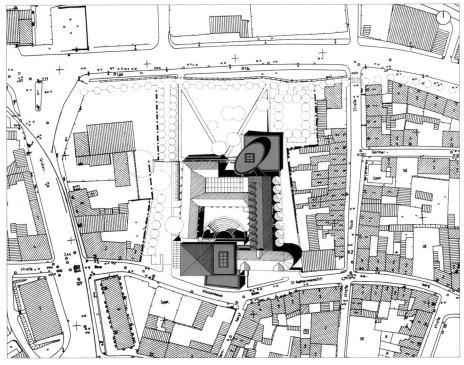

Context plan

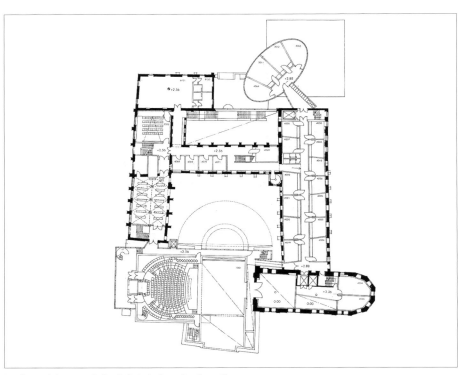

First floor with the concert hall and elliptical rehearsal studio pavilion

MUSIC AND THEATRE SCHOOL
ROSTOCK, GERMANY, 1997

Wilford Schupp Architekten (formerly Michael Wilford & Partners, London and Stuttgart)

The Music and Theatre School respects and reinstates the original ground plan and footprint of the former monastery in which is to be constructed. The design reflects the spirit of the monastery whilst using contemporary architectural elements. Wherever possible use has been made of the historic structures and the modern interventions complement their scale and proportion with a clear distinction made between old and new.

The concert hall re-establishes the former volume of the monastic church and is the focus of the building. It is located within the ruined church walls, leaving them exposed and freestanding. The auditorium has a generous foyer which also provides access by lift and stair to the organ/chamber room located in the unique setting of the monastic double-vaulted Refektorium above. The library is in newly constructed accommodation on the upper floors of the eastern wing and is a double-height space with a main floor and upper gallery for quiet reading areas and listening booths. The new elliptical pavilion has a square base and houses teaching, recording and practice rooms.

The three principal open spaces in the scheme, sequenced on a north/south central axis are: the cloistered courtyard with amphitheatre for outdoor theatrical and musical performances; the glass-covered Wintergarden/cafeteria at the heart of the project; and the monastery garden, a semi-public outdoor room where students and staff can relax.

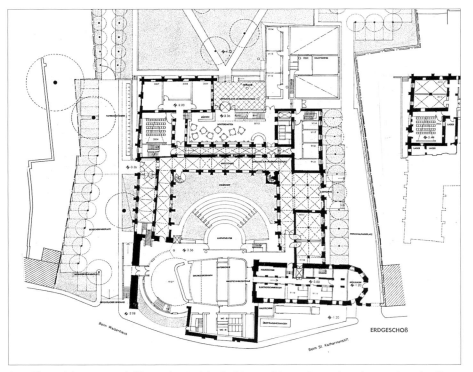

Ground floor with the new concert hall foyer in the ruined church, cloister amphitheatre wintergarden and square rehearsal pavilion

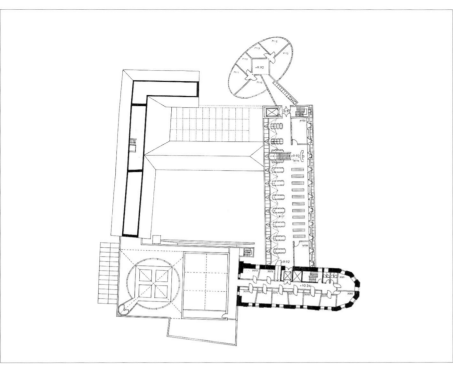

Upper floor plan showing the roof level library addition and elliptical teaching pavilion

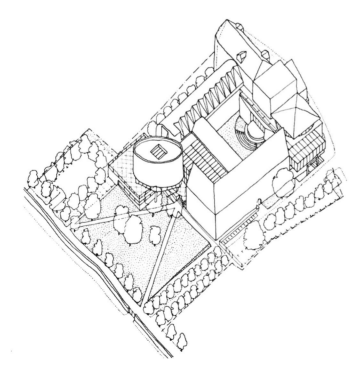

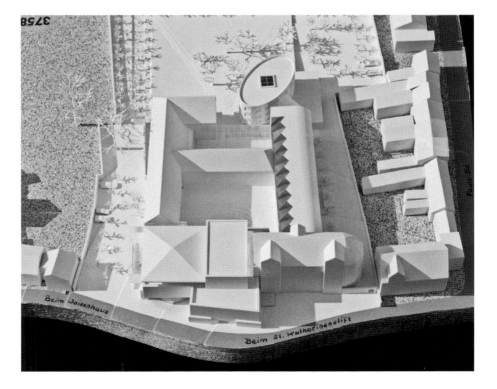

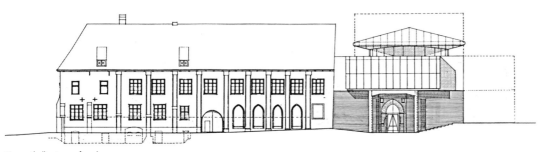

Concert hall entrance facade

Concert hall street facade

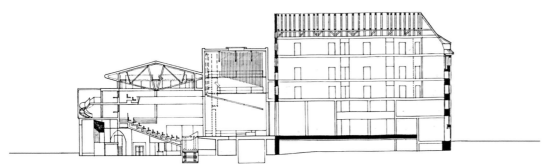

Longitudinal section through the concert hall

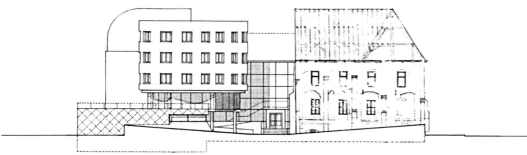

Teaching/rehearsal pavilion facade

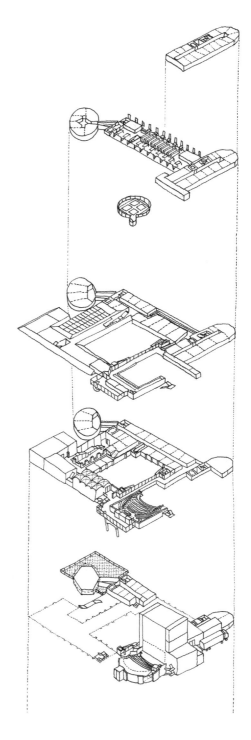

Exploded isometric of the constituent elements of the project

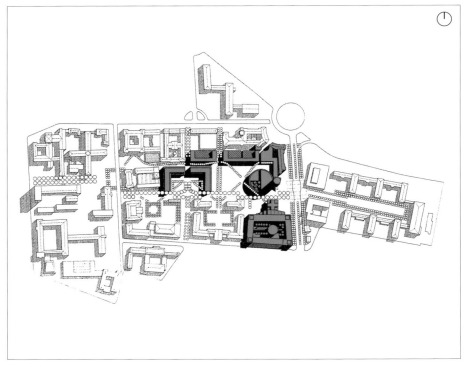

Context plan

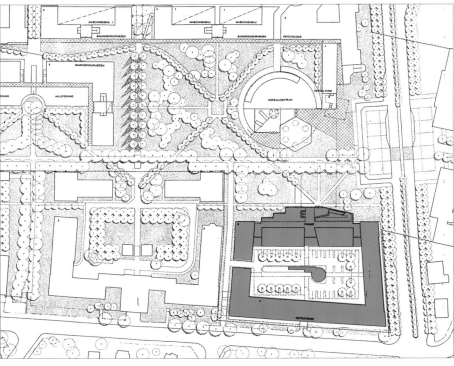

Chemistry department site plan

DRESDEN TECHNICAL UNIVERSITY EXPANSION
DRESDEN, GERMANY, 1994

Michael Wilford & Partners

The campus, situated on the southern edge of the city, lacks a clear organisation and focus, sub-divided by a major street at the intersection of four urban grid patterns. It is without a clear primary entrance. Most buildings are haphazardly arranged and face out of the campus, turning their backs on its centre. In our proposal the separate halves of the campus are united by a new entrance plaza and major pedestrian crossing situated on the junction between the major campus cross-axis and the dividing street. The new administration tower and circular Lecture Theatre cluster enclose one edge of the plaza and signal the presence of the campus on the city skyline. A new central quadrangle establishes a focus to the campus.

The new Chemistry Department is axially organised to face both the central quadrangle and entrance plaza. The cubic pavilion contains the primary Chemistry lecture theatre, library and Dean's office with laboratories accommodated in linear buildings enclosing the rectangular court. Department offices are grouped together in the central drum to encourage close communication between disciplines and linked through the court by bridges to the laboratories.

Other new faculty buildings establish a series of interlocking landscaped courtyard gardens which develop existing minor axes into an all-embracing spatial system enclosing the central quadrangle and focused towards the entrance plaza. New geometric planting reinforces the existing avenues and together with informal tree clusters, establishes an individual character for each faculty garden.

The new faculties respect the scale and materials of the existing buildings with the tower and lecture theatre cluster, surfaced in metal and glass to form 'jewels' in the composition.

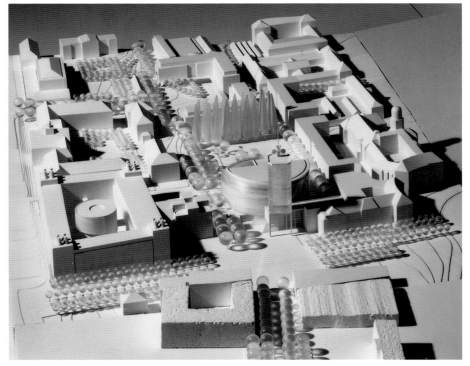

Model view of entrance plaza from the east

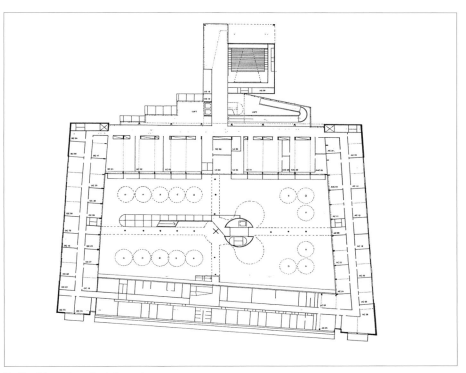

First floor laboratories and main lecture theatre

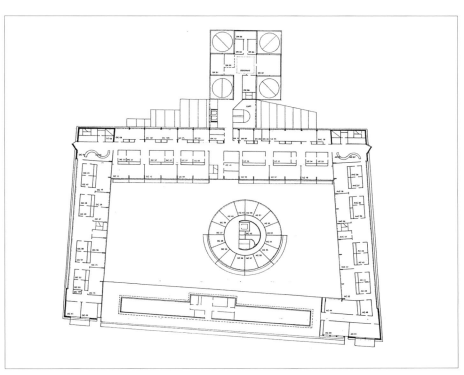

Third, fourth and fifth floor laboratories in the wings and department offices in the central drum

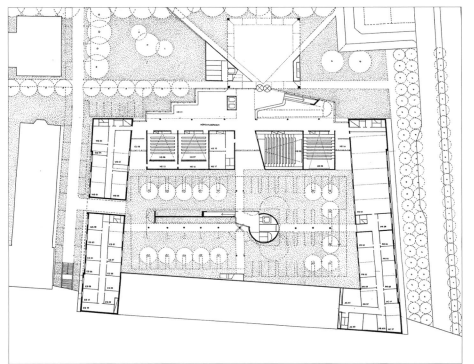

Ground floor entrance foyer, courtyard plan lecture theatres

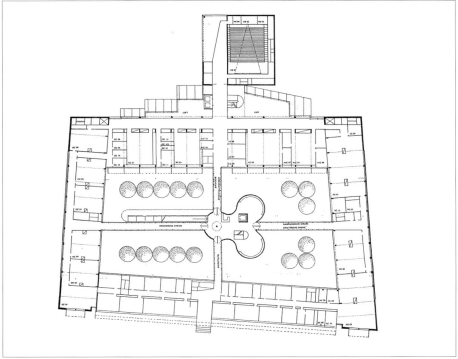

Second floor laboratories and main lecture theatre

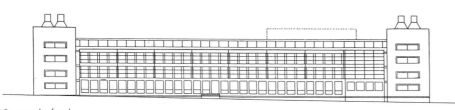

Campus edge facade

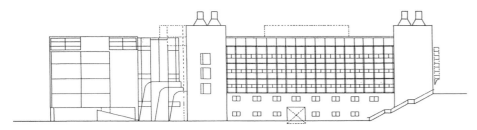

Internal campus facade

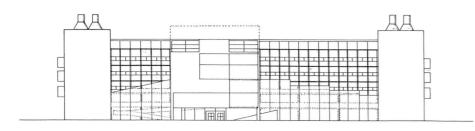

Central quadrangle facade

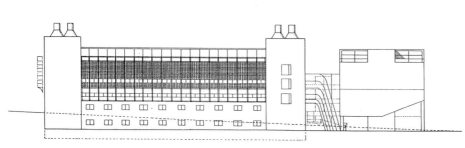

Major street facade at entrance plaza

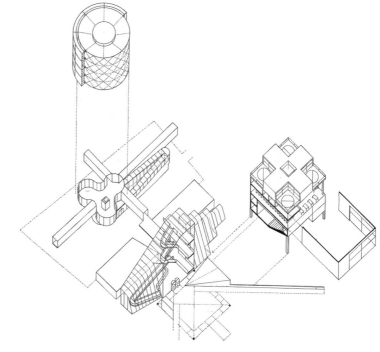

Bird's-eye axonometric views of the chemistry department entrance, main lecture theatre and office drum

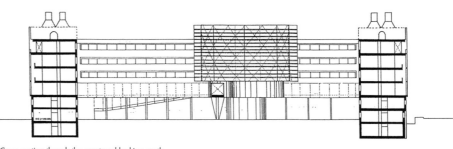

Cross-section though the courtyard looking south

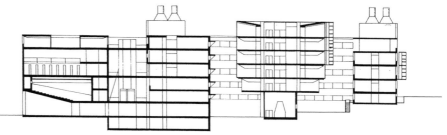

Cross-section through the courtyard looking east

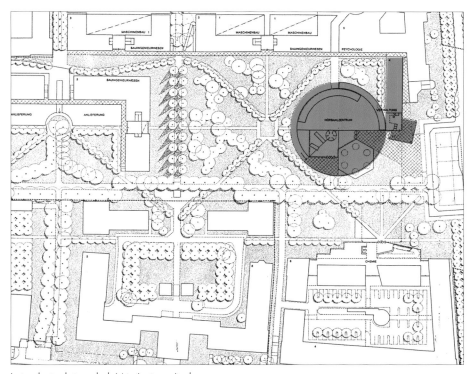

Lecture theatre cluster and administration tower site plan

Entrance plaza facade with the lecture theatre cluster and administration tower in the centre and the chemistry department left

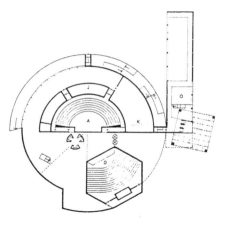

Lower ground floor lecture theatres and administration tower entrances

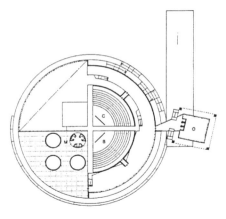

Second floor large lecture theatres

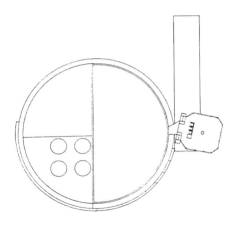

Typical administration tower floor

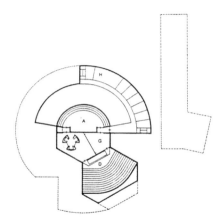

Basement plan

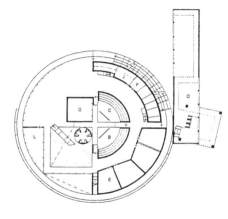

First floor, lecture theatres foyer and seminar rooms

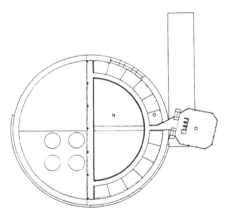

Level four and five meeting rooms

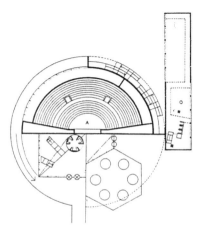

Upper ground floor lecture theatres entrance

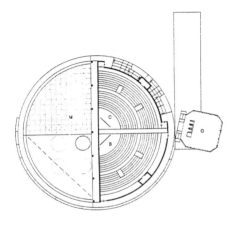

Third floor large lecture theatres

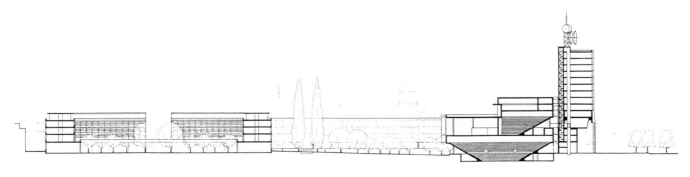

Cross-section looking north

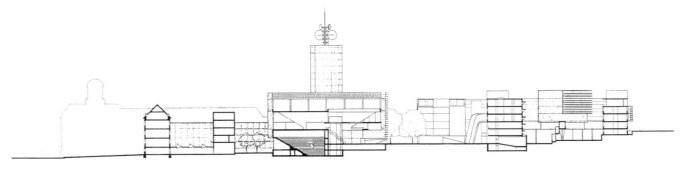

Cross-section looking east

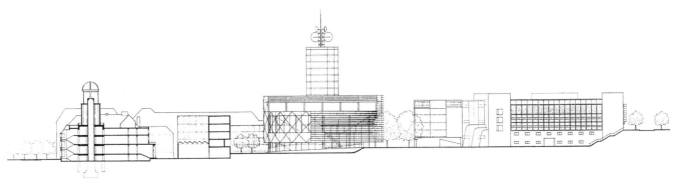

Central quadrangle facade

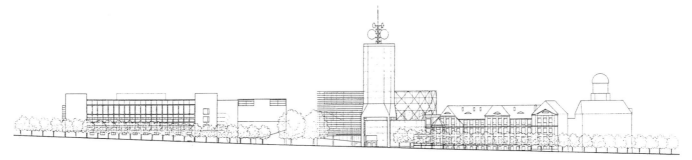

Entrance plaza facade

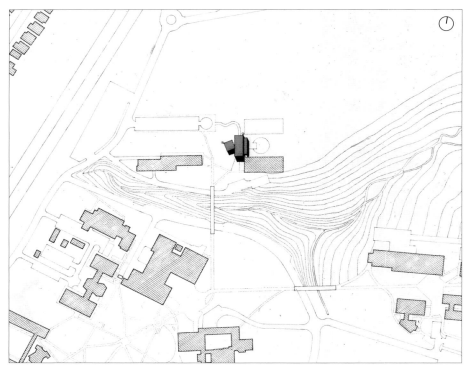

Context plan

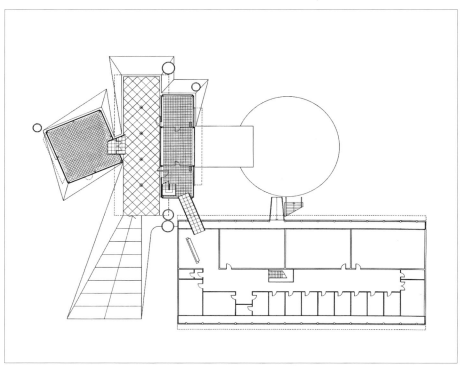

Ground floor plan of the concourse, studio and seminar spaces and upper level of the existing building

SCHOOL OF ARCHITECTURE ADDITION, NEWCASTLE UNIVERSITY
NEWCASTLE, NSW, AUSTRALIA, 1990–1992
Michael Wilford Architects

The school is situated outside the main core of the campus in an attractive arcadian setting amongst mature eucalyptus trees, but visitors had difficulty in identifying the original school building and locating the entrance.

This modest first phase of expansion comprising a large studio, seminar room, classroom and faculty offices housed in two pavilions situated either side of a covered concourse linked to the upper floor of the two-storey existing building by an enclosed bridge. The concourse provides a highly visible and dramatic new entrance to the school as well as a protected outdoor social space.

The square studio comprises the largest pavilion, diagonally related to the concourse and is sized for later use as a lecture theatre when further studio accommodation is built. The linear pavilion accommodates the new entrance, classroom and seminar spaces at concourse level with faculty offices on a second level above. Large sliding doors and internal folding walls enable the lower level to be opened to both the concourse and courtyard for exhibitions and receptions. The pavilions and concourse canopy roof are of steel framed construction, surfaced externally with diagonally ribbed metal panels.

The design was developed with students within the school as a studio-based project under Michael Wilford's guidance as Visiting Fellow.

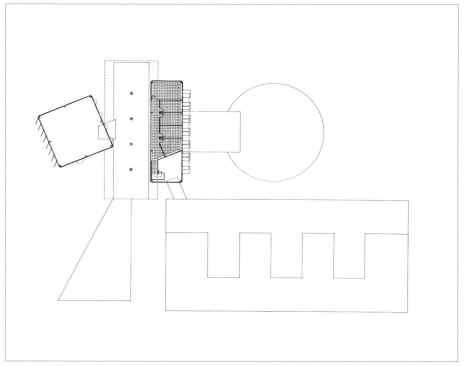

First floor faculty offices plan

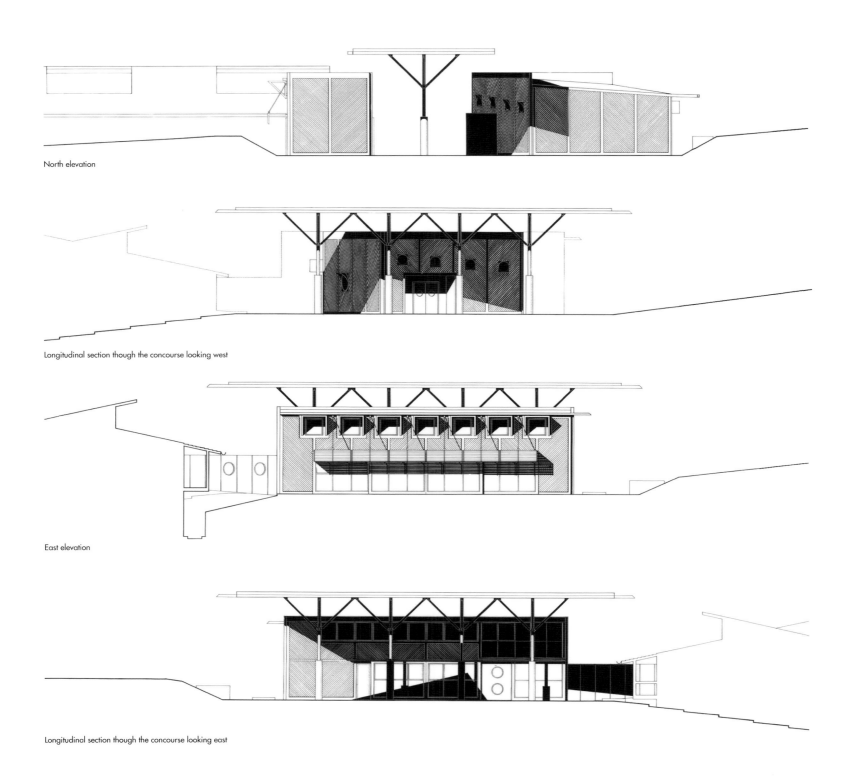

North elevation

Longitudinal section though the concourse looking west

East elevation

Longitudinal section though the concourse looking east

Entrance from north and concourse

East elevation

Entrance from the south and concourse

Seminar rooms

Entrance from the south

Concourse

Entrance from the north

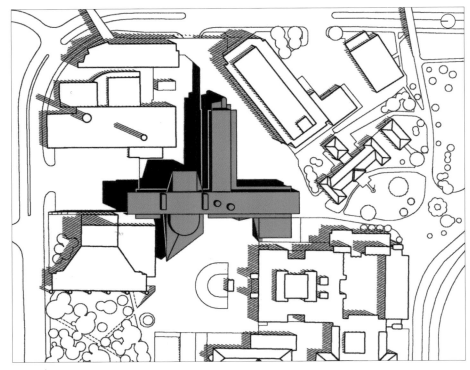

Context plan

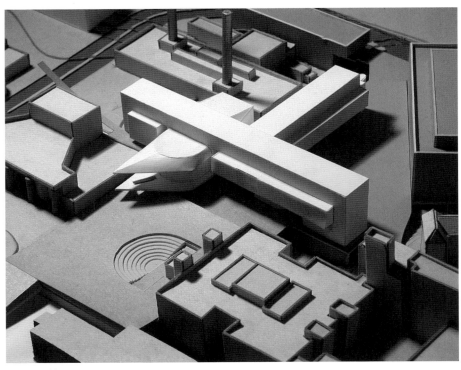

Concept model

THEATER, DRAMA AND UNDERGRADUATE SCIENCE CENTER, UNIVERSITY OF MICHIGAN
ANN ARBOR, USA, 2001–2002

Michael Wilford Architects & MUMA in association with The Smith Group Detroit

Sandwiched between three parking structures, the Power Center Theater and the University power plant, the site is at the interface between the original Ann Arbor urban Campus and greenfield expansion to the east. The parking structures fill a natural hollow in the terrain, providing a horizontal decked extension of the main Campus ground plane. The Center comprises a 450-seat Courtyard Theater, a 175-seat Studio Theater with rehearsal spaces, acting studios, dressing rooms and workshops. The Drama and Science Centers are combined into a T-shaped building providing a visual termination to the Ann Arbor arts axis. It also forms a backdrop to a new public plaza situated over one of the existing parking structure and a gateway between the Arts and Science quarters of the Campus. Pedestrian cross-routes integrate the plaza with surrounding Campus areas.

Situated above a service route and utility lines, the theatre form is an 'air rights' building with limited locations for structural support and service access. The glazed theatre lobby is entered either directly from the plaza or the parking below and the audience rise by escalator to the main foyer above, which provides views over the plaza and is overlooked by balconies serving the upper tiers of the Courtyard Theater. Both theatres are contained within a cantilevered three-dimensional form supported clear of the existing parking structures, trucks and utility routes below.

The Science Center is accommodated in the remainder of the T. The entrance, together with the lecture theatres, resource centre, cafe, lounge and exhibition area is situated at plaza level. Science laboratories and offices are located on the upper levels of the building. The leg of the T, together with the adjacent science building also encloses a new triangular garden.

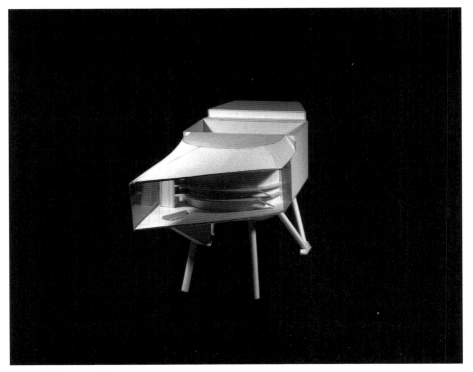

Study model of the elevated theatres

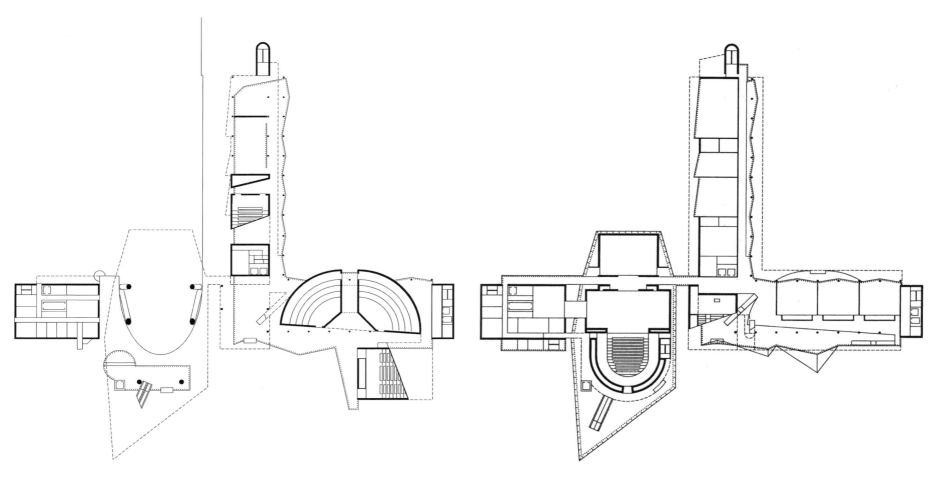

Plaza level entrances and science lecture theatre plan

Elevated theatre auditorium, foyer and support spaces and science laboratories

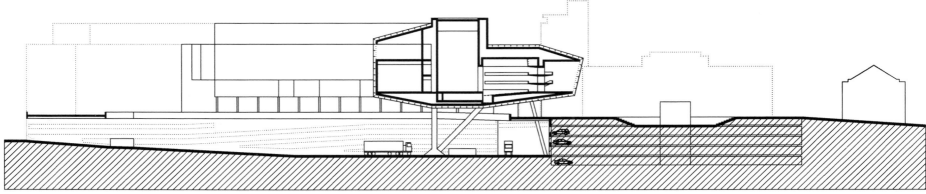

Longitudinal section through the elevated theatres and pre-existing parking structures

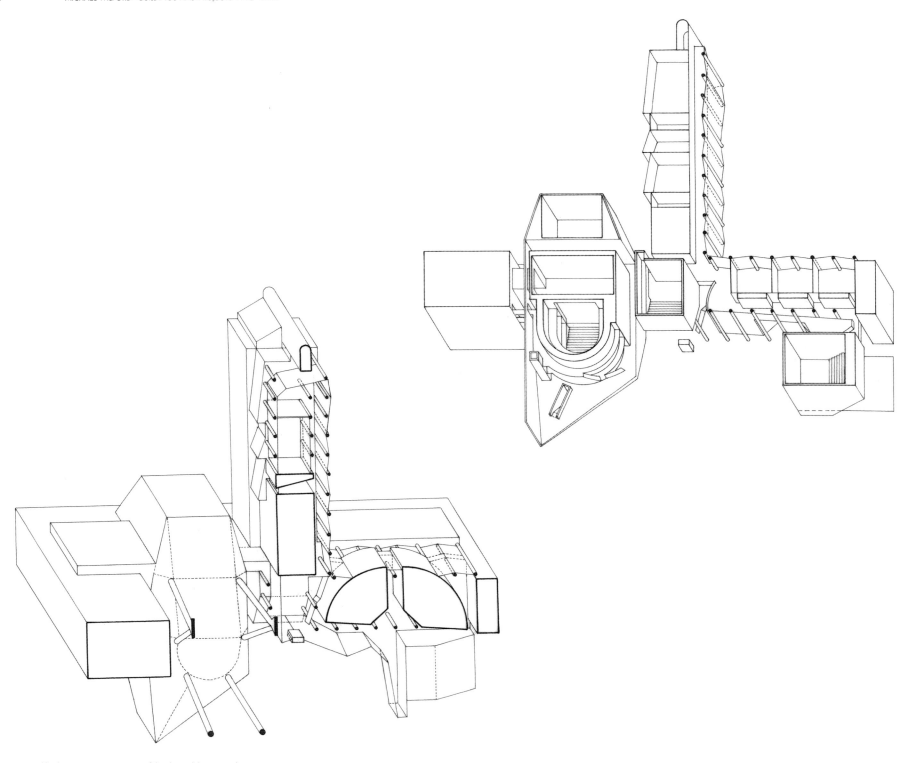

Worm's-eye and bird's-eye axonometric views of the elevated theatres and science wings

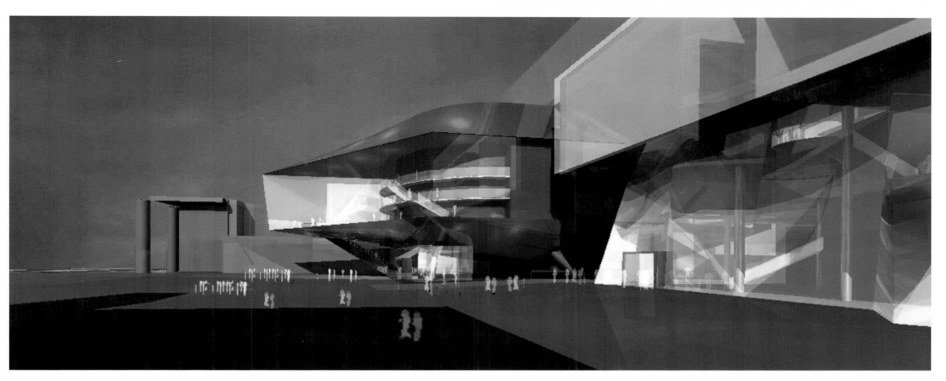

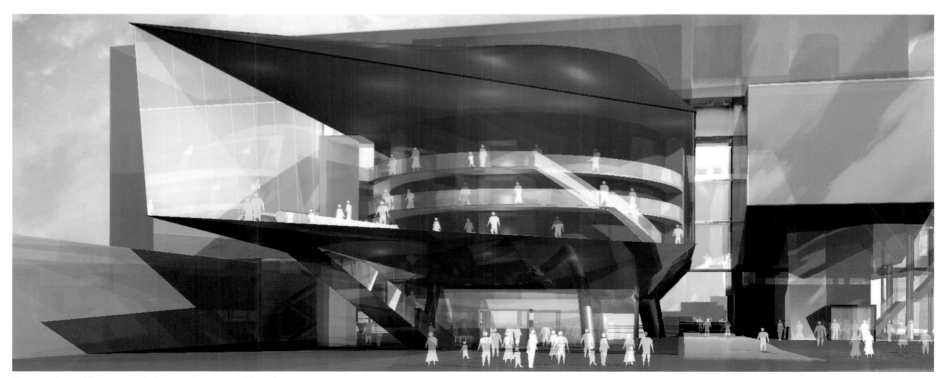

Concept renderings of the entrance to the theatres, science centre and theatre foyer

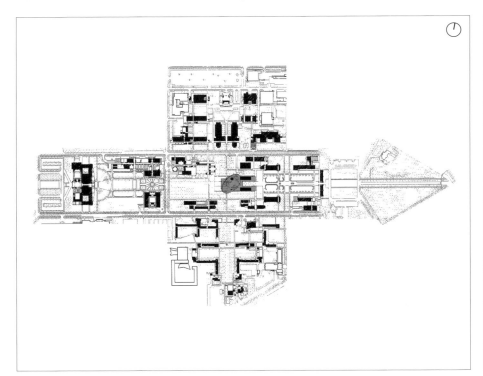

Campus context plan

Concept massing model in context

CAMPUS LIBRARY RICE UNIVERSITY
HOUSTON, USA, 2001–2002

Michael Wilford Architects and MUMA in association with Kendal Heaton Houston

The project presented an opportunity to restore the centre of the university campus to a condition closer to the original Cram, Goodhue and Ferguson Masterplan. The amorphous form of the existing library contravenes the spatial sequence of the Masterplan and disrupts the physical layout of the campus. The new library recovers the spirit of Cram's vision and satisfies the programmatic demands of a twenty-first century university library.

The new building organisation provides opportunities for students and faculty to mix, socialise and study within an intellectual commons. It comprises two parallel linear wings, reflecting the traditional Rice building typology, connected at their western end by a vertical assembly of spaces defined by the immersion concourse and reading room. Within the expanding spatial sequence envisaged by Cram, the building simultaneously offers transparency and spatial flow together with formal closure of the Academic Court. The eastern end of the library is formally rigorous in response to the Academic Court. The smaller courtyard contained between the wings leads to the formal east entrance of the library.

The layered, more relaxed western end of the library responds to the informality of the Great Court. A glazed rotated ellipse containing the Immersion Concourse, reconciles the offset of the primary east/west axis from that of the Academic Court generated by the existing library and subsequent buildings. The reading room is situated above the Immersion Concourse, centred on the cross-axis of the campus and is the dominant element of the composition. Readers can look out over the surrounding tree canopy, prompting a sense of place and a fresh perception of the campus. At night the reading room and Immersion Concourse will act as a beacon reinforcing the library's physical and intellectual location at the heart of the University and its 24 hour activity.

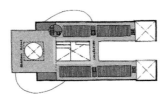

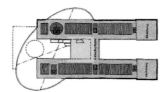

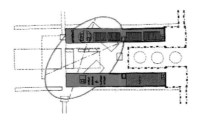

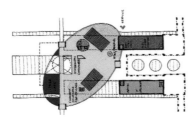

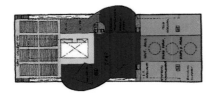

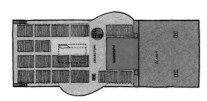

Functional plan stack

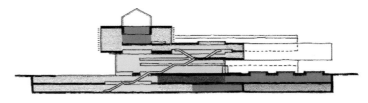

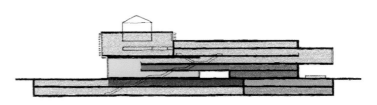

Functional section organisation

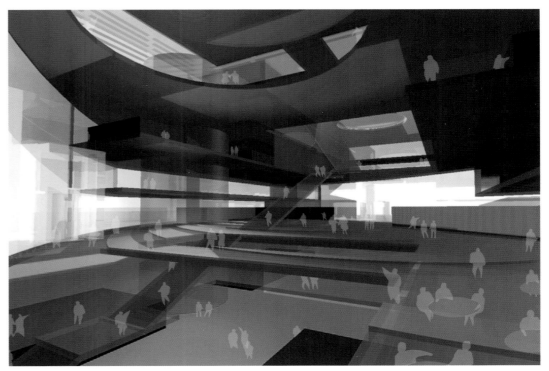

Concept rendering of the immersion concourse

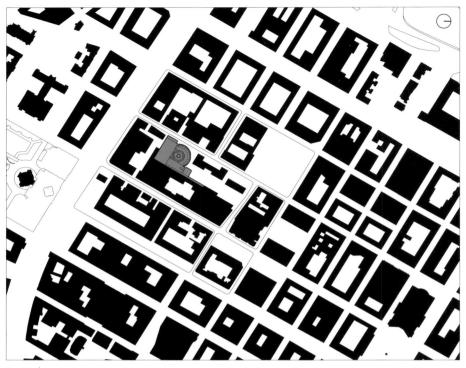

Context plan

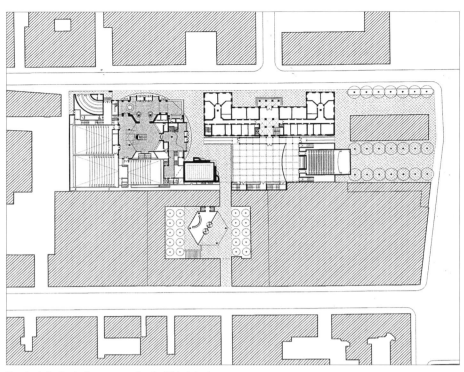

Site plan indicating the future courtyard and mid-block development

MUSIC SCHOOL ADDITION AND CINEMAXX
MANNHEIM, GERMANY, 1995–1999

Wilford Schupp Architekten (formerly Michael Wilford & Partners, London and Stuttgart)

The Music School extension and Cinemaxx are combined into a single building adjacent to the existing Music School within the historic city centre. A circular court at its core unites the three formal elements of the composition—L-shaped Cinemaxx, semi-circular Music School and tower.

An entrance leading to the heart of the new Music School allows entry either from the street or landscaped courtyard behind the existing building. A student cafe, situated at the base of the tower is accessed from the new entrance hall. A grand staircase leads to the Chamber Music and Big Band Rooms on the 'piano nobile' level and to practice studios, seminar rooms and offices on four upper floors.

The tower registers the presence of the school on the city skyline and will form a gateway to a future pedestrian passage through the city block. It contains a stack of three double-height dance studios, topped by a roof terrace for outdoor performance, study and relaxation. Future development of the mid-block courtyard may include a recital hall and small opera theatre.

The Cinemaxx, containing ten cinemas on four levels, is entered directly from the street into a spacious central foyer, lit from a circular court above. A separate restaurant adjacent to the Marienstrasse entrance brings further life to the street and provides an alternative venue to the bars and concessions inside the building. A dramatic staircase climbs through all levels, giving views down to the foyer below.

Although one building, each part is given its own expression through its form and selection of materials and colour.

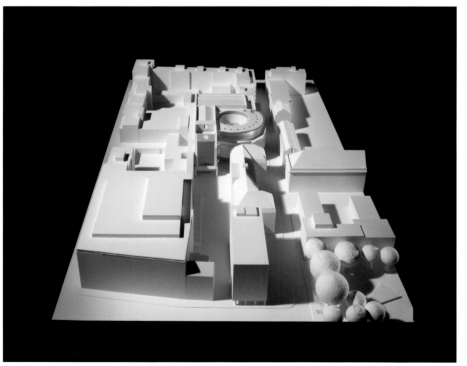

Context model viewed from the north

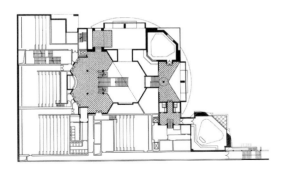

First floor upper foyers

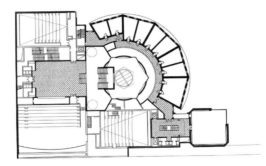

Fourth floor cinemas and music school practice rooms

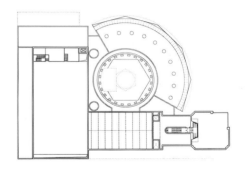

Roof plan

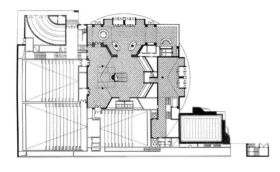

Ground floor cinemaxx and music school entrance foyers

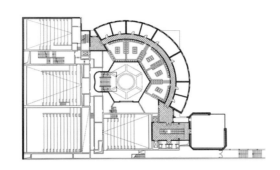

Third floor cinemaxx and music school practice rooms

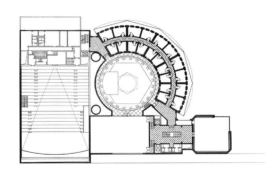

Sixth floor cinemaxx and music school, dance studios and offices

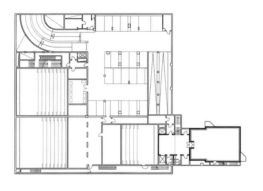

Basement parking and cinema plan

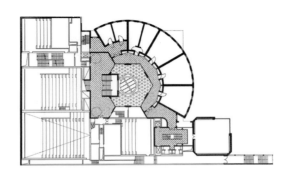

Second floor cinemas and music school rehearsal spaces

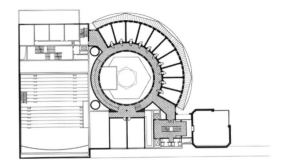

Fifth floor cinemaxx and music school practice rooms

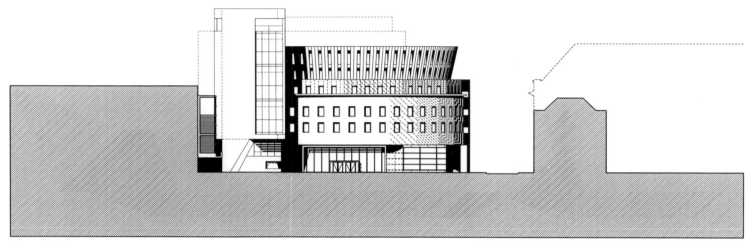

Courtyard facade

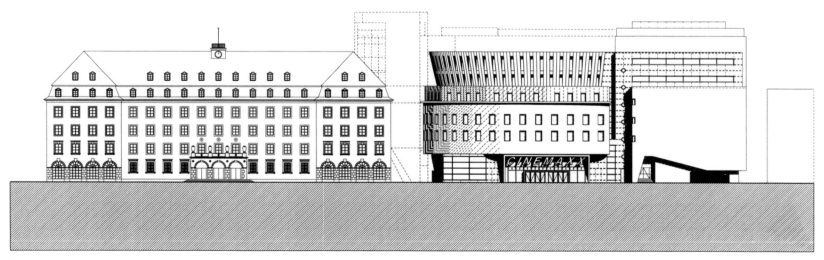

Street facade

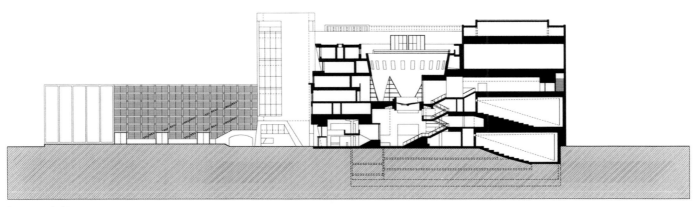

Cross-section looking east

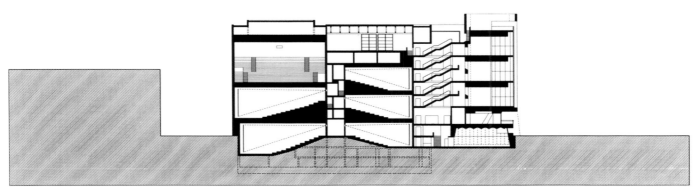

Cross-section looking west

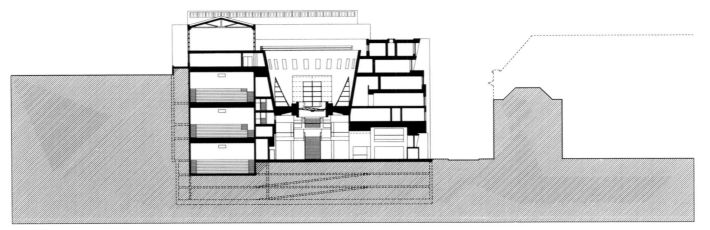

Cross-section looking south

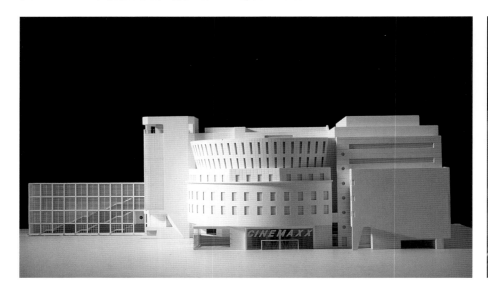

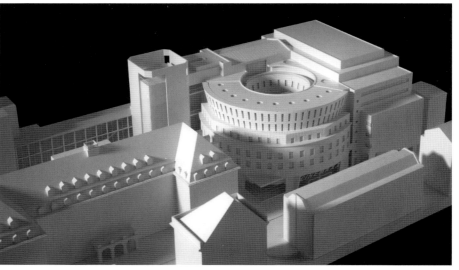

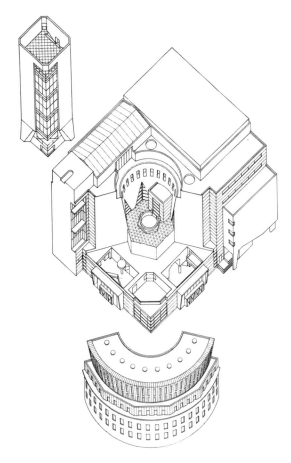

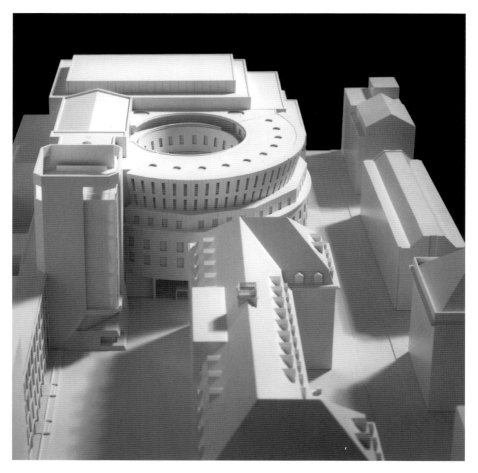

Exploded bird's-eye axonometric view of the primary compositional elements

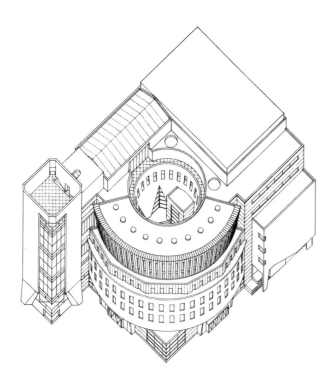

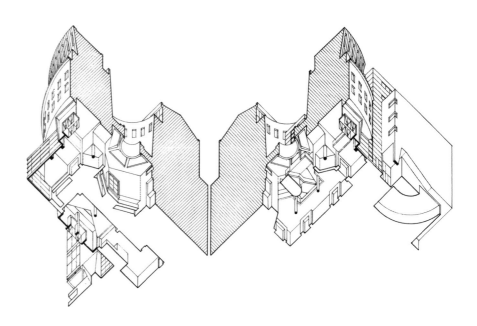

Bird's eye and worm's-eye axonometric views of the street and courtyard facades

Split and hinged axonometric worm's-eye view of the circular central court and music school and cinemaxx entrances

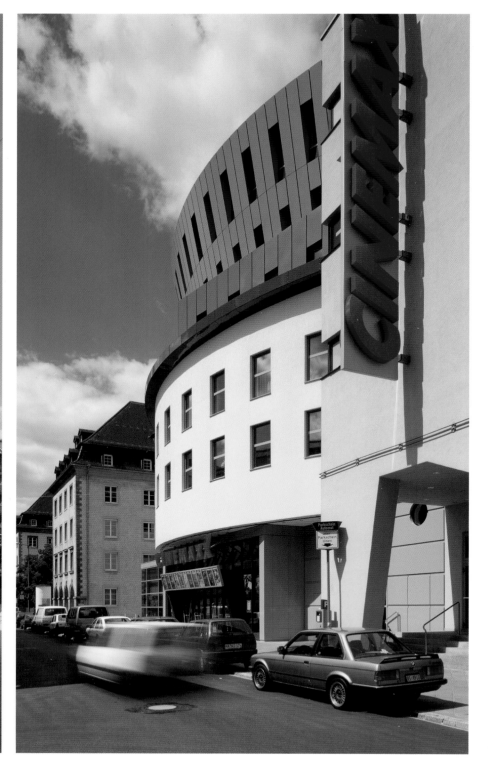

Street facade and cinemaxx entrance

Courtyard facade and music school entrance

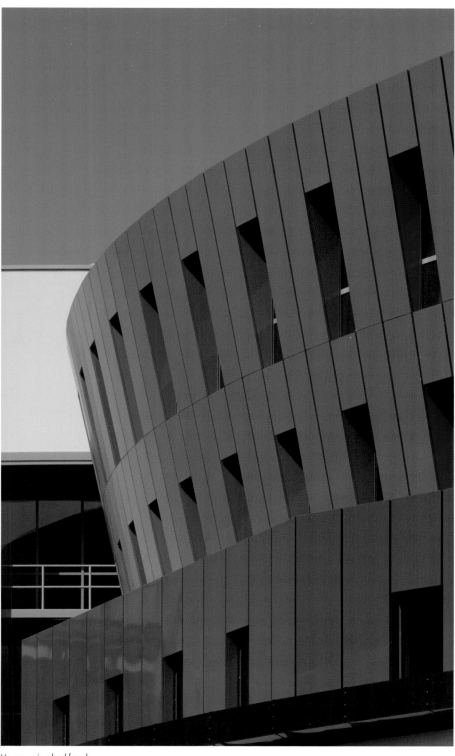

Upper music school facade

Dance studio

Cinemaxx foyer

Big band rehearsal room

Cinemaxx foyer

Music school entrance foyer

Base of the dance studio tower

Circular central court

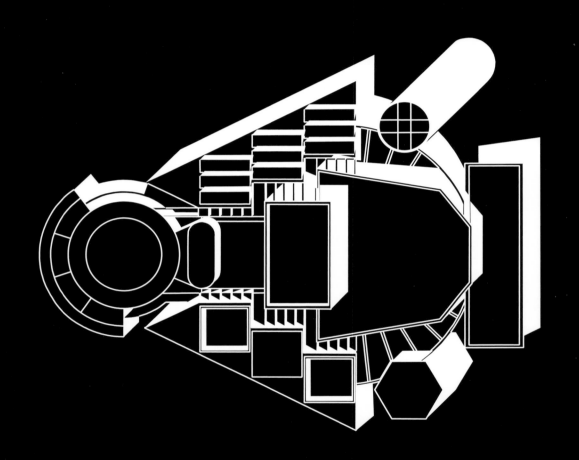

PERFORMANCE

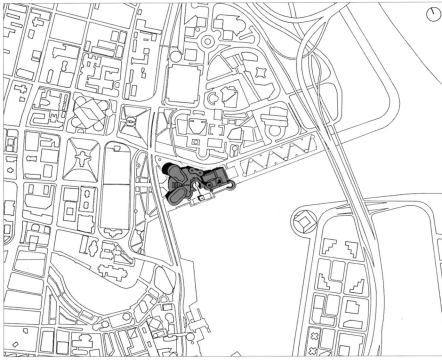

Context plan

THE ESPLANADE, THEATRES ON THE BAY
SINGAPORE, 1992–2002
Michael Wilford & Partners in association with DP Architects Singapore

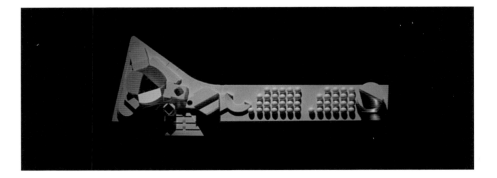

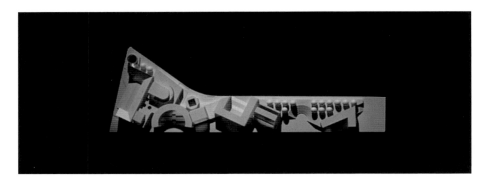

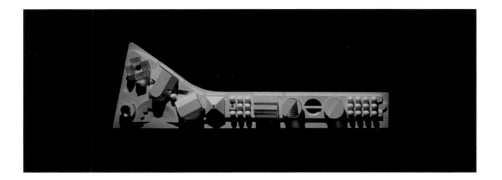

The magnificent Marina Bay location is surrounded by four contrasting urban frontages and overlooked by adjacent hotel and office towers. The unique, tripartite assembly containing a concert hall opera house and four theatres of varying sizes radiates from a central concourse with a clear hierarchy, open and embracing to all approaches and orientations.

The three primary auditoria and their transparent foyers are contained within dramatic three-dimensional forms which echo the traditional soft rounded roof shapes particular to the region and present a memorable roofscape. To exclude direct sunlight and control the internal environment, they are enclosed by an all-enveloping glass and solar shading facade system which changes pattern in response to the varying orientations as well as allowing views in and out.

The concourse is the primary public circulation space of the project. It is connected to the formal entrance hall addressing the Civic Centre, the informal Raffles Avenue entrance and to the Esplanade along the Bay. The dynamic, informal and free flowing foyers and public spaces contrast with the calm ambience of the Auditoria which, in varying scale and character, accommodate the broadest variety of Asian and international performances.

The project is richly landscaped with planting and water to provide spaces for a range of personal experience from private meditation to intensive public interaction.

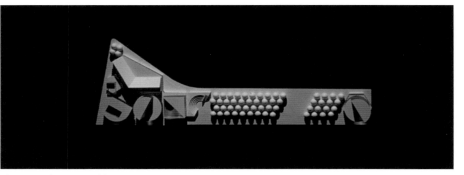

Alternative early concept models

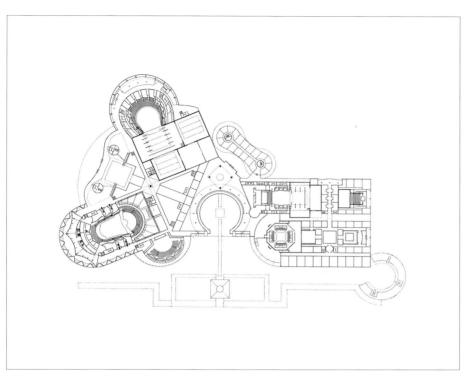

Auditoria first balcony levels and public circulation

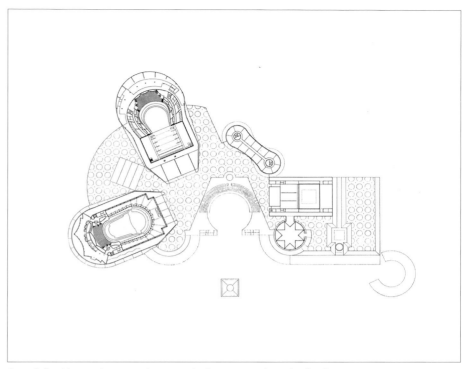

Concert hall and the opera house top audience tiers with administration pavilion and roof gardens

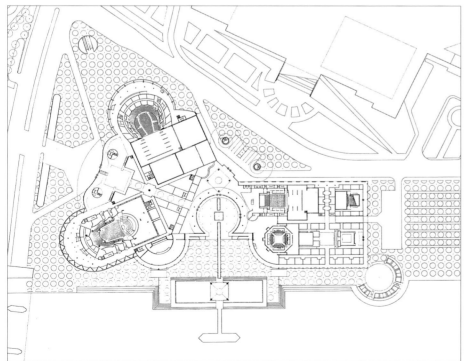

Ground floor level with concert hall, opera house, central circular concourse and four theatres linked by the foyers and public circulation system

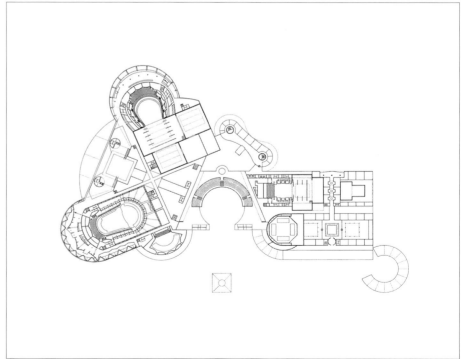

Auditoria second balcony levels and the amphitheatre around the central concourse

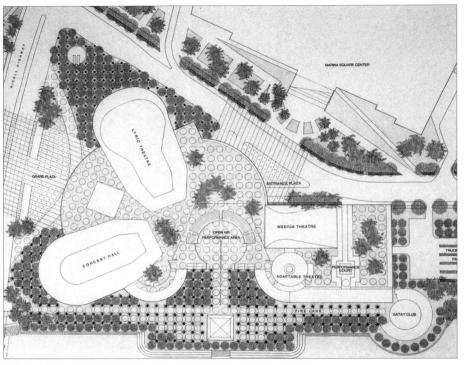

Landscape plan

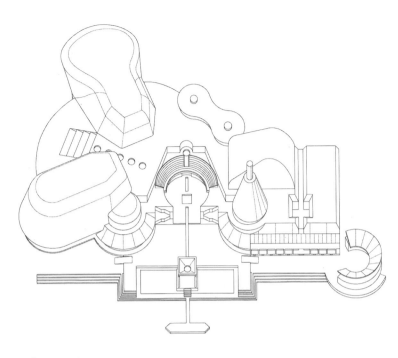

Bird's-eye view above Marina Bay

Photo-montages of massing model in the Marina Bay context

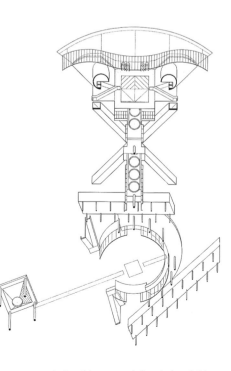

Worm's-eye axonometric view of the promenade from the formal civic centre entrance to the central concourse

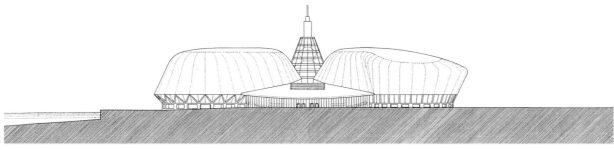

Formal facade to the civic centre

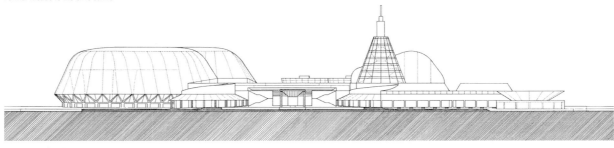

Marina Bay facade

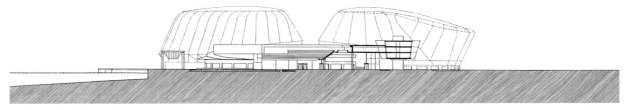

Cross-section through the central concourse and administration pavilion

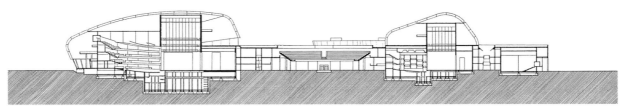

Longitudinal section through the opera house, central concourse, Lyric and studio theatres

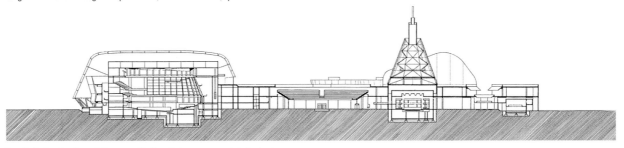

Longitudinal section through the concert hall, central concourse and studio theatre

The relationship to Padang and the downtown financial district

Solar shading facade system responding to the variety of orientations and exposure

Glass and solar shading facade system enclosing the opera house and concert hall foyers

Opera house auditorium

Concert hall interior

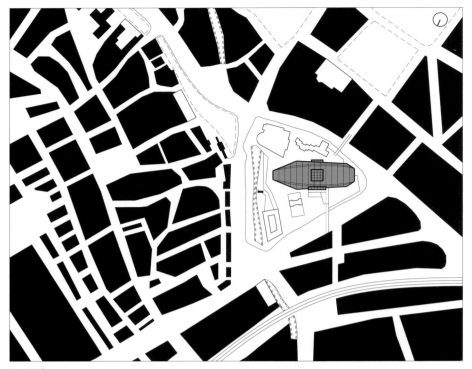

Context plan

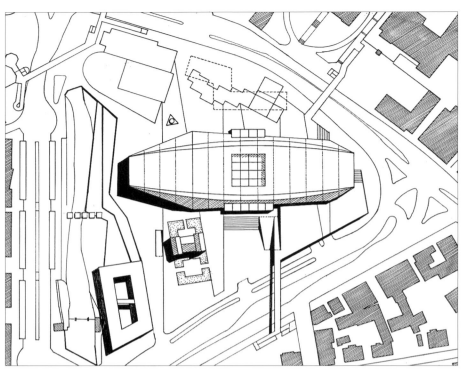

Site plan

CULTURE AND CONGRESS CENTRE
REUTLINGEN, GERMANY, 1999

Wilford Schupp Architekten (formerly Michael Wilford & Partners, London and Stuttgart)

This competition design establishes a social centre for the city at the interface between the Medieval core and more recent residential fringes. The triangular site is bounded on two sides by heavy traffic and on the third by the central bus station. It contains several nondescript buildings which will eventually be replaced but had to be accommodated within our masterplan.

A 1,600-seat Concert Hall and 2,500-seat sub-divisible Conference/Performance Hall are arranged on opposite sides of a top-lit central lobby and exhibition hall in a dynamic linear form focused towards the city centre. An adaptable theatre is located beneath the lobby and office levels above.

To improve pedestrian connections to the city centre the building forms the centrepiece of a new urban park linked by bridges across the surrounding streets to the neighbourhoods beyond. The existing stream is dammed to establish a small lake lined with stepped terraces.

The building's form and orientation establishes it as a prominent landmark—a powerful solitaire, glowing at night and registering its cultural activities at the heart of the city. A cloak of stainless steel, pierced by windows as required, encloses separate geometric figures containing the major spaces.

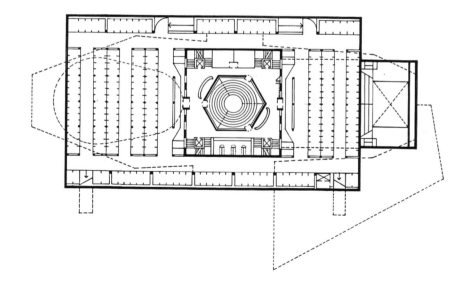

Basement adaptable theatre and parking plan

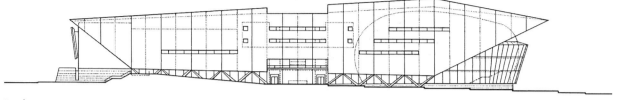

Facade

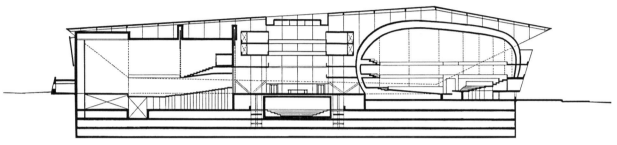

Longitudinal section looking north

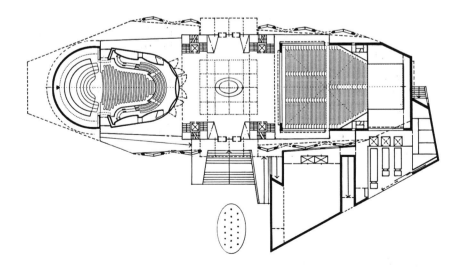

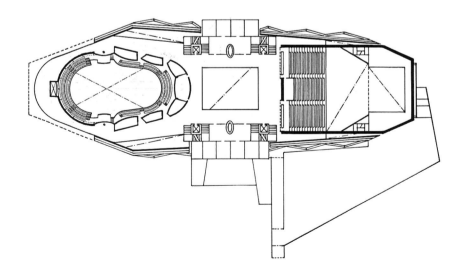

Ground floor foyer, concert hall, central foyer/exhibition and conference/performance hall

Auditoria balcony levels

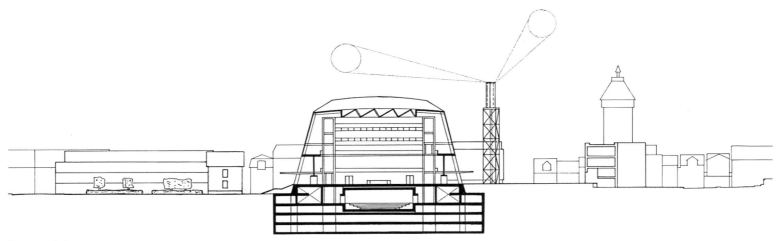

Cross-section looking east

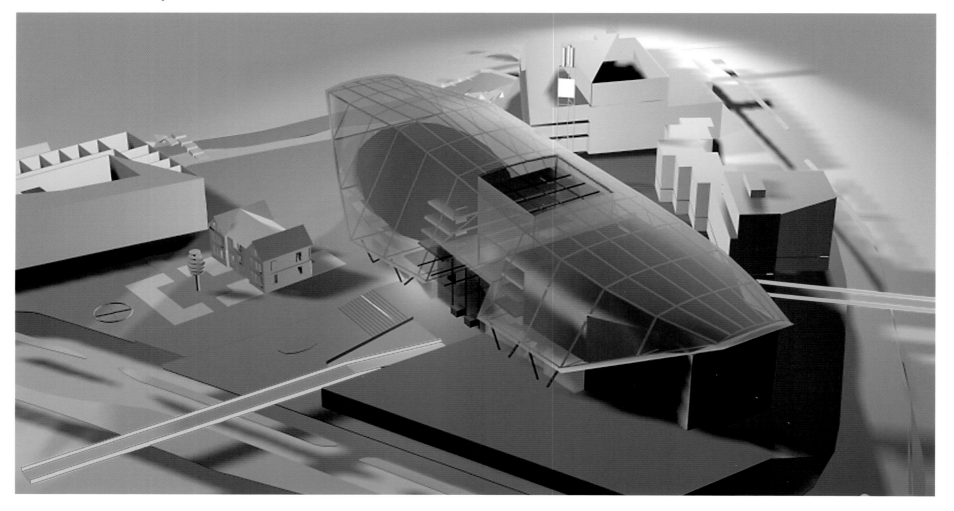

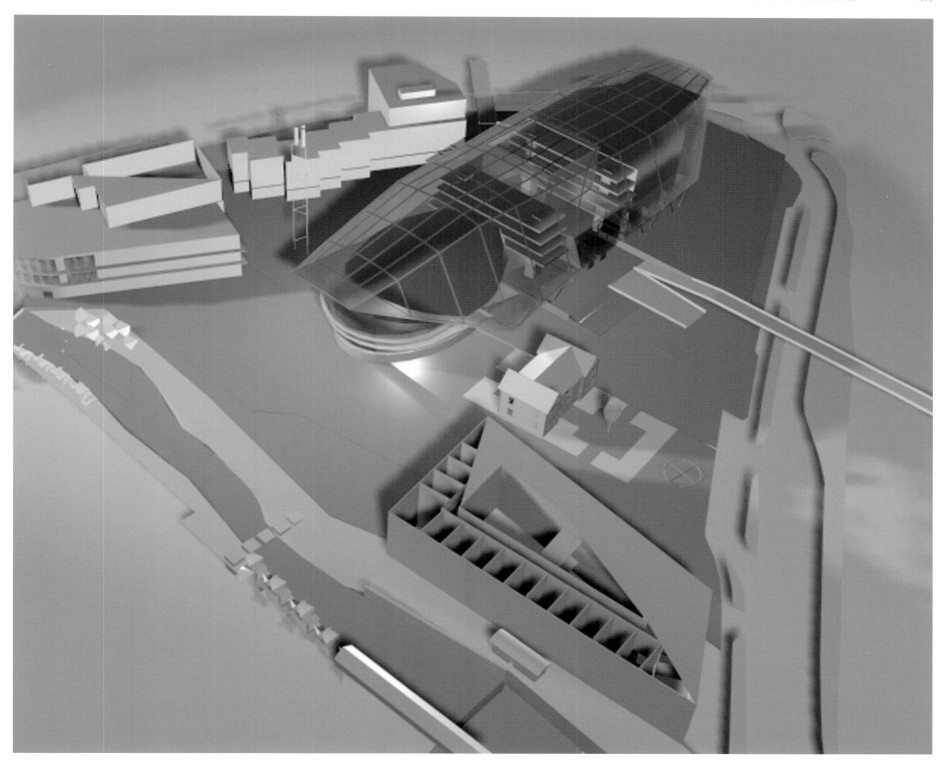

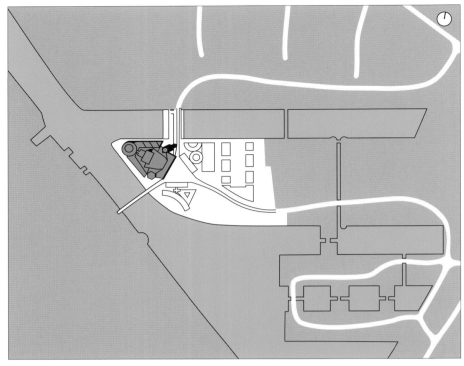

Context plan

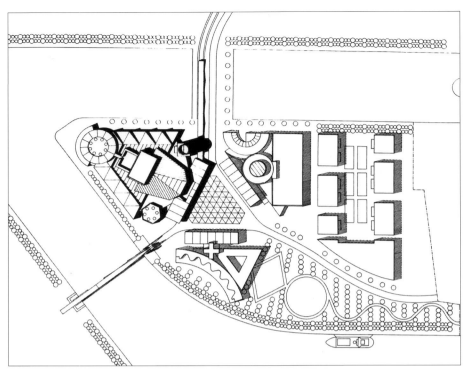

Site plan and masterplan proposal

THE LOWRY
SALFORD, ENGLAND, 1992–2000

Michael Wilford & Partners

The Lowry, combining facilities for the visual and performing arts, provides an exciting, stimulating venue for recreation and education. Bordered by the Manchester Ship Canal and facing a new triangular public plaza, it is the focus of the regeneration of the derelict dockland into Salford Quays. The plaza is a sheltered venue for community activity which, together with the waterside promenades, gathers all primary approaches to the building.

The building contains a 1,650-seat Lyric Theatre, a 400-seat flexible theatre with rehearsal and dressing room facilities, art galleries to display the city's collection of LS Lowry paintings and changing exhibitions together with a Children's Gallery.

The foyer, open to the public throughout the day, surrounds the Lyric Theatre and leads into an internal promenade around the entire building enabling visitors to browse and access all activities throughout the day. Bars, cafes, restaurant and lounges are distributed around the promenade and help to establish the building as a community focus.

The Lyric Theatre forms the heart of the building with stairs and balconies within the foyer providing direct access to three auditorium seating levels. The adaptable theatre on axial alignment with the Lyric Theatre and scene store has a courtyard form to suit proscenium, traverse, thrust and in-the-round performances. The roof-lit Lowry Galleries provide a flexible suite of rooms of varying scale and ambience with views out across the water.

The archive, picture vault and conservation studios are situated in the tower which also registers the presence of the Lowry on the Salford skyline. Rehearsal spaces and dressing rooms are provided adjacent to both theatres beneath the Lowry Galleries and a secure truck dock at the centre of the plan services the scenery and gallery stores.

Salford Quays before substantial re-development

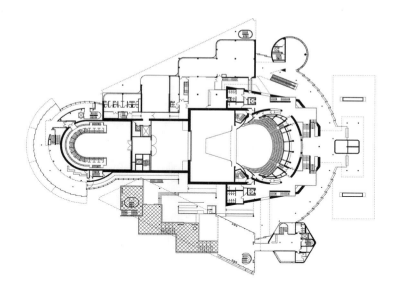

First floor auditoria balconies, south promenade and offices

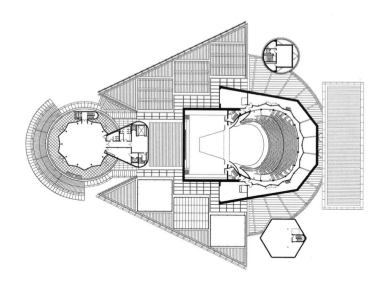

Third floor upper Lyric Theatre balcony and rehearsal studios

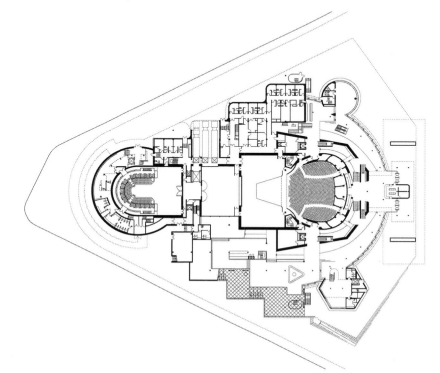

Ground floor entrance foyer, theatre auditoria, south promenade and dressing rooms

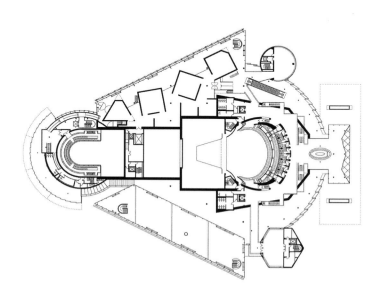

Second floor Lowry and children's galleries, top auditoria balconies and north promenade

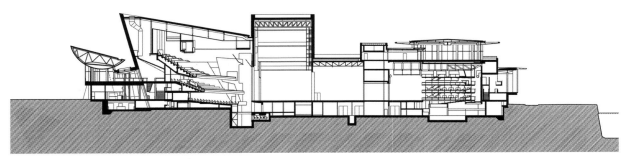

Longitudinal section through the theatres looking southwest

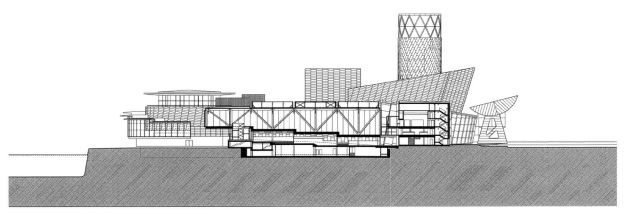

Longitudinal section through the children's gallery looking northeast

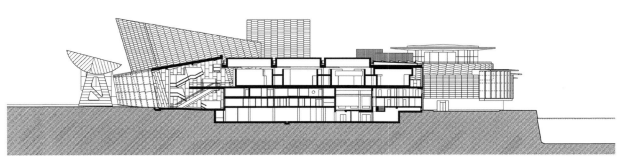

Longitudinal section through the Lowry galleries looking southeast

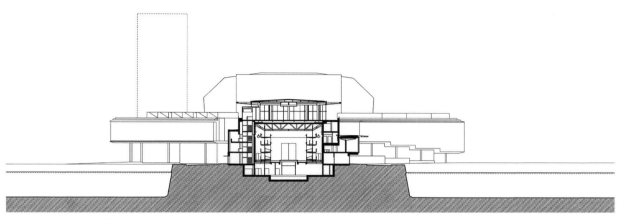

Cross-section through the flexible theatre looking east

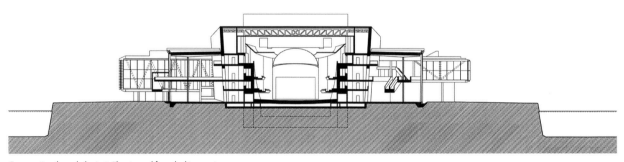

Cross-section through the Lyric Theatre and foyer looking west

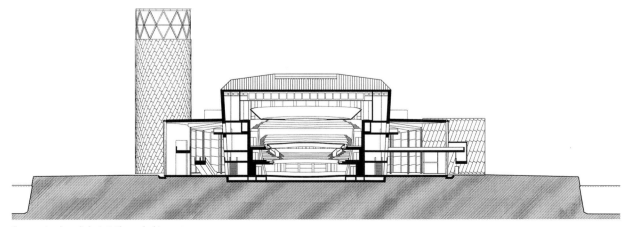

Cross-section through the Lyric Theatre looking east

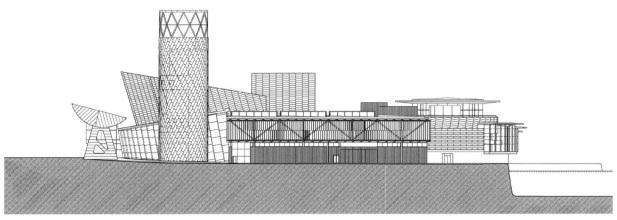

North facade

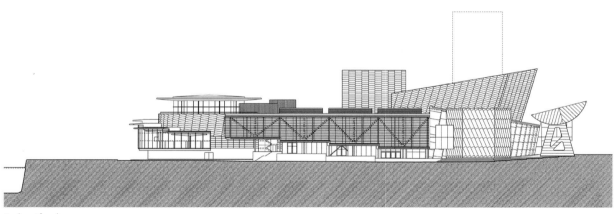

Southwest facade

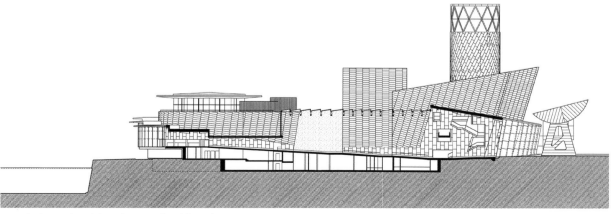

Longitudinal section through the south promenade and theatre foyers

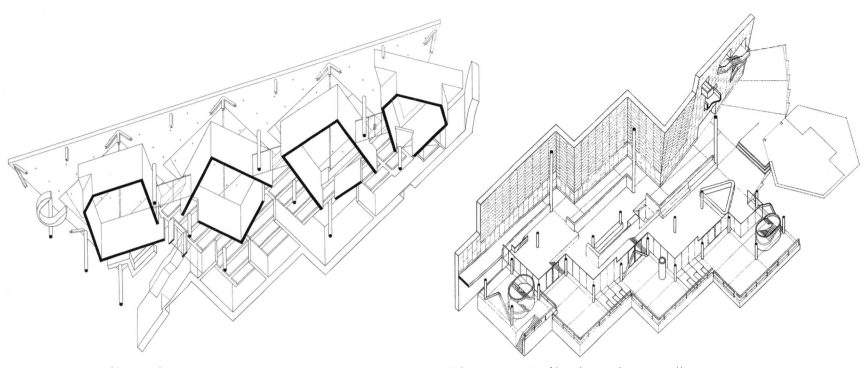

Worm's-eye axonometric view of the Lowry galleries

Bird's-eye axonometric view of the south promenade, restaurant and bar

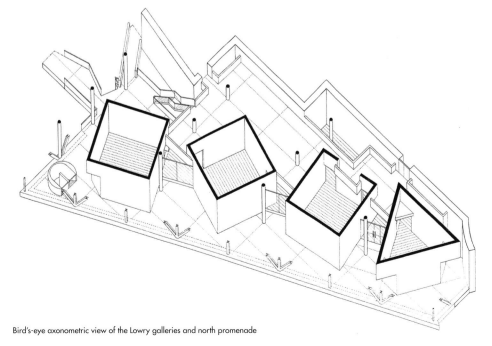

Bird's-eye axonometric view of the Lowry galleries and north promenade

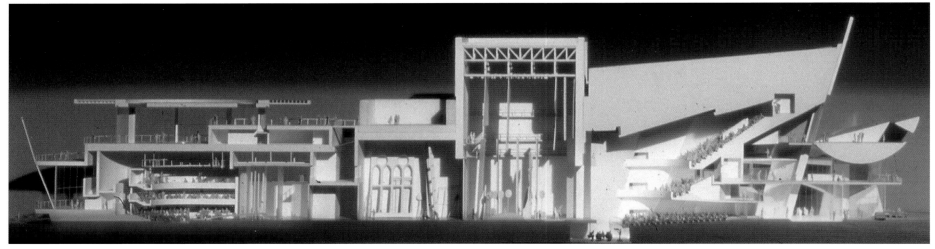

Longitudinal section model through the theatre foyers, auditoria, stages and central scenery store

Model view from the northwest

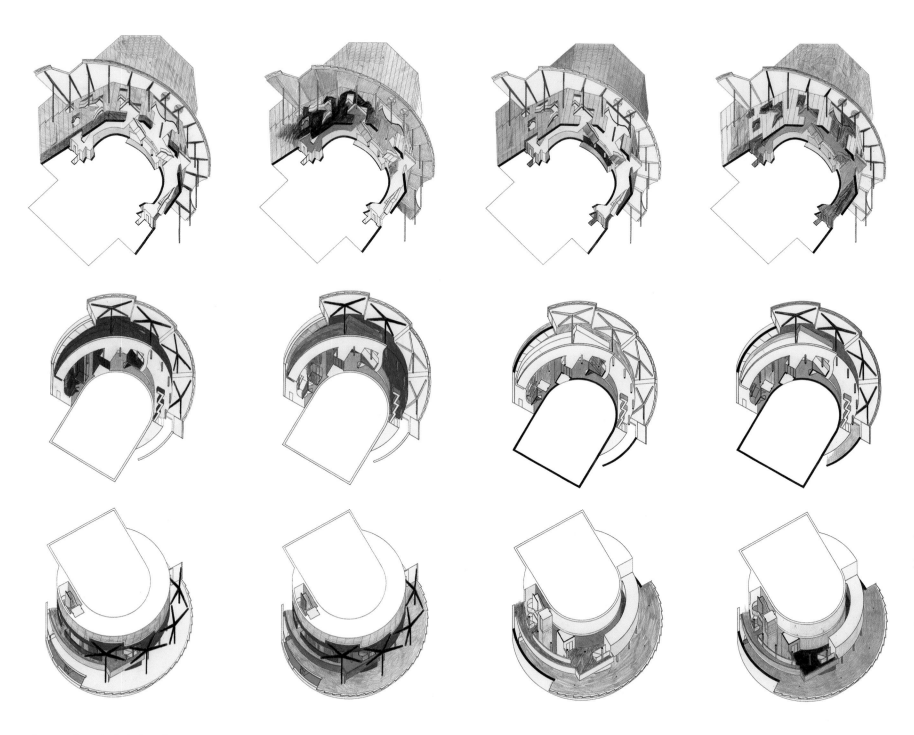

Alternative colour studies for the theatre foyers

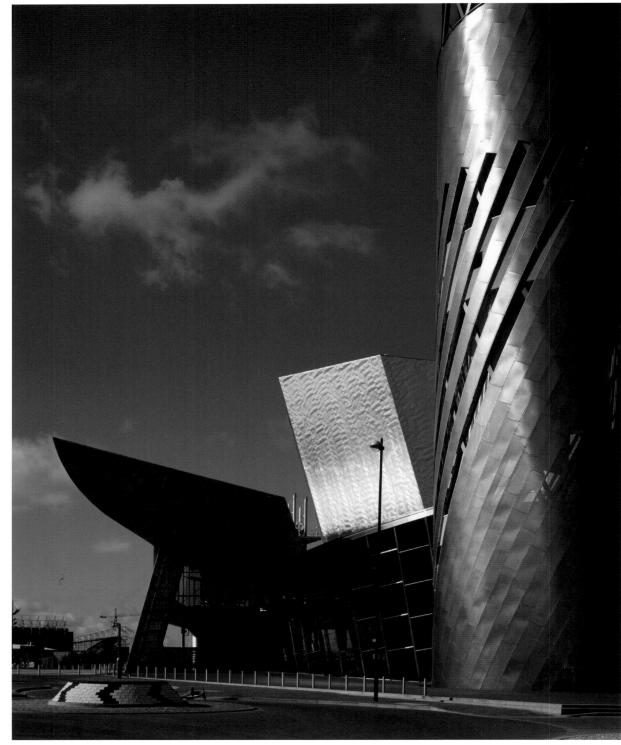

Entrance canopy, Lyric foyer and archive tower

North promenade facade

Flexible theatre foyer and rehearsal studio above

North facade

Southwest facade

Children's gallery

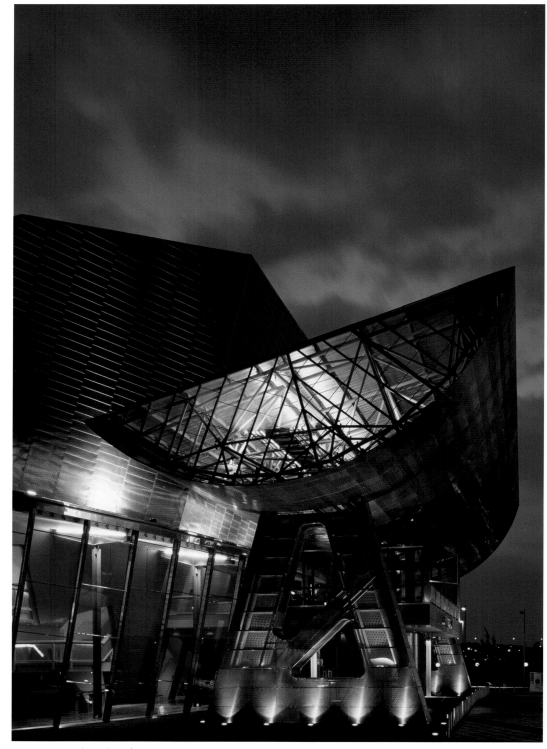

Entrance canopy and Lyric Theatre foyer

Lyric Theatre foyer and entrance

Flexible theatre foyer

Children's gallery above the south promenade and bar

" I feel more strongly about these people tha

Lowry galleries and north promenade

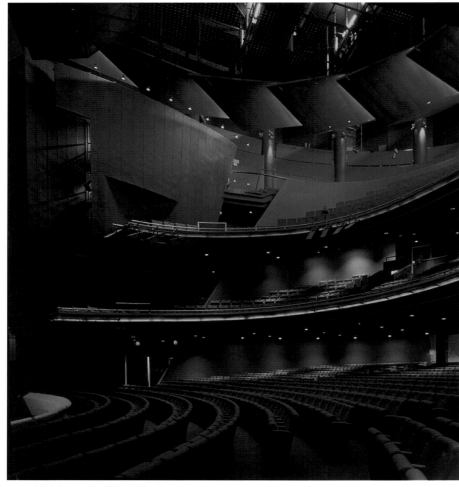

Lyric and flexible theatres' audiences and auditoria

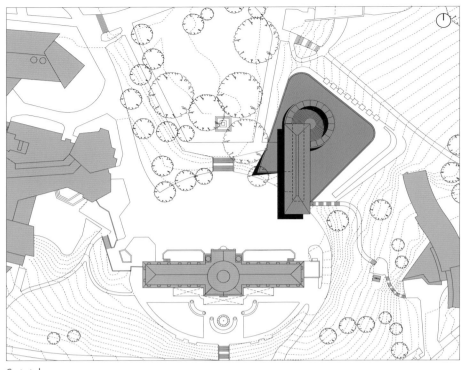

Context plan

LITERATURE MUSEUM
MARBACH, GERMANY, 2001
Wilford Schupp Architekten

The new building is an addition to the Schiller National Museum situated on the Schiller Hills overlooking the River Neckar amongst an ensemble of buildings of different architectural periods and styles. In order to avoid competition with the earlier buildings the new Museum takes advantage of its elevated site and steep crossfall. It is hidden in the southern face of the Schiller Hills as an integral part of the landscape. It registers itself in the museum garden with a modest linear entrance pavilion, recessed amphitheatre and terrace. The crossfall is also used to introduce daylight into the outer perimeter of the library beneath the terrace.

The design of the Museum comprising rotunda, exhibition galleries and entrance pavilion responds to the three axes (but not the form) of the German Literature Archive, National Museum and Collegiate Building. The rotunda expresses the centre of the Exhibition Galleries below and relates directly to the axis of the Schiller Monument.

The Exhibition Galleries are grouped around the rotunda, accessed from a gentle spiral ramp which leads into the depth of the building, to the lower exhibition spaces and underground connection to the Schiller Museum.

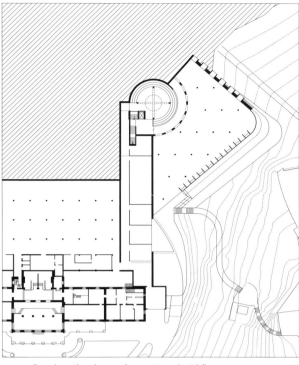

Lower gallery plan with underground connection to the Schiller Museum

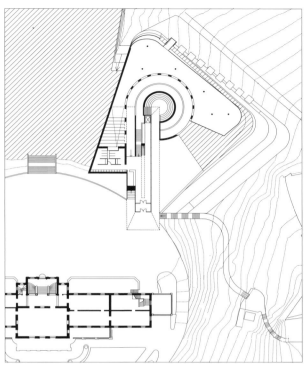

Lecture theatre, library and gallery entrance spiral

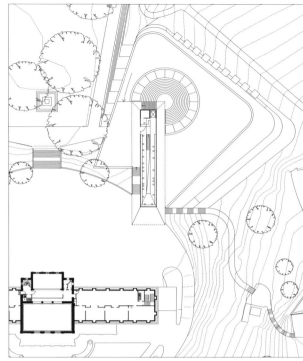

Entrance pavilion and amphitheatre

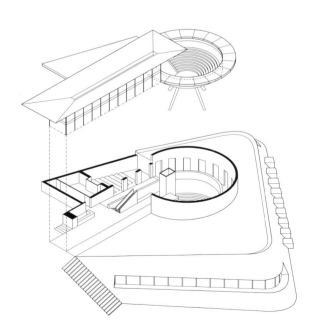

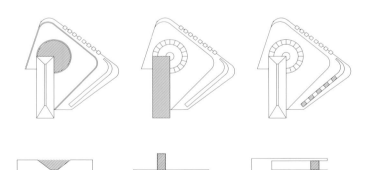

Plan and section diagrams of the compositional elements

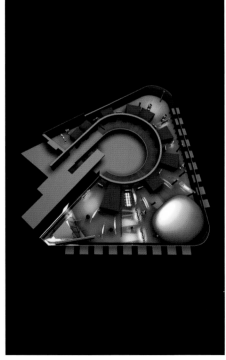

Aerial view of the museum spiral and galleries

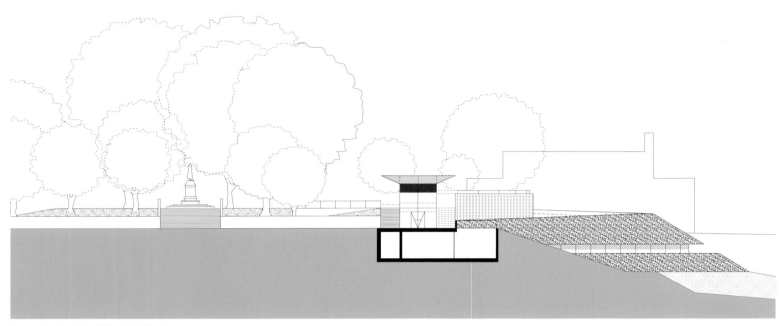

Cross-section through the link to the Schiller Museum

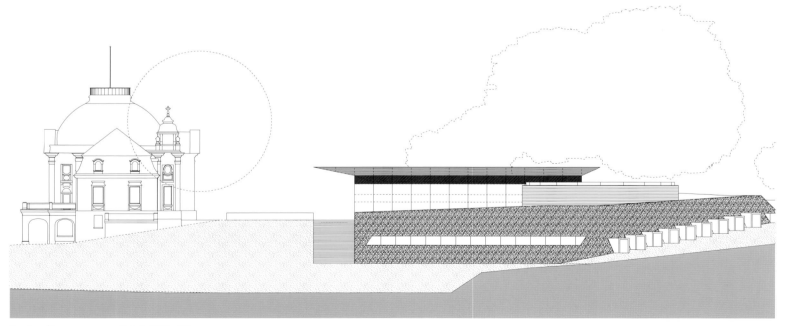

Elevation of the museum recessed into the Schiller Hills

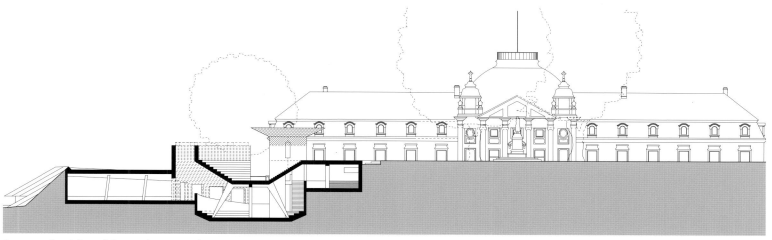

Cross-section through the amphitheatre and museum spiral

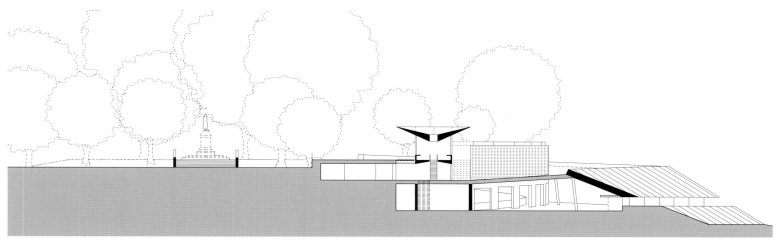

Cross-section looking through the entrance pavilion, museum and library

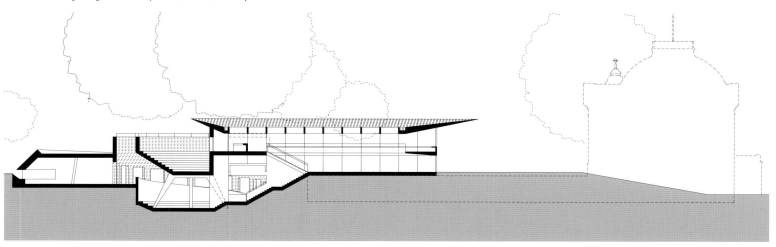

Longitudinal section looking through the entrance pavilion, amphitheatre and museum spiral

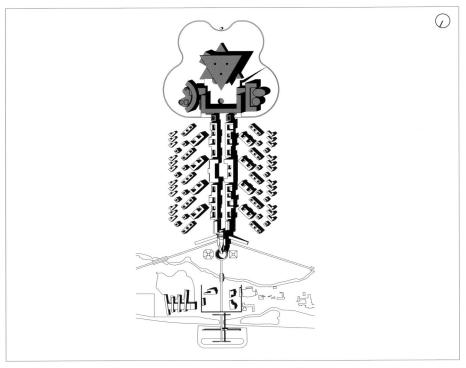

Context plan

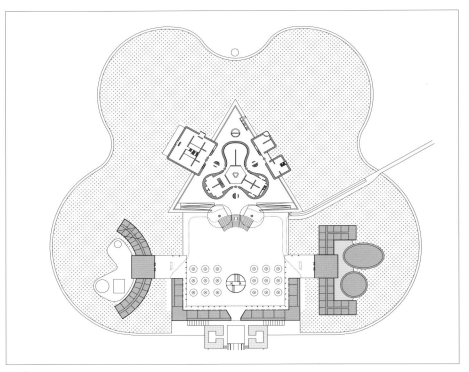

Site plan

MUSEUM OF AFRICA
STELLENBOSCH, SOUTH AFRICA, 2003–2004
Michael Wilford Architects & Chris Dyson Architects

The masterplan for the development of the Spier Wine Estate comprises an Artists' Village and promenade connecting the historic winery in the valley with a new Cultural Plaza on the hill crest above. The plaza, as the principle outdoor public space for performances and exhibitions, terminates the new Village axis and is enclosed by the Performing Art Centre, hotel, bars and cafes with car parking below.

To express the diversity of African culture and establish a unique presence, the Museum comprises a triple-layered composition comprising triangular plinth, gallery pavilions and roof canopy.

The plinth, containing lecture theatre, library and audio visual spaces, roots the building in the landscape. The terrace which extends over it has commanding views over the surrounding vineyards and links a cluster of exhibition pavilions whose form, material and colour represent indigenous African building typologies and materials. Each pavilion contains a series of independent galleries for exhibitions of a wide range of size and layout.

The soaring triangular canopy, set in counter orientation to the plinth below, provides shading to the pavilions and terrace which, together with hilltop breezes, ensures an ambient micro climate. The ribbed sculptural form of the canopy comprises layered multi-directional timber lattices allowing controlled daylight to penetrate to the interior of the building.

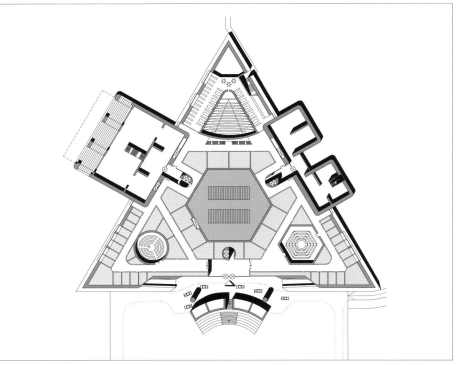

Ground level plinth containing the library, lecture theatre and audio visual spaces

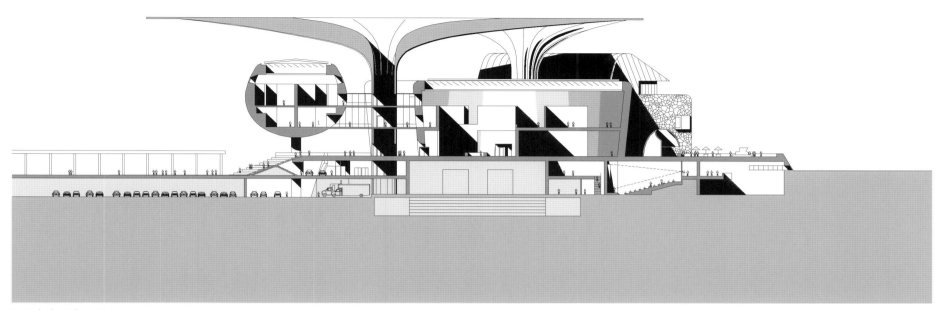

Longitudinal centreline section

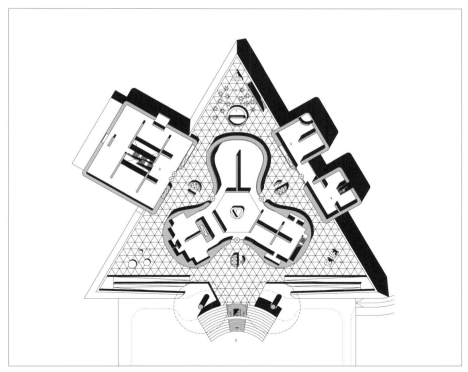

First floor terrace linking the exhibition pavilions

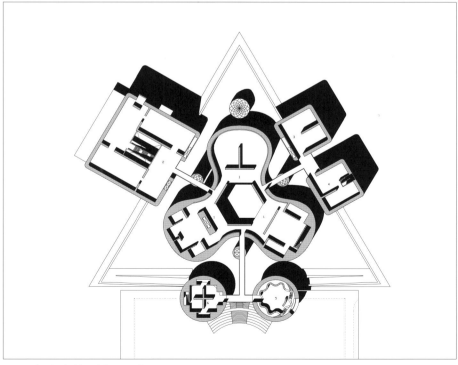

Upper gallery level of the exhibition pavilions

Entrance elevation sketch from the north

View from the southeast

Side elevation sketch from the south

View from the northwest

Street facade illumination

Foyer/Gallery One

Florence Hall

WILFORD/STIRLING/WILFORD RIBA EXHIBITION
LONDON, ENGLAND, 1996
Michael Wilford and Partners

Gallery One/foyer

The 30 year old Partnership of James Stirling, Michael Wilford and Associates was an internationally renowned architectural practice and ended with the death of James Stirling in 1992.

The exhibition was mounted in 1996 in the headquarters of the Royal Institute of British Architects in London and traced the evolution of that Partnership into the practice of Michael Wilford and Partners.

Completed projects designed by James Stirling, Michael Wilford and Associates and featured in the exhibition were Temasek Polytechnic Singapore, Stuttgart Music School and the Science Library at the University of California, Irvine, as well as No.1 Poultry, an office building in the City of London which was under construction at that time.

Work by Michael Wilford and Partners included the Lowry Salford, Abando Passenger Interchange Bilbao, the British Embassy Berlin and four industrial projects for Sto AG in Germany. Recent competition entries and schematic designs were included alongside 11 major projects to illustrate work in progress at that time.

The exhibition comprised sketches, drawings, models and photographs to explain the interlocking architectural strategies which underlie the projects and the evolving design philosophy of the practice.

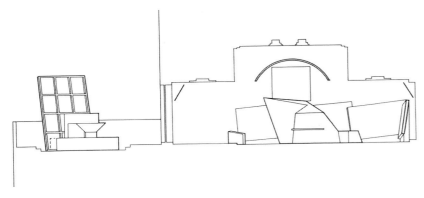

Cross-section through the terrace and Florence Hall

Longitudinal section through Gallery One, the foyer and Florence Hall

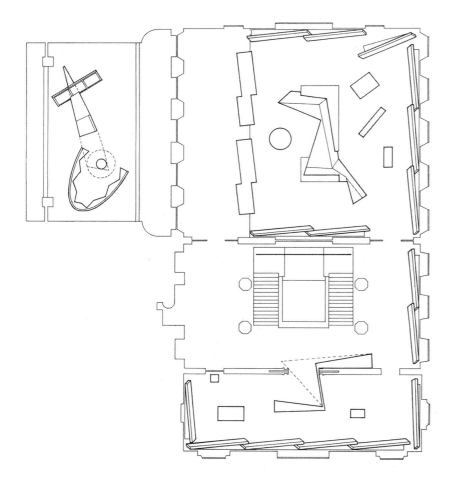

Florence Hall, terrace, foyer and Gallery One floor plan

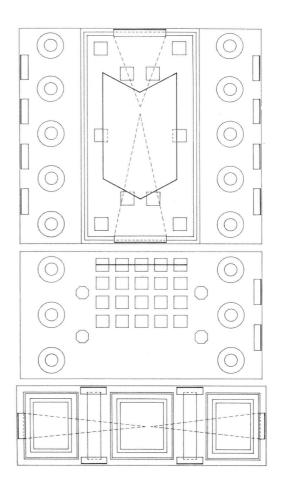

Reflected ceiling plan

Gallery One

Florence Hall

Florence Hall

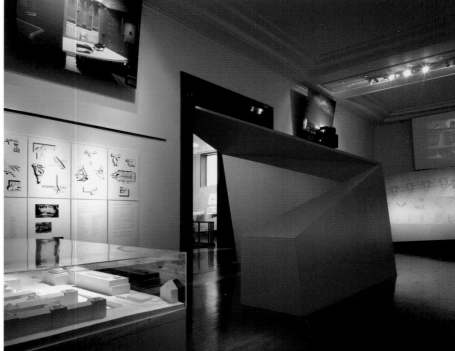

Gallery One

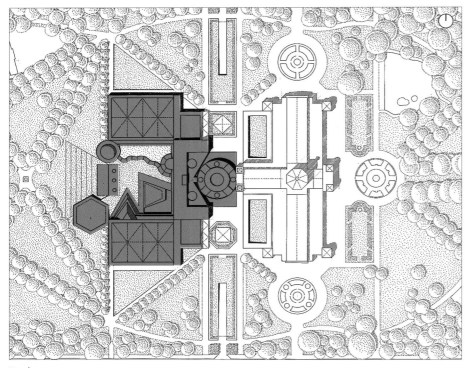

Site plan

MUSEUM OF VICTORIA EXTENSION
MELBOURNE, AUSTRALIA, 1993
Michael Wilford & Partners

The brief required an extension significantly larger than the original Victorian building and functionally integrated without compromising the historic structure. The new U-shaped building addresses the western half of the park and is in balance with, and counterpoint to, the linear form of the existing museum.

A grand circular loggia situated on the intersection of the longitudinal and cross-axes of the park, forms a new combined entry point for both pedestrians and vehicles at the heart of the extended building. Its form minimises any detrimental physical and visual impact on the historic building leaving it essentially intact, still to be experienced as a large villa in the park. A circular connecting ring within the upper level of the loggia ensures an uninterrupted promenade around the whole expanded museum.

The extension encloses a central garden to assist orientation and provide a lively focus for the museum. A series of geometric pavilions accommodating special activities and social functions are disposed informally in the garden to animate the primary circulation route around its perimeter and contrast with the flanking black box exhibition galleries required by the brief.

Intrusion of this large new intervention into the park is ameliorated by its fragmented and articulated massing and its low profile defers to the cupola and grand hall of the original building.

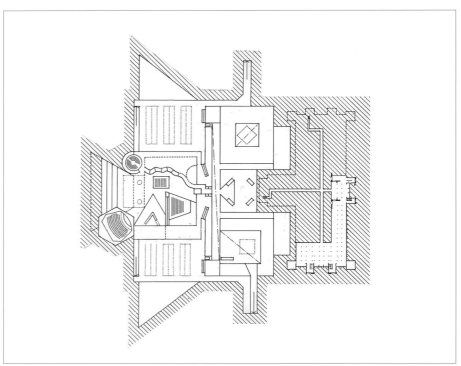

First basement and lower courtyard plan

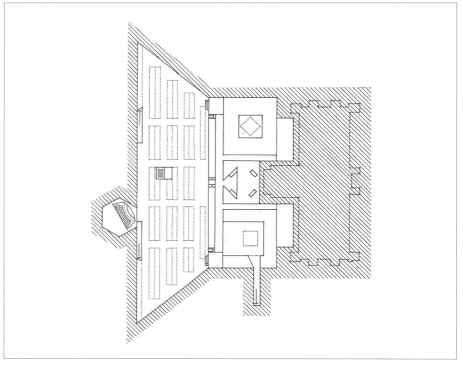

Second basement parking, storage and service plan

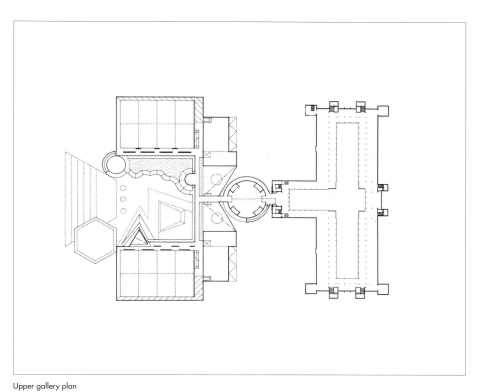

Upper gallery plan

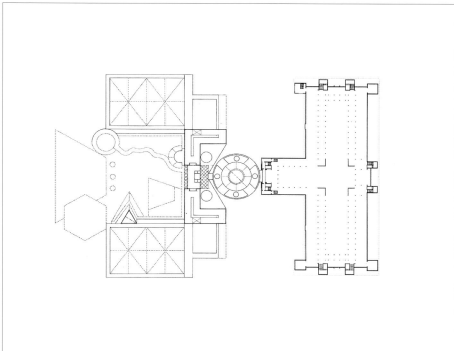

Roof plan

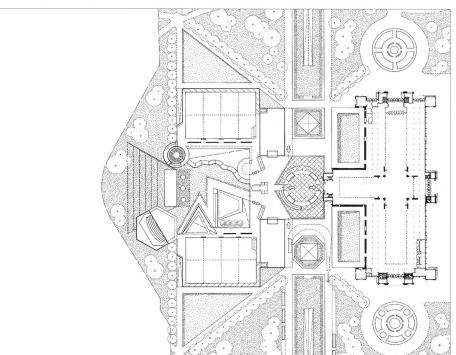

Ground floor gallery plan

Sketch view of the garden

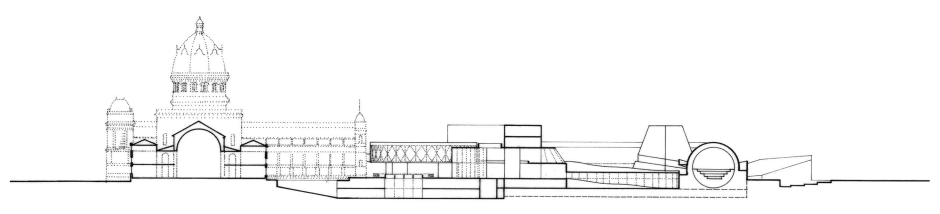

Longitudinal section through the gallery connecting wing and the planetarium looking south

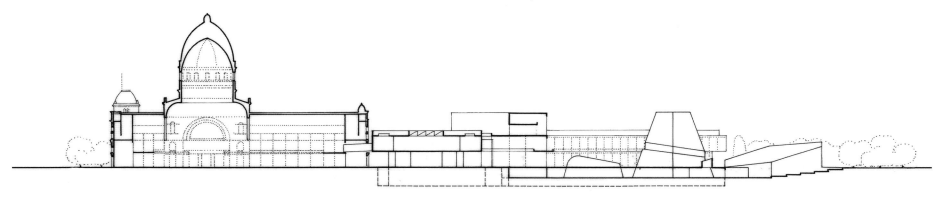

Longitudinal centreline section through the garden looking south

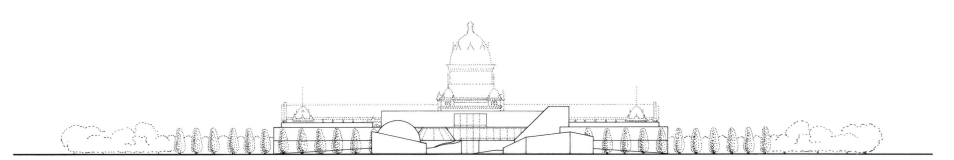

West facade

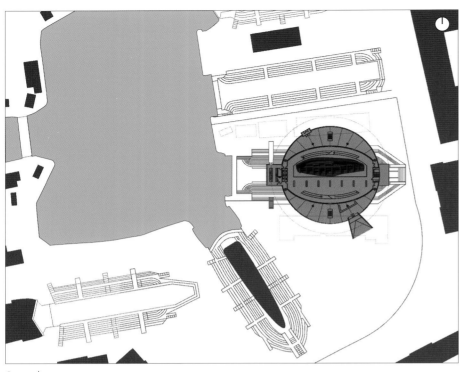

Context plan

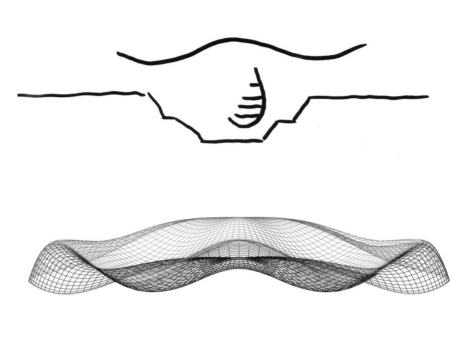

Concept sketch and roof development

MARY ROSE MUSEUM
PORTSMOUTH, ENGLAND, 2005

Wilford Schupp Architekten and Chris Dyson Architects

This competition design is for a special conservation museum to house, preserve and display the fragile historic hull of the *Mary Rose*—a wooden Tudor warship—together with the large collection of artefacts recovered with her from the seabed. The building is located in Portsmouth Dockyard over an historic dry dock, alongside *HMS Victory*.

The building is organised concentrically around the hull which forms the focus of the Museum, overlooked and surrounded by a multi-level array of open galleries interpreting aspects of the hull and life on board the ship. The artefacts are displayed relative to their respective locations of use on board the ship.

Gentle curving ramps define a primary route through all exhibition levels, allow more detailed special interest detours and provide long and close-up views of the hull. The brief required that the hull should be open to public view throughout its extended drying out and restoration procedure. It is therefore cocooned within a glazed hall—a room within a room—to satisfy conservation requirements that its humidity should be maintained within strict limits in order to control timber degradation.

The circular plan form encapsulates all accommodation and its undulating roof evokes marine life and the deep from where the hull and its artefacts were recovered. Its horizontality contrasts with the vertical masts of *HMS Victory* without dominating it. It also provides an appropriate climax to the visitors' procession through Portsmouth's historic naval dockyard.

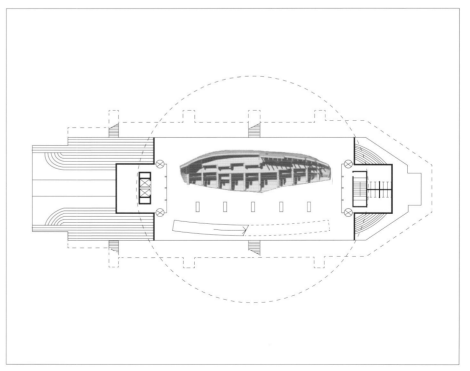

Lower level plan

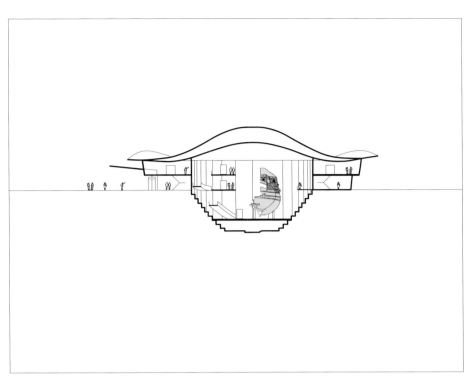

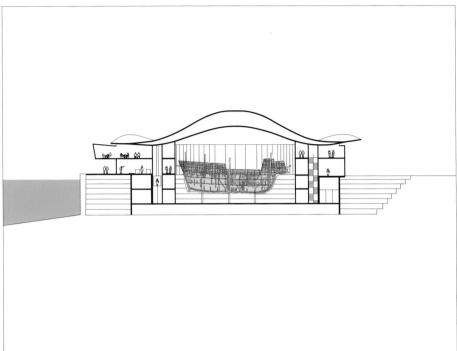

Cross-section looking west

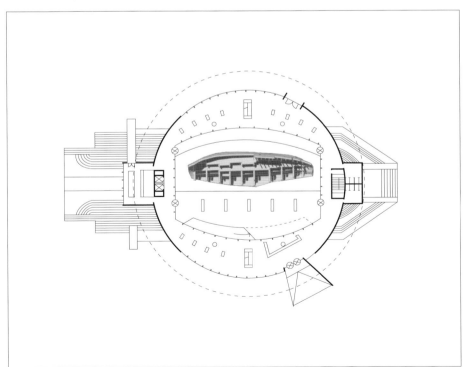

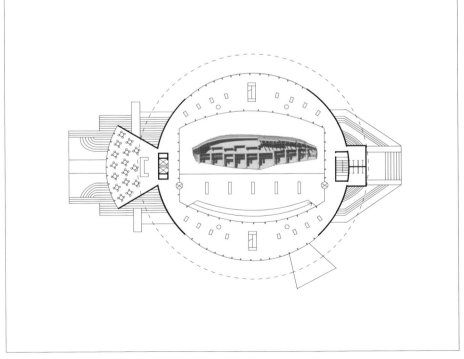

Ground level plan

First floor plan

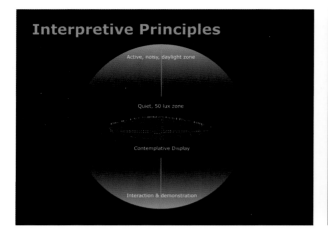

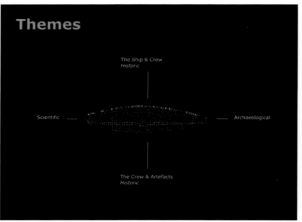

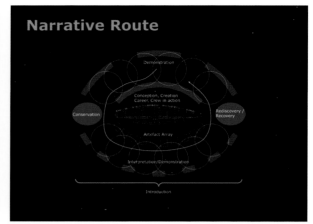

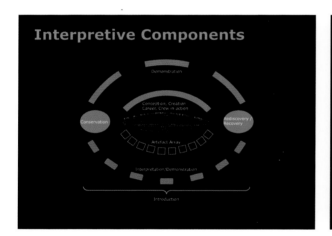

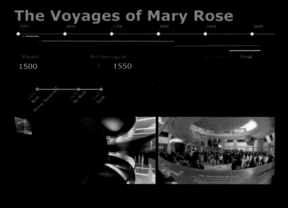

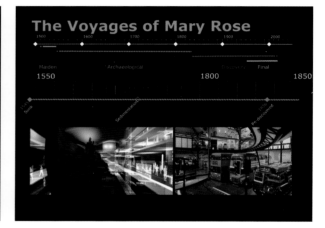

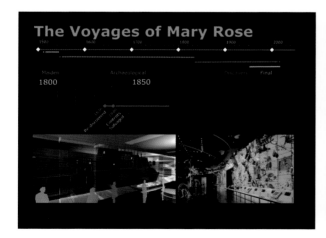

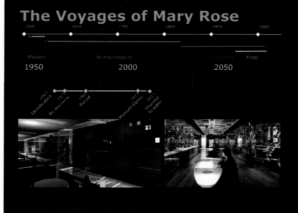

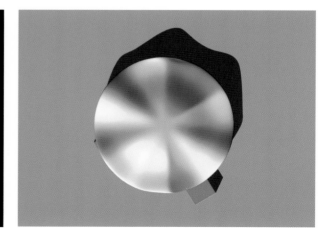

Exhibition concept

Roof model

Museum entrance adjacent to HMS Victory

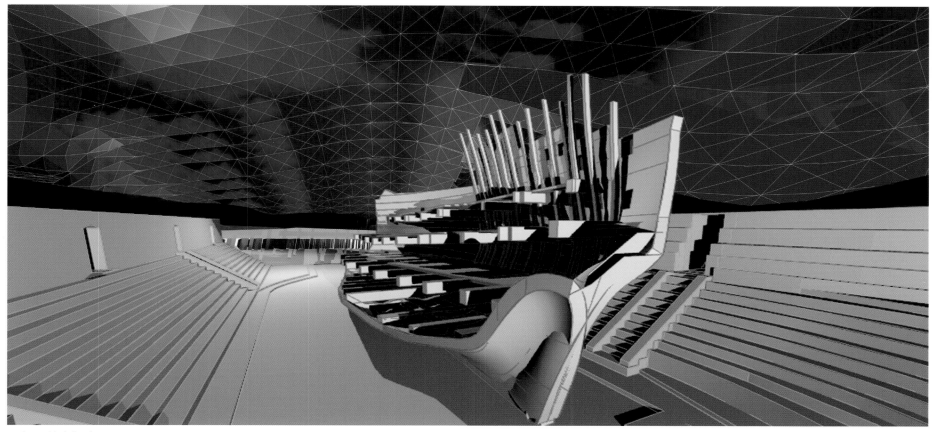

Rendering of the hull enclosure

Context plan

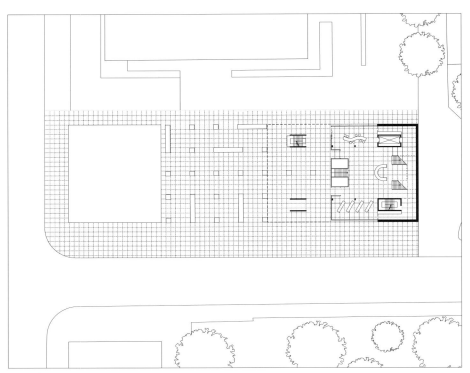

Ground floor plan

NATIONAL SOCIALISM DOCUMENTATION CENTRE
MUNICH, GERMANY, 2007

Wilford Schupp Architekten

The rectangular footprint of this competition design relates to the surviving base of one of a pair of Neo-Classical pavilions marking the entrance from the city into the ceremonial parade ground which formed the symbolic heart of National Socialism. The new building is oriented towards the former parade ground and together with the pavilion base, defines an entrance courtyard and outdoor exhibition space.

Within the building, flexible column-free gallery floor plates supported on four structural service cores allow curatorial definition of a variety of volumes for a wide range of relationships between exhibition, research and debate.

The building cantilevers beyond the ground level entrance lobby to provide a covered outdoor assembly space and accommodate a major footpath across the site. Vitrines extend from this covered porch to encompass the courtyard and give an impression, outside opening hours, of the exhibition and activities within the building. A lecture theatre and changing exhibition gallery are situated on the lower ground level.

The building has large windows at key locations around its perimeter which, together with the large roof terrace, provide views to other adjacent monumental buildings which played significant roles in the National Socialist Movement and survived World War Two. The red gridded facade symbolises the ubiquitous Party membership books so closely associated with National Socialism. Sections of the facade can be opened for views out of the building and closed as required for audio-visual presentations and sun-shading.

Lower ground floor plan

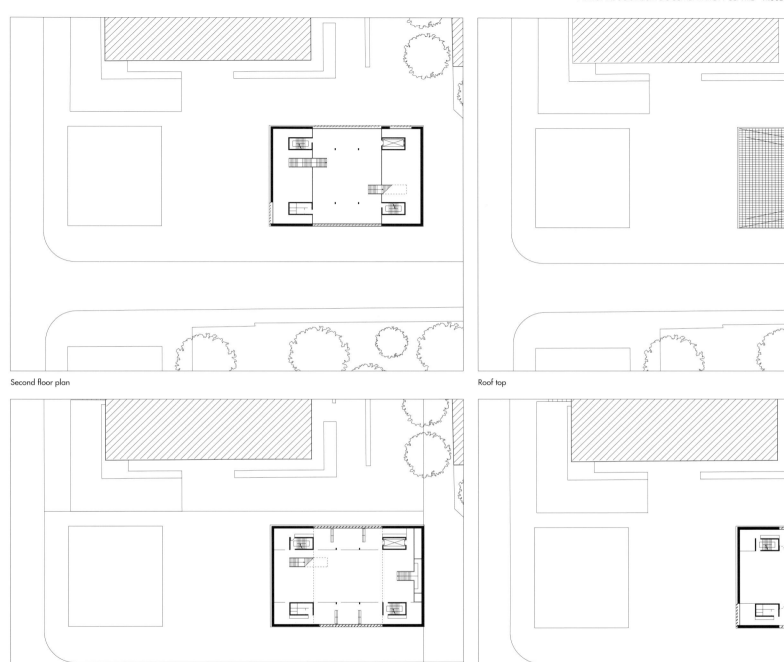

Second floor plan

Roof top

First floor plan

Third floor plan

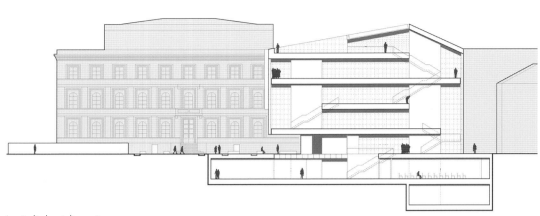

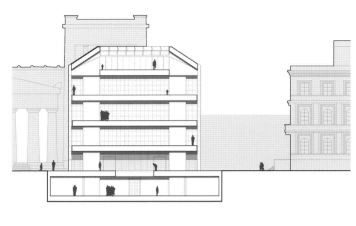

Longitudinal centreline section

Cross-section

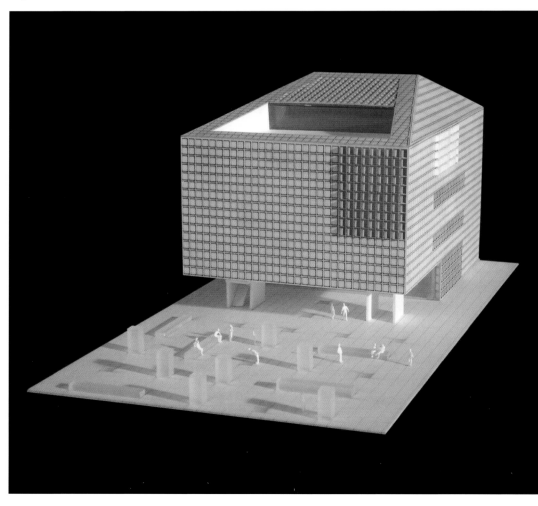

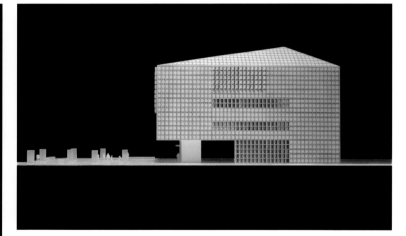

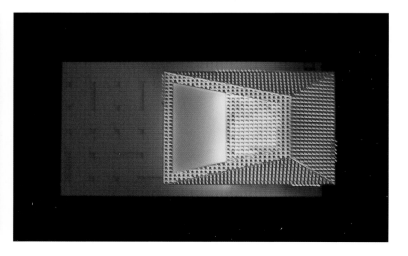

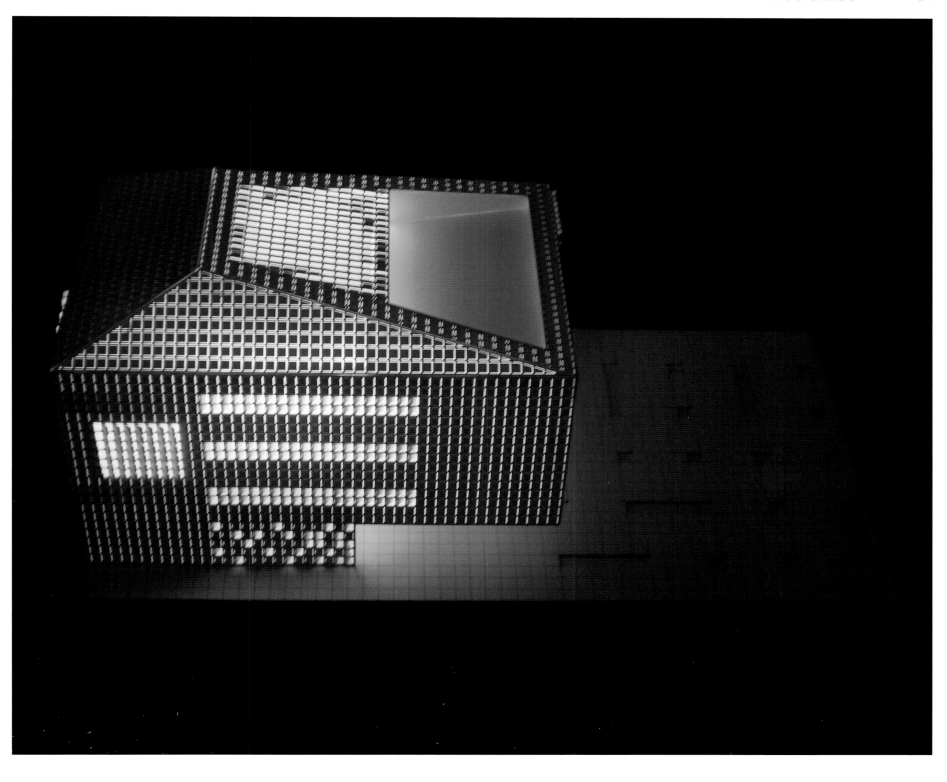

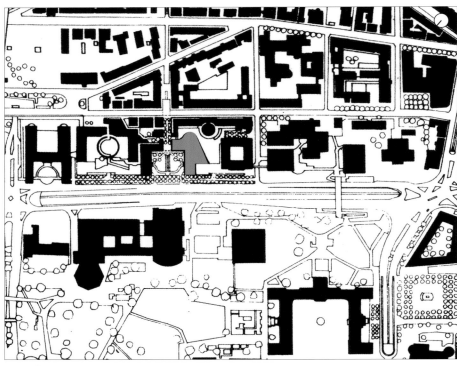

Context plan

BADEN-WURTTEMBURG HISTORY MUSEUM
STUTTGART, GERMANY, 1999–2002

Wilford Schupp Architekten (formerly Michael Wilford & Partners, London and Stuttgart)

The Museum, which also contains an extension of the Music School, is the final phase of construction which, together with the Staatsgalerie and Music School, completes the ensemble of three buildings envisaged by James Stirling, Michael Wilford & Associates in their masterplan for Stuttgart's 'Cultural Mile'. On one side its L-shaped form, mirroring the Kammertheatre, completes Museumsplatz centred on the Euganstrasse and Opera House axis. On the opposite side, together with the circular Music School tower and Parliament offices, it defines an additional plaza which completes the public route under the Music School from Urbanstrasse to Konrad Adenauerstrasse.

The galleries comprise a series of neutral, stacked 'black box' spaces, set either side of a top-lit cascading staircase connecting all levels and forming the spine of the building. Visitors enter from a wide passage through the building which continues the raised pedestrian promenade along the 'Cultural Mile'. The glazed foyer overlooking Museumplatz, leads directly to the main staircase, cafeteria and shop.

The permanent exhibition unfolds as visitors rise up through three gallery levels and culminates in a glazed conservatory and roof terrace. A special corner window on the street frontage overlooks the city skyline, and forms a climax to the processional route through the museum. A changing exhibition gallery and lecture theatre are situated on the lower level. In contrast to the introverted ambience of the exhibition experience, the circulation spaces celebrate daylight, views and colour.

Whilst using a similar palette of materials to the Staatsgalerie and Music School the facades are more abstract, reflecting the internal organisation of the building and providing a distinct identity to the museum within the whole ensemble.

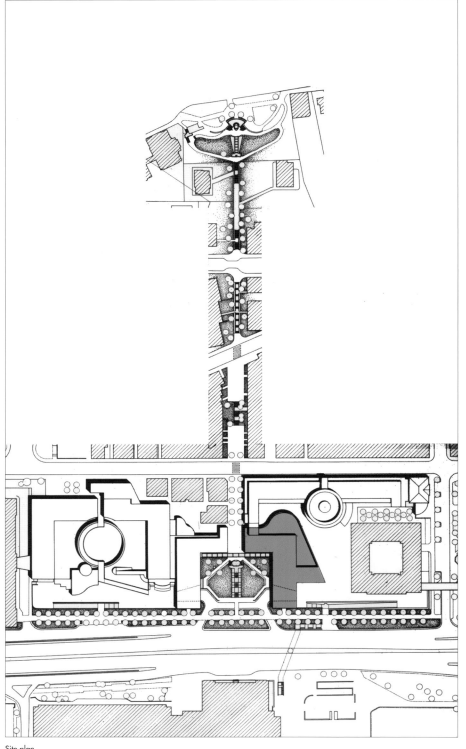

Site plan

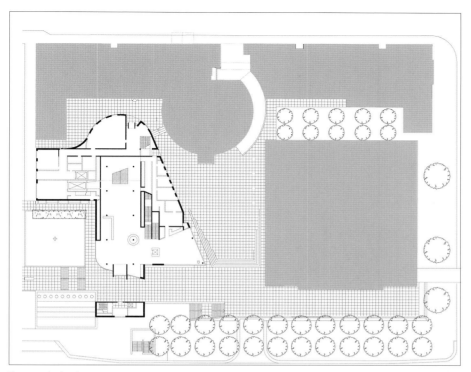

Plaza entry level and restaurant

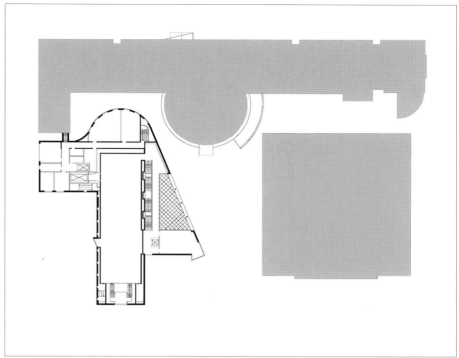

Third gallery and roof terrace level

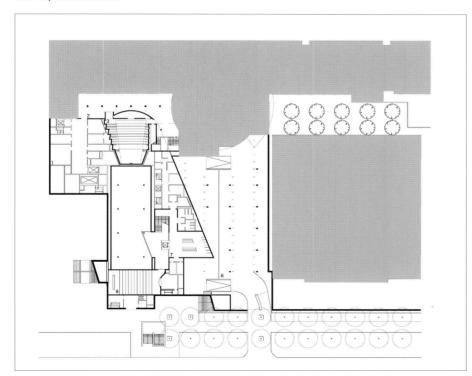

Street level plan with changing exhibition gallery, audio-visual theatre and parking

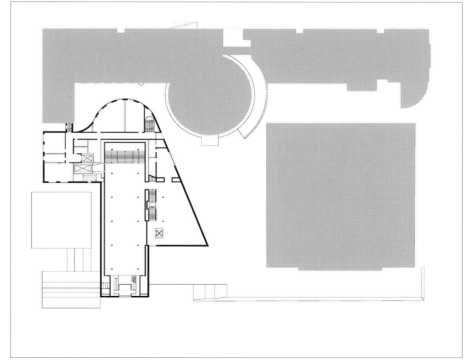

Second gallery level

Museumplatz facade

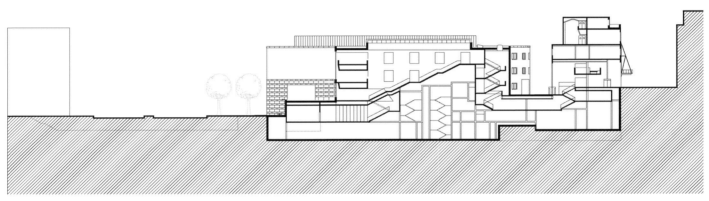

Longitudinal section through the staircase

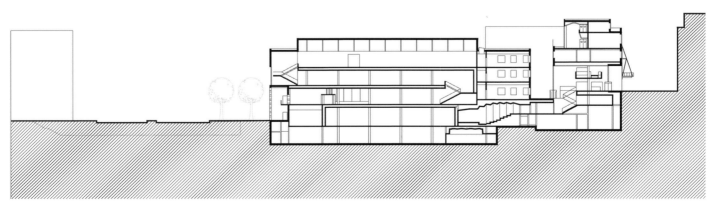

Longitudinal section through the entrance and galleries

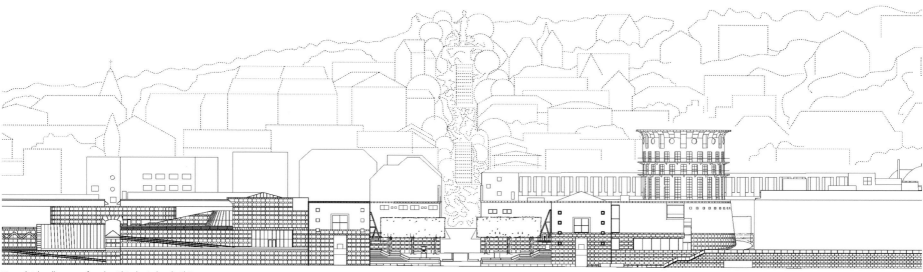

Konrad Adenallerstrasse facade within the 'cultural mile'

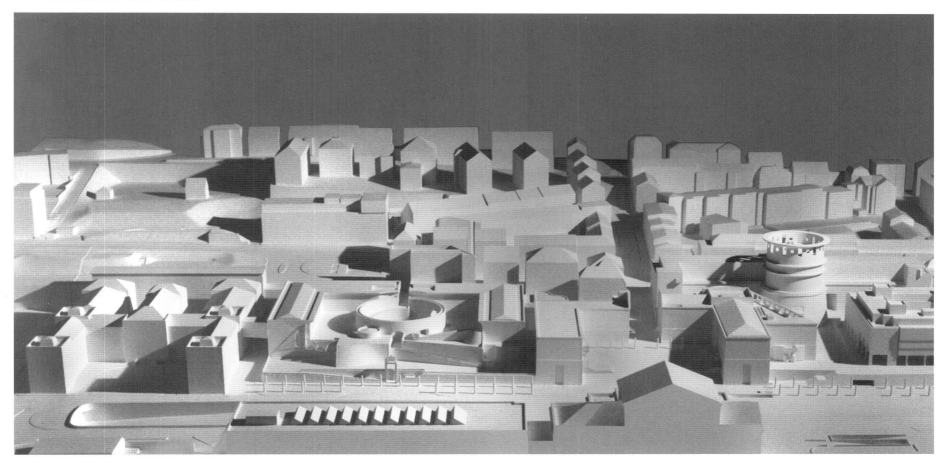

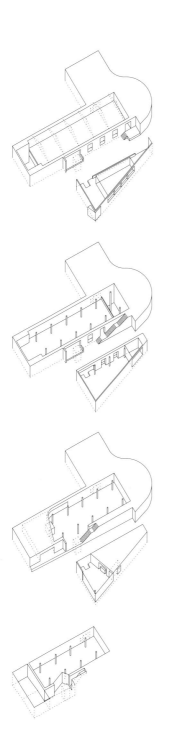

Exploded isometric diagram of the gallery stack

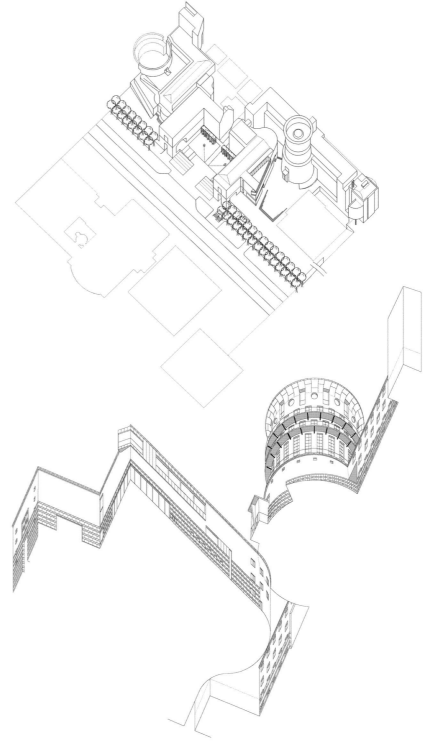

Worm's-eye upview of the south facade of the history museum and west facade of the music school

Museumsplatz from the west

Stuttgart city centre observation window in the third floor gallery

South facade and the music school plaza

Museum entrance from the raised promenade

Entrance hall and base of the cascading stair

Introduction to the permanent exhibition

Typical upper exhibition gallery

Central stair and roof terrace

THE WORK OF MICHAEL WILFORD

WITH MICHAEL WILFORD & PARTNERS, WILFORD SCHUPP ARCHITEKTEN AND OTHERS

ROBERT MAXWELL

Glancing through this enormous body of work, I find much that is familiar.

The Lowry Centre Salford Quays, Abando Passenger Interchange, the National Centre for Literature at Swansea, the Masterplan for Dresden Technical University, the Sto AG Headquarters at Weizen, the British Embassy in Berlin: all these designs by Michael Wilford and his colleagues appeared in my book with Birkhauser of 1998 on *James Stirling/Michael Wilford*. I have also written some other texts on Michael Wilford's work: the Hamburg Depot ["*Über Alles*", in *RIBA Journal,* July 1994], the *Peace Palace Library* at The Hague [in *Architectural Review*, June 2008] and the new entrance for Braun Melsungen [in *Architecture Today*, September 2010]. In many cases the buildings have been completed a little differently, but they are essentially the same. Moreover, the work now presented by Michael Wilford and his Partners is a continuation of what Wilford did when he was a partner of Stirling. There is considerable consistency, along with a sense of something different. Just what that difference is will probably become clear as we consider the variety of the projects presented here.

There is just one of these projects with which I am familiar, from having visited myself: the Lowry Centre at Salford Quays, on the Manchester Ship Canal. That seems an appropriate place from which to start appraising more recent work.

Stirling was still alive when work was started on this design, and in the Birkhauser book of 1998 it appears under the heading of James Stirling/Michael Wilford and Associates, showing that he participated in it. Professor Alan Short, while Head of the Cambridge University School of Architecture, analysed the sketches, and showed how Stirling was consulted when Wilford made the crucial decisions that pulled the design together. The completed building is identical in style to the rest of Michael Wilford's work, which is the subject of this book.

The Lowry commemorates the famous northern artist who depicted mainly working class people, and who then came to stand for a more democratic aspect of fine art. The Centre combines facilities for the visual and performing arts in such a way as to embody this democratic view by providing what is clearly intended to be an exciting and stimulating venue for recreation and education.

I have said elsewhere [in *Ancient Wisdom and Modern Know-how*, Artifice books on architecture, 2013, Chapter 8] that two important things motivated Stirling at the end of his life: privately, how to be a modern mannerist; publicly, how to give shape and continuity to the city. I shall go on to consider how much these intentions still show in the new work by Michael Wilford.

The city became important for Stirling after Leon Krier spent some time in the office, starting with the Stirling/Wilford design for Derby Civic Centre, and continuing with the designs for museums in Cologne and Dusseldorf, both of 1975. The city is clearly important for Michael Wilford too, as is shown by the following quotation from him:

I am interested in exploring the combination of function and economy with new strategic permutations of the monumental and the informal... as part of a broader and more profound search for a robust modern architecture which contributes to the evolution of the city and contemporary culture.

The importance that city space came to have for Stirling/Wilford is primary in the design for the Lowry. With canals on two sides of a triangular site, the third side opens up to a new public plaza at the confluence of the three approaches. It was intended to be connected to a new metro terminus linking it to Manchester.

The building itself contains the Lyric Theatre (1,650 seats), a flexible theatre (400 seats), art galleries, a Children's Gallery, together with shops, bars and a waterfront restaurant. A high foyer lines the whole width of the plaza frontage.

What one notices on a visit is the clear sculptural impact of the principal forms. The entrance canopy has a heroic scale, which does not stop it acting as a canopy, but also tells you how important this building is going to be. The logo tower, which earlier, with a cylinder rising out of a faceted base, bore a resemblance to a tower in the Canary Wharf project, now is a cylinder all the way down to ground. All the forms have the same sculptural strength. Inside, however, the scene is more varied, with the structure often expressed soberly by the use of Corb-like cylindrical concrete columns; but also in more spritely mode, with small-bore brightly painted steel tubes set at angles, as if caught dancing. Is there a touch of mannerism in all this? It may be better to reconsider this aspect later. There is certainly much in this that is new and exciting.

Of the other works familiarised by their inclusion in the Birkhauser book, the Abando Passenger Interchange at Bilbao has been designed in greater detail. Stirling Wilford had done a preliminary design for it in 1985 and, after Stirling died in June 1992, Michael Wilford was confirmed as the architect for the new design, which was on a much larger scale.

They drew lucky! Wilford and his team have produced a design for a huge building in the centre of the city which, dominated by its office tower, looks like an aircraft carrier, and becomes a presence on the city's skyline. It brings a massive improvement of transport problems, bringing together a car park, a bus station and two railroad stations, one of which accommodates high-speed trains. But it does more. Situated between the Mediaeval and nineteenth century quarters of the city, it also works to draw these together by providing a network of pedestrian links, a big step towards making the whole city walkable. The bus and train stations are covered by a large vaulted concourse, also linked by arcades to adjacent streets. In the concourse are located a trade centre, offices, a hotel and apartments, with many cafes and restaurants, and of course, a ticket hall. It provides a place for passengers to relax while waiting for their train or bus, or perhaps, with no transport in mind, just a convenient place for local people to meet. In short, it makes the city as a whole more liveable. It is far more comprehensive than the original scheme of 1985. It is a great pity that disagreement between the various political parties has so far stymied the realisation of this scheme.

Of the others, the design for the National Centre for Literature and City Library in Swansea was among the first major schemes undertaken by Michael Wilford after Stirling's death, his response to a limited competition. Two separate buildings enclose a small public plaza that links two parallel streets at the western edge of the town centre, and their entrances face each other across this square. This space can be approached up a broad flight of stairs from the adjoining tree-lined boulevard. The Literature Centre includes a top-lit exhibition gallery, which is contained in a rotunda that faces the boulevard, and has outwardly canted sides for maximum impact. Within the library a grand staircase leads to a central reading room overlooking the square, and leading on to the reference library above. The crisp forms comprise a complete language, which will be consolidated in subsequent work.

However, more important for Wilford at this stage in his career was the British Embassy in Berlin, work on which was started in 1995. It reoccupies its original pre-war site in Wilhelmstrasse. This was a good-sized area, big enough to allow the introduction of two large courtyards: one for the entrance, where cars can enter and put down guests before passing round a newly planted oak tree, symbol of Britannia; a second that is covered by a roof with top-lights forming a wintergarden at lower level: this is the social space where the public is welcomed. Both allow daylight and natural ventilation into the heart of the Embassy. The use of internal courtyards also renews the local tradition of grand pre-war villas in this part of Berlin.

The design was the winner of a limited competition, and the main change made since it was adopted has been to remove the Ambassador's office from public scrutiny. Where the building as a whole is very plain and traditional, as required by the city development regulations, it has two elements that stand out by shape and colour: the Ambassador's office and the circular Conference Room. These elements are revealed through a large opening in the regular grid of repeating windows, and the very existence of this opening, as well as how big it could be, was the subject of intensive negotiation with the city fathers. The fact that this was achieved at all establishes Michael Wilford as a force to be reckoned with, an architect who believes in what he is doing, and can get his vision built.

In the event, the clients preferred, for security reasons, to have the Ambassador's office discretely tucked away among the other offices, so the projecting triangular space was used instead for an information centre, perfectly appropriate to its position just above the entrance gates. It's especially strong because these gates make a single entrance to the building and are used by everyone. Because of this change, when in 2002 there was a hostile demonstration in front of the building, with rocks being thrown and glass shattered, none of the disturbance reached the Ambassador.

But the change, while sensible, leaves the architectural image intact. The two special shapes relieve the plainness of the rest, bringing interest to anonymity, as was originally intended, and emphasising the special public face of an embassy situated in a neighbourhood of ordinary buildings. That the triangular projection should draw attention to a public function rather than the head of the organisation is, if anything, more appropriate.

The most dramatic sequence in this design must be the grand staircase that leads up from the car set-down to the space of the wintergarden on the piano nobile, providing immediate access to the conference and dining room, and ready access to the information centre, where the public (including any British visitors) can learn about Britain. A pair of lifts behind the reception desk allows for wheelchairs. In the wintergarden many events occur: receptions, banquets, conferences, exhibitions, parties. Most of these call for celebration, for showing off, so the grandeur is appropriate.

The grand staircase narrows as it ascends into a narrowing space, so where near the bottom you pass between two columns, higher up two similar columns come close together, making a barrier, and you turn instead to the right, where the high light of the wintergarden draws you on. The sequence is intensified by having a bright red ceiling. It's an effect that I'm sure Stirling would have enjoyed.

Since the work contains two embassies, there is an opportunity to appraise both together, and see if we learn something. By comparison the design for the British Embassy at Tbilisi, Georgia, is more modest, but also more comprehensive, since it includes the Ambassador's residence. This is a two-storey block rising above the rest, and distinguished by a cladding of anodized 10 mm aluminium panels, with a decorative pattern of small openings, which runs over the window shutters as well as the solid walls. The residence has its own car entrance courtyard at the high end of the site, a long way removed from the public entrance at the low end. This separation is possible because of the sloping site, which extends far beyond the limits of the Embassy.

The chancery is faced in stone veneer, instead of decorative panels, speaking of more serious work, perhaps referring to the rhetoric of plain speaking. The working offices form a two-storey block rising above the one-storey part open to the public for issuing visas and similar work. This relationship repeats the way the two-storey Residence rises above the working offices, giving a pleasing unity to the overall design, apparent in the site layout. There is a two-storey high atrium rising through the chancery, terminating in a roof-light, with the staircase and the glazing bars both set at an angle that reconciles axes, which adds a touch of liveliness.

Comparing these two embassies, one becomes aware of the way a functionalist approach based on asserting the workings of the plan have led to two quite different buildings, each adapted to its particular site and context. This approach, where practical requirements are met without allowing them to take over completely, leaving them subservient to the overall sense of form, can only be described as masterly.

The Campus Masterplan for Dresden Technical University was a competition project that fell by the wayside. It is still of interest to note that in this design the administration tower carries a reminiscence of the administration tower in Leicester Engineering, in the transition between the facetted form above and the rectangular structure below.

The Sto Masterplan concerns a site at Weizen, Baden Wurttemburg, that we have encountered before, in dealing with the first phase of realisation of the masterplan—the Communication Building [Robert Maxwell: *James Stirling Michael Wilford*, Birkhauser Verlag, 1998, p.186]. This masterplan draws together the different buildings done at different times by relating them to an overall structure, just above the point where a tributary joins the River Wutach.

The Sto Production and Exhibition Building falls into the second phase of the masterplan. Two rectangular buildings are placed together in a Z-formation: a tower on one contains a cluster of raw materials storage silos, gravity-fed down through a vertical production sequence. The other building contains the horizontal production facilities. In an ensemble somewhat dominated by functional requirements, it is a relief to find in the proposal some variety in the less demanding forms of entrance and exhibition spaces. The use of a trefoil shape creates architectural interest here. As with the fan shapes beloved by Alvar Aalto, the trefoil appears elsewhere in Wilford's work (for example The Museum of Africa, Wilford House, Dresden Technical University).

The Sto Communication Building, was the first building to be completed on this site, destined to grow into the campus of new buildings. It has an oval entrance hall leading down to a square two-storey base containing training facilities, and upwards to a four-storey lineal superstructure containing offices for the marketing department. This sounds simple enough, but it is rendered eye-catching by the fact that the offices slide towards the road as they go up, so that they lean over the visitor in a way that emphasises the STO logo carried at their peak, effectively making an entrance to the site; while at the other end the succeeding set-backs allow a sunny sitting-out terrace for each office floor. The effect is to increase the drama of the building as it rakes out over the road, while adding to the amenity of its use. The structure adds to the drama by employing a couple of A-frames under the overhang; while the colours—white with strip windows above, earth colours for the square base, complete the story.

A new Sto AG Office Building A/B is planned for the western periphery of the campus, in a linear form bent into a V. There will be three floors of offices, carried on zig-zag columns, allowing the undulating landscape with its meandering river to flow beneath the building. Above, offices line each side of a central corridor, connected by more flexible meeting rooms, with a central reception area. The lift shaft pins the two wings together, and, beyond, a café opens on to a riverside terrace with views across the lake.

The Sto Hamburg Depot is located on a corner site in a light industrial park. The chief element is the warehouse, occupying most of the site and following its rectangular geometry. The other elements, one square and red (containing training rooms), one rectangular and yellow (containing offices above, exhibition space below), are set at an angle, making a small triangular courtyard between them, the focus of the office block terrace above, and the location of the main order desk below. A wall in the form of an arc struck approximately from this courtyard unifies the exhibition space and relates the group to the curve of the road at the corner of the site. A tower exhibiting the company logo stands beside the termination of this arc. A square store for finished Styrofoam panels is freestanding just beyond the warehouse.

The usual British answer to the question: how to make a dumb structure interesting, is to put art into the structure, as is done all the time by the 'high-tech' school: but this makes it expensive.

Here, none of the buildings is expensive, the warehouse is as dumb as they come; the other buildings are made interesting by their juxtaposition, and by the spaces they make with each other. They are also given extra punch by being finished in primary colours—red, yellow and blue, which is a selling point for the panels. Naturally, the bright colours here are made of the same panels.

The Sto group at Weizen provides an example of a client's faithfulness to their architect's design approach. Wilford is clearly devoted to the art of architecture, as was his partner James Stirling: but this does not preclude giving attention to the functional problems, the comfort of those who occupy the buildings, the practical questions of cost and benefit. A good architect can satisfy all the important aspects simultaneously. Conversely, to the extent that some aspects escape from the overall concept, they may benefit from the accidental effects that intervene. There are many architects today who no longer worry about a unifying concept, but are happy to accumulate accidents. The accidental may appear unexpected, surprising, strange. It may come to be seen by some as a way of being different, of identifying their work as avant-garde. For a more rational architect, like Michael Wilford, it can still provide an element of surprise on top of the basic humanity of his endeavours.

None of the projects cited were carried out before Stirling's death. Of the work illustrated in this book only the initial concept of the Lowry was a joint Stirling/Wilford initiative. The rest were entirely due to Wilford, his partners and collaborators. This is certainly the case with the two embassies we have already considered, the Abando Interchange, and the work for Sto AG at Weizen and Hamburg. Nevertheless Wilford's work undoubtedly shows complete continuity with the work of the two partners, indicating that Wilford already contributed a full share of the ideas that went before.

The Music School extension and Cinemaxx are combined in a single building next door to the old music school, in Mannheim city centre. It is made up of three parts: an L-shaped block containing many cinemas, a semi-circular Music School and a tower carrying a stack of three double-height dance studios, finishing with a roof terrace, with high reflecting walls to allow open air performances. From the street an entrance underneath the semi-circular overhang leads on to a circular court, co-axial with the wider circle. It is actually hexagonal in its lower levels, but becomes smoothly circular above.

The semi-circular mass of the Music School, under which the entrance occurs, creates an effect similar to the entrance of the Centre for Literature at Swansea, accentuated by the outward cant of the upper floors. In a way Wilford carries a set of preferred forms in his head, and every project gives an opportunity for using some of them. (Alvar Aalto worked in a similar way, looking always for a chance to apply his favourite fan shape.) The curved shape restores a certain prominence to the function of the Music School, otherwise it risks being overwhelmed by the rectangularity of the cinemas. There are no less than ten cinemas of different sizes. Three levels of car parking lie under the full extent of the plan.

The History Museum of the Land of Baden-Wurttemberg at Stuttgart completes the group of buildings designed by James Stirling/Michael Wilford between 1977 and 1994, centred around the Staatsgalerie and the Music Academy. It retains the essential features of the earlier design, with minor modifications. Access to the galleries is by means of a "cascading" stair, as in the Sackler Gallery at the Fogg, Harvard. The interior is made dramatic by the use of strong colours—red and purple in this instance.

The LBBW Regional Headquarters at Karlsruhe conforms to a masterplan put forward by the city with the aim of regenerating disued railway lands east of the city centre. The main feature of the masterplan is a new park, and this building helps to define its northern boundary. The accommodation of mainly offices is divided into three layers: a fairly solid service plinth, two stories of highly glazed offices and foyers, and above, four stories of standard offices, in a linear block animated by zig-zagging at two points. The upper offices are given more definition by being carried on dramatic groups of cylindrical columns drawn together at the ground. This motif is even further emphasised by a huge cantilever at the end, where the entire four stories of offices juts out to form a gateway to the park.

After all this drama it is quite a pleasure to pass next to a small, modest building: the Peace Palace Visitors' Centre at The Hague. I already wrote about this group [the Peace Palace Library at The Hague in *Architectural Review*, June 2008]. The new building has its own unique personality while taking its place in the total composition. The building serves two functions: control of access by vehicles and pedestrians and providing an introduction to interested visitors and tourists. Trucks and cars admitted through an outer set of gates are "trapped" under the scrutiny of the officials before being admitted through a second set of gates. The entrance court provides parallel entry and exit for judges, VIPs and other visitors.

In the larger wing an exhibition sequence telling the story of the Peace Palace rises by shallow ramp to an observation area from which the Palace and its gardens can be viewed. Visitors return to ground level by a short stair, where they can buy souvenirs, pass on through security for a conducted tour, or leave the building. The functions are handled efficiently but discreetly, the building is both modern and deferential to its setting.

The Trossingen Music School is another small and relatively simple building. It provides additional rehearsal rooms and offices for several departments of the existing Music School. The entrance is marked by a reddish metal portal set into a highly glazed foyer at a sharp angle to the street frontage. This angle leads the eye through towards the left, and towards the existing Music School beyond. The walls of the building are covered with large Sto AG composite and metallic lacquered panels finished in bright blue. The general proportions of wall and window are beautifully judged, giving the building a compact, jewel-like character. Philosophers have difficulty in explaining the power of beauty: here it is evident.

The Wilford House in Sussex is unexpected in its emphasis on the roof. It might almost be designed by Frank Lloyd Wright. As with Wright, it is thoroughly integrated into nature. It enjoys panoramic views to the west across a wooded valley towards heath-land beyond. The master bedroom, the living room and the kitchen/dining room on the principle floor all have large windows and share in the extensive views. Because the site is on a slope it is possible to give both ground and first floor immediate contact with the outside by means of ramped bridges.

On the lower floor are the guest bedrooms and a plunge pool with a large round-headed window facing south. Utility rooms are located in the basement. Up under the roof is a balcony fitted out as a house office, with space for a drawing board, which may occasionally help to resolve a crisis in the work of the firm! Otherwise the roof space is packed with insulation.

The windows, in Wrightian mode, are all of timber, but the two special forms which partly show on the outside of the trefoil containing bathroom and shower, and the warped cube containing the kitchen food store are both clad in stainless steel. They enliven the entrance approach, in a way not unlike the way special forms are used to enliven the Embassy in Berlin. In this they bring a modern note, along with the modern furniture and minimalist aesthetic of the main rooms, providing modern know-how along with ancient wisdom. It was Adolf Loos who first made the distinction, employing traditional forms outside and soft carpet in Lina's bedroom inside.

It seems appropriate to discuss next the only other house illustrated in this book: the Stotmeister House in Balhausen. This was done in 1990, well before the Wilford house in Sussex, so it is possible that it was through this design that Wilford came to appreciate the power of the roof form. It is a complete renovation of a traditional farmhouse set on a sloping site in a small village in the Black Forest. From the outside, the old roof dominates; inside, a completely modern interior has been made. Immediately below the roof, the old hayloft becomes a double-height space containing lounge, dining area and kitchen, a T-formation in plan just as in the Wilford house. Windows in the three gable ends allow light to penetrate and provide wide views. A wide platform connects living room to the high ground above the house, while an inclined bridge from the drop-off circle leads directly to the main spaces. The interior is indeed a sophisticated play of modern forms: the kitchen is contained in a semi-circular form, which even projects to the outside. Bedrooms and staff quarters, and a large garage, occupy the lower levels. There is a clear sense of enjoying the play of the new with the old. The building was commissioned by the son, initially against the wishes of his father: why would you expect a British architect to know how to build in the Black Forest? Now, the old man is delighted with the result.

The National Socialism Documentation Centre at Munich occupies a rectangular site adjacent to the ruin of a Neo-Classical pavilion that marked the entrance from the city into the parade ground where the Nazis learned their trade. The entire building is covered in a close grid which itself symbolises the Party membership books, forever associated with National Socialism.

The entire building is carried on four major service cores, which act as structure. On one side the building is cantilevered to cover a shaded open-air assembly space. Beyond this covered space there is a whole series of glazed vitrines, which already give some idea of the exhibition and activities going on inside. The lower level contains a lecture theatre and a variable exhibition space. The surface of the building is covered by a uniform structural grid. Sections can be opened for views out, or closed for audio-visual presentations, or for sun-shading. The same grid covers most of the roof and gives the building an impressive homogeneity. It rises to a ridge closer to one end, and only at night, when the internal lights are on, is one aware of a pattern of smaller windows within the grid. There is a large roof terrace, from which one can see other monumental buildings important for National Socialism. One feels that if it had not been for Hitler's manic anti-Semitism, the party might even have done some good.

One is so used to associating B Braun with Melsungen, where the company originated, that it is almost disconcerting to find B Braun in Malaysia. But after all Stirling/Wilford was a global firm, with work in America as well as in Europe and the Far East. In Japan there was the project for the Tokyo International Forum of 1989, the Kyoto Centre of 1991, and the Temasek Polytechnic in Singapore, a project that was built and complete by 1986, and was strongly related to the large unbuilt project for British Telecom Headquarters of 1983. Now we have the B Braun Expansion and Masterplans, in Malaysia and Vietnam.

The masterplan envisaged replacing some of the existing buildings with higher ones that would free more site. The first building will be a linkage of two new production wings, fanning away from each other to make a garden between them. Each wing is aligned on the adjacent urban grid, which changes at this point. Where the two plants meet is the administration tower, attached to one wing, with a staff canteen in a separate pavilion between the two. Each side of the wings has a covered promenade, providing protection from the sudden downpours and intense sun that are features of the climate here. The form of two fanning wings is similar to the form used in the design of the Sto AG A/B Office Building described above.

With the Visitors' Centre and Production Expansion for B Braun Melsungen one is on familiar ground again. I wrote about this new entrance to the entire plant [in *Architecture Today*, September 2010]. After the "city of industry" (Ludwig Georg Braun's affectionate term for the new campus) was in use for some time it was better understood by both architect and client that most of the visitors were primarily interested in the production (of plastic items for medical use), so visitors' facilities are now attached to the end of the original production plant, under a high portico formed by the overhang of the main roof. Further expansion can still be accommodated at the other end of the building. In the new position visitors are closer to the canteen where they can have lunch. As I said in my article for *Architecture Today*, there is a clear reference here to the AEG Turbine Factory in Berlin, 1908, by Peter Behrens, itself a building of symbolic significance. In the site plan we can judge the improvement to function that results.

That site plan also shows the new Administration Building A2, now completed in the position included in the original Stirling/Wilford masterplan. The strategy from the beginning was to break up the overall requirements into a series of separate buildings to avoid monotony. In this spirit, the need for further admin places is achieved by adding a triangular mass (less bulky than a square building) approached through the entrance hall of the original curved building, by means of a ramped bridge containing a permanent exhibition (in wall boxes) of the history of the company. From that level a pair of lifts and double interlocking staircases connect to all levels. The upper levels in the triangular formation have bands of open workstations and enclosed 'cockpit' offices around the periphery, separated from the circulation by structural columns, but flexible in relation to each other: this is anyway a company policy to promote transparency in personal relations between staff.

The B Braun Swiss Headquarters is a relatively modest building located in the industrial fringe of Sempach. It consists of a ground-hugging Z-shaped block surmounted by a two-storey bar of offices. The ground floor contains entrance hall, exhibition and conference facilities. Two arms of the lower building define a square garden, a further side enclosed by trees, which functions as a quiet cloister for both workers and visitors. The office floors contain some open work-spaces, together with lounges and coffee bars, to stimulate social relations between employees. The windows look out on a typical Swiss landscape, with lake and snow-covered peaks. The programme is thus nicely balanced between the inward and the outward look

In Stuttgart, a research building used by the Max Planck Institute became redundant, leading to a proposal to convert it to residential use. The district is partly filled by university, partly by residential uses. The building was therefore stripped back to its structural frame, extended in places, and given new facades and windows. It has six storeys; these are divided into three separate vertical elements, each having its own entrance, allowing a perception by the owners of belonging to a relatively small community. Car parking is in a basement under the open part of the site.

Bright colours are again used to give individuality to each apartment. Large windows, balconies and roof terraces provide extensive views: but what strikes the visitor is the uniform whiteness of the exterior: it seems to be a re-incarnation of 1930s architecture.

I have left until last my comments on the Museum of Africa, a design so far unrealised. It was to be located on land belonging to the Spier Wine Estate, on a hilltop in Stellenbosch, South Africa. It would have been spectacular. A promenade mounts the hill above the historic winery below, arriving at a plaza contained by a performing arts centre, a hotel, bars and cafes, with car parking below; and on the fourth side, the Museum of Africa.

This is made up of three elements: a fairly solid plinth containing lecture theatres, a library and audio-visual facilities, which reads as part of the ground formation, and provides a terrace with a number of separate exhibition buildings showing themes relating to indigenous African building technologies. Between these buildings we have space for outdoor exhibitions and a cafe.

But what makes this design spectacular is the enormous canopy. It is cantilevered from three huge columns, set in counter orientation to the plinth below, and providing extensive shade without interrupting the hill-top breeze. It counters the hot sun to restore an enjoyable micro-climate. The ribbed form of the canopy contains timber lattices, which allow controlled daylight to be admitted to the interior as required. And the resulting appearance is remarkable: it reminded me of a herd of charging elephants! Africa, out of which humanity emerged, is itself an enormous subject, a subject recognised by David Attenborough in numerous television programmes on its wild-life, but also, with unresolved conflicts in Mali and Somaliland, of increasing concern to the world community. Here, for Africa, its importance is recognised, justice is done.

This concludes my comments on individual designs. I turn now to a consideration of the work as a whole.

James Stirling was, in my view, a great architect, probably the best British architect of the second half of the twentieth century; but he was not good with words. When he had to explain his work, he assembled just enough words by summarising the clients' brief, as received by the office; then included words from the report made to the client. Finally, he turned to comments made by the critics, particularly Charles Jencks or myself. In contrast, Michael Wilford is very articulate, and must have been responsible for many of the words used by Stirling in the procedure I have just described.

Indeed, he has produced a paper on what he does as an architect: he calls it "An Evolving Design Philosophy".

This gives us an indication not only of his feelings about modern architecture, but also his views on the whole process of designing buildings, how the client is involved, how the building will relate to the constraints placed upon it, how it will relate to the shape of the city, what it will contribute to the city, the physical context, the historical context, and so on. His attitude is so comprehensive that it would have been a godsend to myself in the early 60s, when I moved to the Bartlett at University College, and began to consider more seriously the theory of design: the two big subjects of those days were Design Method and Design Psychology. Wilford knows a lot about both.

He certainly, like Stirling, sees architecture as an art, but he appreciates the constraints placed upon the role of the architect, in contrast to the relative freedom enjoyed by author, playwright or composer, and the amount of collaboration required to process all the information needed to deal with a building.

Working with intuition, imagination and as many ideas as we can muster, we seek to achieve an architecture of order, proportion and balance which provokes exploration and creative interaction amongst those who use and visit our buildings and in the process provide aesthetic pleasure.

Nothing could be more comprehensive than that. He also has some interesting things to say about the aesthetic aspect, particularly the question of style:

Confusion between style and quality continues to undermine the development of a truly contemporary architecture and I believe a distinction has to be made between them in the architectural debate. For example, the ongoing war of words between architects historians and conservationists over the respective merits of Modernism and Classicism seems to me to be one of extremes and polarities. I believe it is possible to combine elements of both and achieve a richer, inclusive architectural language relative to the twenty-first century, which synthesises historical precedent and modern abstraction.

These extracts are enough to explain how a design like the Museum of Africa can come about. Wilford is global in his compass, with work in Georgia, Singapore, Malaysia, Australia, as well as throughout Europe. He thinks big, he thinks free.

And then, what about the question of mannerism: a style that depends on irony, on a pessimistic view of the world, on the idea of "as if …" In discussing the Sackler Gallery at the Fogg (which in my view is a thoroughly mannerist building) with Michael Dennis, Stirling stated: "Nowadays one can draw equally, without guilt, from the abstract style of modern design and the multiple layers of historical precedent."

That is a view that seems to comply with what Wilford believes he himself does in practice, and it would be natural to suppose that in working with Stirling, Wilford will have absorbed many of his ideas. But the idea of becoming a modern mannerist came to Stirling from Colin Rowe, and I don't think impinged on Wilford directly. So, mannerist aspects may cling to some of Wilford's work. But I don't believe his work can be seen as mannerist in intention.

The character of his work is far too positive to be seen as mannerist. It expresses a straight-forward *joie de vivre* that is too complete in itself to leave any room for mannerist doubt. Mannerism is about doubt. Wilford is about hope. Hope for the future, the expectation of betterment. He has no doubt.

I have come to believe that mannerism is, possibly, a universal condition of art; but it did develop as part of a historical sequence, arising in the *Cinque Cento* after a brief period of High Classicism (Bramante, Rafael), and before a protracted period of classicism done with mannerist doubt (Julio Romano, Palladio, Pontormo, El Greco); most art historians still think of it as a purely historical phenomenon. Yet, there is another possibility: what if it happens as a sort of mega-sequence that occurs in *all* historical developments? In this case, modern mannerism will be seen as succeeding the original style of Modernism, the white-walled style of the 30s: in other words it corresponds to the protracted years of postmodernism, now presumably drawing to a close.

And, if so, what, historically speaking, comes after mannerism? What came, in the original sequence, was Baroque. Are we already living in an age of modern baroque?

If we think of Michael Wilford's work in this way, it suddenly makes sense. It is too flexible to be mannerist. It has none of the tortuous sequences that occur in mannerism. It flows. It measures up to the many kinds of expressionism that are prevalent today: Hadid, Libeskind, et al. It has the exuberance of baroque, the forward momentum. This is what I believe Wilford has brought to Stirling: a way forward.

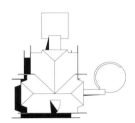

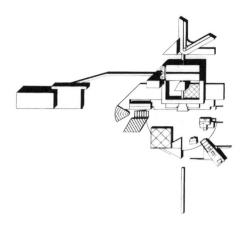

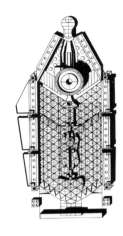

SCHOOL OF ARCHITECTURE ADDITION, NEWCASTLE UNIVERSITY
NEWCASTLE, NSW, AUSTRALIA, 1990–1992
Michael Wilford Architects

Michael Wilford
Steven Proctor
Andrew Matthews
School Student Studio

STOTMEISTER HOUSE
BALZHAUSEN, GERMANY, 1990–1992
Michael Wilford Architects

Michael Wilford
Karenna Wilford
Steven Proctor
Andrew Matthews

STO AG HEADQUARTERS AND PRODUCTION PLANT MASTERPLAN
WEIZEN, GERMANY, 1992
Michael Wilford & Partners

Michael Wilford
Laurence Bain
Russell Bevington
Charlie Sutherland
Chris Dyson
Stuart McKnight
Ian McMillan
Claudia Murin
Manuel Schupp

ABANDO PASSENGER INTERCHANGE
BILBAO, SPAIN, 1992–1993
Michael Wilford & Partners

Michael Wilford   Christina Garcia
Laurence Bain   David Jennings
Russell Bevington   Kirsten Lees
Chris Dyson   Ian McMillan
Paul Barke - Asuni   John Munro
Darren Caple   Manel Pares
Iain Clavadetscher   Simon Whiting
Jeremy Emerson
Kenny Fraser

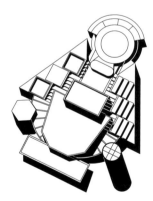

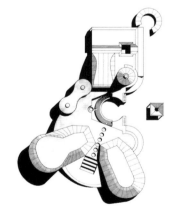

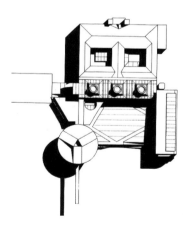

THE LOWRY
SALFORD, ENGLAND, 1992–2000
Michael Wilford & Partners

Michael Wilford   David Jennings
Laurence Bain   Chris Matthews
Russell Bevington   Alison McLellan
Charlie Sutherland   Ian McMillan
Gillian McInnes   Andrew Pryke
Stuart McKnight   Peter Ray
Simon Usher   Leandro Rotondi
Paul Barke - Asuni
Liam Hennessy

THE ESPLANADE, THEATRES ON THE BAY
SINGAPORE, 1992–2002
Michael Wilford & Partners in association with DP Architects Singapore

Michael Wilford   Charlie Hussey
Laurence Bain   Chris Matthews
Russell Bevington   Stuart McKnight
David Turnbull   Ian McMillan
Chris Dyson   John Munro
Paul Barke – Asuni   Leandro Rotondi
Kenny Fraser   Karenna Wilford
Liam Hennessy   Gareth Wilkins

NATIONAL LITERATURE CENTRE AND CITY LIBRARY
SWANSEA, WALES, 1993
Michael Wilford & Partners

Michael Wilford   Andrew Pryke
Laurence Bain   Gareth Wilkins
Russell Bevington
Chris Dyson
Charlie Hussey
Charlie Sutherland
Paul Barke - Asuni
Liam Hennessy

ROYAL LIBRARY EXTENSION
COPENHAGEN, DENMARK, 1993
Michael Wilford & Partners

Michael Wilford
Laurence Bain
Russell Bevington
Chris Dyson
Bjork Haroldsdottir
Andrew Pryke
Simon Whiting

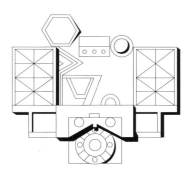

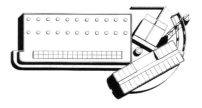

MUSEUM OF VICTORIA EXTENSION
MELBOURNE, AUSTRALIA, 1993
Michael Wilford & Partners

Michael Wilford
Laurence Bain
Russell Bevington
Charlie Sutherland
Stuart McKnight
Ian McMillan

STO AG OFFICE AND TRAINING BUILDING A/B
WEIZEN, GERMANY, 1994
Michael Wilford & Partners

Michael Wilford
Laurence Bain
Russell Bevington
Charlie Sutherland
Stuart McKnight
Ian McMillan
Manfred Klemt
Manuel Schupp
Simon Whiting

DRESDEN TECHNICAL UNIVERSITY EXPANSION
DRESDEN, GERMANY, 1994
Michael Wilford & Partners

Michael Wilford   John Munro
Laurence Bain   Jonathon Rose
Russell Bevington   Simon Whiting
Charlie Sutherland
Stuart McKnight
Chris Dyson
Jeremy Emerson
David Haseler
Ian McMillan

STO AG REGIONAL DEPOT PROTOTYPE
HAMBURG, GERMANY, 1994–1995
Michael Wilford & Partners

Michael Wilford   Ian McMillan
Laurence Bain   Stuart McKnight
Russell Bevington   Jutta Simpfendorfer
Charlie Sutherland
Manuel Schupp
Jurgen Engelhardt
Kenneth Beattie
Klaus Gruebnau
Markus Mangold

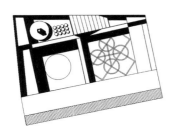

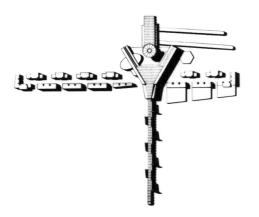

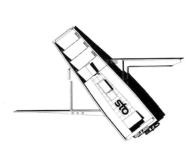

BRITISH EMBASSY BERLIN
BERLIN, GERMANY, 1994–2000
Wilford Schupp Architekten
(formerly Michael Wilford & Partners London and Stuttgart)

Michael Wilford   Gillian McInnes
Laurence Bain   Thomas Rupp
Russell Bevington   Simon Usher
Charlie Sutherland   Ian Clavadetscher
Manuel Schupp   Juergen Engelhardt
Chris Dyson   David Reat
Heike Andrees   Thomas Weiss
Stuart McKnight   Ulrike Wilke

EXPO 2000 RAILWAY STATION
HANNOVER, GERMANY, 1995
Michael Wilford & Partners

Michael Wilford   David Jennings
Laurence Bain   Chris Matthews
Russell Bevington   Alison McLellan
Charlie Sutherland   Ian McMillan
Manuel Schupp   John Munro
Darren Capel   Simon Usher
Iain Clavadetscher   Ulrike Wilke
Chris Dyson
Liam Hennessy

**RARE LIMITED RESEARCH
AND DEVELOPMENT CENTRE**
TWYCROSS, ENGLAND, 1995
Michael Wilford & Partners

Michael Wilford
Laurence Bain
Russell Bevington
Chris Dyson
Darren Capel
Ian McMillan
Brian Reynolds

STO AG COMMUNICATIONS BUILDING K
WEIZEN, GERMANY, 1995–1997
Wilford Schupp Architekten
(formerly Michael Wilford & Partners, London and Stuttgart)

Michael Wilford   Irmgard Gassner
Manuel Schupp   Daphne Kephalidis
Laurence Bain   Heike Lentz
Russell Bevington   Stuart McKnight
Charlie Sutherland   Ian McMillan
Stephan Gerstner   Daniel Seibert
Jurgen Engelhardt   Andy Strickland
Heike Andrees   Richard Walker

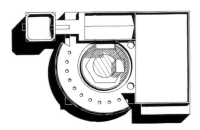

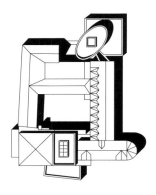

MUSIC SCHOOL ADDITION AND CINEMAXX
MANNHEIM, GERMANY, 1995–1999
Wilford Schupp Architekten
(formerly Michael Wilford & Partners London and Stuttgart)

Michael Wilford   Heike Andrees
Manuel Schupp   Darren Capel
Laurence Bain   Borbala Csicsely
Russell Bevington   Klaus Gruebnau
Charlie Sutherland   Stuart McKnight
Stephan Gerstner   Alison McLellan
Ralf-Peter Haussler   Ian McMillan
Gudrun Ahrens   Axel Overath

WILFORD / STIRLING / WILFORD RIBA EXHIBITION
LONDON, ENGLAND, 1996
Michael Wilford & Partners

Michael Wilford
Laurence Bain
Russell Bevington
Mika Burdett
Thomas Hamilton
Thomas Manss & Company

MUSIC AND THEATRE SCHOOL
ROSTOCK, GERMANY, 1997
Wilford Schupp Architekten
(formerly Michael Wilford & Partners, London and Stuttgart)

Michael Wilford   Alison McLellan
Manuel Schupp   Manel Pares
Laurence Bain
Russell Bevington
Charlie Sutherland
Stephan Gerstner
Chris Dyson
Nicole Grobecker

WILFORD HOUSE
SUSSEX, ENGLAND, 1997–2000
Michael Wilford & Partners

Michael Wilford
David Guy
Suzanne Garrett

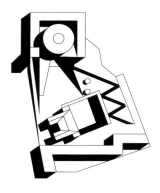

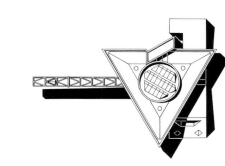

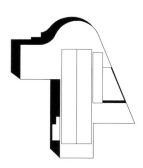

SCOTTISH PARLIAMENT
EDINBURGH, SCOTLAND, 1998
Michael Wilford & Partners

Michael Wilford
Laurence Bain
Russell Bevington
Chris Dyson
Stuart McKnight
Gillian McInnes
Ian McMillan
Alison McLellan
Claudia Murin
David Reat

CULTURE AND CONGRESS CENTRE
REUTLINGEN, GERMANY, 1999
Wilford Schupp Architekten
(formerly Michael Wilford & Partners, London and Stuttgart)

Michael Wilford   Chris Matthews
Manuel Schupp   Claudia Murin
Laurence Bain
Russell Bevington
Chris Dyson
Christian Bocci
Carsten Engel
Liam Hennessy

B BRAUN AG ADMINISTRATION BUILDING A2
MELSUNGEN, GERMANY, 1999–2002
Wilford Schupp Architekten
(formerly Michael Wilford & Partners, London and Stuttgart)

Michael Wilford   Martin Braun
Manuel Schupp   Borbala Csicsely
Laurence Bain   Frauke Goldammer
Russell Bevington   Susanne Lorch
Charlie Sutherland   Claudia Murin
Chris Dyson   Sabine Schlempp
Stephan Gerstner   Denis Wolf
Axel Overath

BADEN-WURTTEMBERG HISTORY MUSEUM
STUTTGART, GERMANY, 1999–2002
Wilford Schupp Architekten
(formerly Michael Wilford & Partners London and Stuttgart)

Michael Wilford   Christoph Bohsung
Manuel Schupp   Wolfgang Heckmann
Laurence Bain   Mike Reissner
Russell Bevington   Sivija Saronovic
Chris Dyson   Holger Schmidt
Stephan Gerstner   Franziska Seemann
Klaus Grubnau   Katrin Trimborn
Gillian McInnes   Alexander Witte

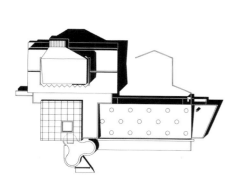

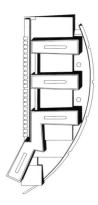

STO AG PRODUCTION AND EXHIBITION BUILDINGS
WEIZEN, GERMANY, 1999–2003
Wilford Schupp Architekten
(formerly Michael Wilford & Partners London and Stuttgart)

Michael Wilford   Martin Braun
Manuel Schupp   Frank Maurer
Laurence Bain   Claudia Murin
Russell Bevington   Carsten Philippin
Chris Dyson   Hanna von der Kall
Stephan Gerstner
Joachim Carle
Christoph Bohsung

DGF STOESS AG HEADQUARTERS
EBERBACH, GERMANY, 2000
Wilford Schupp Architekten
(formerly Michael Wilford & Partners, London and Stuttgart)

Michael Wilford
Manuel Schupp
Laurence Bain
Russell Bevington
Chris Dyson
Carsten Engel
Gabi Mettenleiter
Bjorn Zimmermann

B BRAUN AG SWISS HEADQUARTERS
SEMPACH, GERMANY, 2000
Wilford Schupp Architekten
(formerly Michael Wilford & Partners, London and Stuttgart)

Michael Wilford
Manuel Schupp
Laurence Bain
Russell Bevington
Chris Dyson
Paul Barke-Asuni
Martin Braun
Carsten Engel

KRYSTALTECH LYNX AG, EUROPEAN HEADQUARTERS, PRODUCTION AND DISTRIBUTION BUILDING
REUTLINGEN, GERMANY, 2000
Wilford Schupp Architekten
(formerly Michael Wilford & Partners, London and Stuttgart)

Michael Wilford
Manuel Schupp
Laurence Bain
Russell Bevington
Chris Dyson
Axel Overath
Denis Wolf

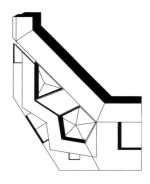

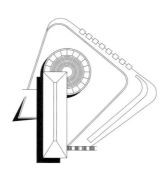

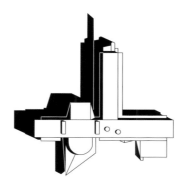

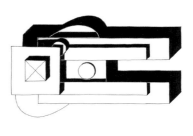

LEIPZIGERPLATZ OFFICE, APARTMENT AND RETAIL DEVELOPMENT
BERLIN, GERMANY, 2001
Wilford Schupp Architekten
(formerly Michael Wilford & Partners London and Stuttgart)

Michael Wilford
Manuel Schupp
Charlie Sutherland
Klaus Grubnau
Georg Ackermann
Borbala Csicsely
Bjorn Zimmermann

LITERATURE MUSEUM
MARBACH, GERMANY, 2001
Wilford Schupp Architekten

Michael Wilford
Manuel Schupp
Charlie Sutherland
Thomas Rupp
Bjoern Zimmermann

THEATER, DRAMA AND UNDERGRADUATE SCIENCE CENTRE, UNIVERSITY OF MICHIGAN
ANN ARBOR, USA, 2001–2002
Michael Wilford Architects and MUMA
in association with The Smith Group Detroit

Michael Wilford   Sonia Grant
Gillian McInnes   Monika Lenkmann
Simon Usher   Andrew Llowarch
Stuart McKnight   Ben Paul
David Artis   Helle Westergaard
Simon Branson
Pamela Campbell

CAMPUS LIBRARY RICE UNIVERSITY
HOUSTON, USA, 2001–2002
Michael Wilford Architects and MUMA
in association with Kendal Heaton Houston

Michael Wilford
Gillian McInnis
Simon Usher
Stuart McKnight
David Artis
Andrew Llowarch
Helle Westergaard

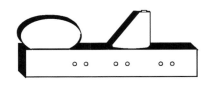

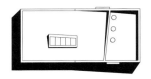

ADIDAS FACTORY OUTLET
HERZOGENAURACH, GERMANY, 2002
Wilford Schupp Architekten

Michael Wilford
Manuel Schupp
Peter Bauhofer
Malve Kaschner
Frank Maurer
Thomas Rupp

MUSEUM OF AFRICA
STELLENBOSCH, SOUTH AFRICA, 2003–2004
Michael Wilford Architects & Chris Dyson Architects

Michael Wilford
Chris Dyson
Karenna Wilford
Angelito Jr Wang

PEACE PALACE LIBRARY AND ACADEMY
THE HAGUE, NETHERLANDS, 2003–2007
Wilford Schupp Architekten

Michael Wilford   Vincent Geisel
Manuel Schupp   Tamara Giesberts
Stephan Gerstner   Oliver Hilt
Charlie Sutherland   Frank Maurer
Klaus Gruebnau   Jens Mueller
Kahlid Atris   Stephan Wurster
Christoph Bohsung   Mariya Yankulova
Martin Braun
Michael Enste

MUSIC SCHOOL ADDITION
TROSSINGEN, GERMANY, 2003–2007
Wilford Schupp Architekten

Michael Wilford
Manuel Schupp
Stephan Gerstner
Martin Braun
Claudia Maas
Katrin Meincke
Natalie Port

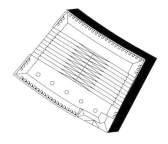

LANDESBANK OFFICE BUILDING
KARLSRUHE, GERMANY, 2004
Wilford Schupp Architekten

Michael Wilford   Carsten Philippin
Manuel Schupp   Alexandra Vassilakou
Charlie Sutherland   Marija Yankulova
Frank Maurer

LBBW REGIONAL HEADQUARTERS
KARLSRUHE, GERMANY, 2004–2007
Wilford Schupp Architekten

Michael Wilford   Vincent Geisel
Manuel Schupp   Wolfgang Heckmann
Stephan Gerstner   Frank Maurer
Charlie Sutherland   Jens Michalke
Christoph Bohsung   Thomas Rupp
Silvia Antal   Alexandra Vassilakou
Martin Braun   Sonja Walossek
Isabel Fleischer Derouiche   Stephan Wurster

RESIDENTIAL CONVERSION
STUTTGART, GERMANY, 2004–2007
Wilford Schupp Architekten

Michael Wilford
Manuel Schupp
Stephan Gerstner
Thomas Rupp
Nicole Baumbusch
Vincent Geisel
Frank Maurer
Alexandra Vassilakou

MARY ROSE MUSEUM
PORTSMOUTH, ENGLAND, 2005
Wilford Schupp Architekten & Chris Dyson Architects

Michael Wilford
Manuel Schupp
Chris Dyson
Claudia Maas
Mark Coles
Anna Kubelik
Frank Maller
Marlene Probst

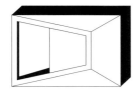

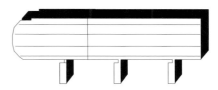

BRITISH EMBASSY
TBILISI, GEORGIA, 2006–2010
Wilford Schupp Architekten

Michael Wilford
Manuel Schupp
Stephan Gerstner
Vincent Geisel
Martin Braun
Jakob Dreher
Christian Kirchner
Tilman Raff

**NATIONAL SOCIALISM
DOCUMENTATION CENTRE**
MUNICH, GERMANY, 2007
Wilford Schupp Architekten

Michael Wilford
Manuel Schupp
Sian Brehler
Vincent Geisel
Christian Kirchner
John Milligan
Andreas Ried

**B BRAUN VISITOR CENTRE AND
PRODUCTION EXPANSION**
MELSUNGEN, GERMANY, 2007–2009
Wilford Schupp Architekten

Michael Wilford   Max Schlentner
Manuel Schupp   Daniel Spies
Stephan Gerstner   Natalie Zabrocka
Christoph Bohsung   Vesna Zaneta
Martin Braun
Jakob Dreher
Michael Enste
Christian Kirchner

PEACE PALACE VISITOR CENTRE
THE HAGUE, NETHERLANDS, 2008–2011
Wilford Schupp Architekten

Michael Wilford
Manuel Schupp
Vincent Geisel
Markus Brucker
Sandra Pallmann

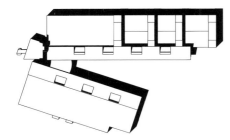

**B BRAUN AG CAMPUS ONE MASTERPLAN
AND PRODUCTION BUILDING EXPANSION**
PENANG, MALAYSIA, 2009–
Wilford Schupp Architekten in association
with BYG Architects Penang

Michael Wilford   Michael Enste
Manuel Schupp   Vincent Geisel
Stephan Gerstner   Christian Kirchner
Christoph Bohsung   Andreas Ried
Natascha Baksic
Martin Braun

IN ADDITION TO THOSE MENTIONED IN THE TIME LINE, THE FOLLOWING ARCHITECTS HAVE CONTRIBUTED TO
THE PROJECTS INCLUDED IN THIS MONOGRAPH WHILST WORKING IN THE OFFICES OF MICHAEL WILFORD AND
PARTNERS AND WILFORD SCHUPP ARCHITEKTEN:

Sarah Adams
Aleksandra Antkowiak
Sandra Bosch
John Bowmer
Simon Branson
Marcus Brucker
Mark Bunting
Pam Campbell
Chris Chong
Hilary Clarke
Robiel Debrezion
Soinibhe Diamond
Robert Dinse
John Dorman
Mark Emms
Sabine Ferre Nerbot
Jane Frank

Burkhardt Franke
Soren Fricke
Wolfgang Fuchs
Jennifer Gerber
Beate Gockeritzeffs
Aleksandra Hollibowska
Kate Iverson
Hanna Jacob
Mark Jeffs
Wei Jiang
Norbert Jobst
Nina Kenntner
Anna-Maria Koebcke Friedrich
Johannes Landsdorfer
Petra Lebson
Kirsten Lees
Hanna Lepiorz

Toby Lewis
Tess Mahoney
Giles Martin
Gareth McGuire
David McKenna
Alan Mee
Kerstin Monkemeyer
Joscha Oberndorfer
Jess Paul
Annette Paulick
Cornelia Renner
Brian Reynolds
Jutta Rheinlander
Jonathon Rose
John Ryan
Roberto Sanna
Max Schlentner

Sven Schmedes
Zorica Seremet
Maurice Shapiro
Philip Smithies
Johanna Sutherland
Jason Syrett
Melanie Tempel
Kit Wallace
Chaoa Wang
Megan Williams
Silke Wolff
Udo Wrede
Gary Wyatt
Gulten Yilmaz
Eric Yim

In over 50 years of professional practice
I have had, and continue to have, the
privilege of working with many excep-
tional architects who have demonstrated
the talent and dedication to practice
architecture as an art rather than a mere
business. They have occupied key roles
in the development and evolution of
the concerns, objectives and strategies
underlying the designs contained within
this monograph. Together we have been
constantly exploring and pushing boundaries to achieve better and more interesting
ways of designing and constructing buildings which stimulate, intrigue and, I hope,
delight all who use and experience them.
I am especially grateful for the support of
my partners, Laurence Bain and Russell
Bevington in Michael Wilford & Partners
and Manuel Schupp in Wilford Schupp
Architekten, together with key associates,
several of whom have subsequently
formed their own successful practices and
for the stimulation and enthusiasm of the
current team with whom I am working on
the various projects currently in hand at
Wilford Schupp Architekten in Stuttgart.

MICHAEL WILFORD & PARTNERS, LONDON
AND STUTTGART.
MICHAEL WILFORD, LAURENCE BAIN
& RUSSELL BEVINGTON.
ASSOCIATES: CHRIS DYSON, ANDREW PRYKE, PETER RAY,
MANUEL SCHUPP, CHARLIE SUTHERLAND AND DAVID
TURNBULL.

WILFORD SCHUPP ARCHITEKTEN, STUTTGART.
MICHAEL WILFORD, MANUEL SCHUPP.
ASSOCIATES: STEPHAN GERSTNER, VINCENT GEISEL,
CHRISTOPH BOHSUNG AND MARTIN BRAUN.

BIOGRAPHY

PERSONAL
Born 1938, Surbiton, Surrey, England.
Married 1960.
Two sons and three daughters.
Resident Sussex, England.

EDUCATION
Kingston Technical School, 1950–1955.
Northern Polytechnic School of Architecture,
London, 1955–1962.
Honours Diploma with Distinction in Thesis
(Buildings for Secondary Education).
Regent Street Polytechnic Planning School,
London, 1967.

PROFESSIONAL PRACTICE
Senior Assistant with James Stirling and James
Gowan, 1960–1963.
Senior Assistant with James Stirling,
1963–1965.
Associate Partner in James Stirling and
Partner, 1965–1971.
Partner in James Stirling Michael Wilford
and Associates, 1971–1992.
Sole Practitioner in James Stirling
Michael Wilford and Associates,
1992–1993.
Senior Partner in Michael Wilford and
Partners, 1993–2000.
Senior Partner in Michael Wilford Architects
from 2001.
Managing Director of Michael Wilford
Gmbh 1997–2001.
Managing Director of Wilford Schupp
Architekten Gmbh from 2001–2013.

PROFESSIONAL MEMBERSHIPS
Royal Institute of British Architects.
Honorary Member Bund Deutscher
Architekten, Germany.
Honorary Fellow American Institute of Architects.

DECORATIONS
Honorary Doctorate of Literature, Sheffield
University, UK. 1989.
Honorary Doctorate of Science, Newcastle
University, NSW, Australia 1993.
CBE (Commander of the British Empire) for
services to architecture 2001.
Honorary Doctorate of Letters, Salford
University, UK. 2002.
Honorary Doctorate of Science, Leicester
University, UK. 2011.

AWARDS
Various projects have received Royal Institute
of British Architects UK and European
category awards and been short-listed for the
Stirling Prize Building of the Year.

TEACHING EXPERIENCE
Tutor, Visiting Critic and Visiting Professor at
University Schools of Architecture throughout
the UK, Europe, USA, Canada and Australia.
Addressing standards of architectural
education as External Examiner and Royal
Institute of British Architects Visiting Board
Member to UK Schools of Architecture,
including service on the RIBA Education and
Professional Development Committee.
Lecturing on architecture at Schools,

Institutions and Conferences throughout the
UK, Europe, USA, Canada, South America,
South Africa, Australia and New Zealand.

GENERAL
Professional Advisor and Committee Member
on architectural appointments, building
renovation and urban design.
Jury Member and Assessor of numerous
architectural competitions, awards and prizes
throughout the UK, Europe and USA.

PUBLISHED ARTICLES/BROADCASTS
"CRITIQUE OF THE BURRELL MUSEUM
GLASGOW"
Architects Journal, 19 October 1983
"OFF TO THE RACES OR GOING TO
THE DOGS"
An appraisal of the London Docklands
Development Corporation's guide to design
and development opportunities for the Isle of
Dogs. *Architectural Design*, January 1984
REVIEW OF "CONCEPTS OF URBAN
DESIGN" by David Gosling and Barry
Maitland published by Academy Editions/
St Martins Press, *Architecture Review*,
January 1987
"INSPIRED PATRONAGE"
A review of the RIBA 1990 National
Awards, *RIBA Journal*, April 1991
"A SENSE OF PLACE IN MILTON KEYNES"
A critique of the Milton Keynes Magistrates
Court. *Architecture Today*, September 1991
"AN EVOLVING DESIGN PHILOSOPHY"
"Architectural Monographs No. 32.

James Stirling and Michael Wilford"
Academy Editions, 1993. Introductory Essay.
"BUILDINGS AND PROJECTS 1975–1992
JAMES STIRLING MICHAEL WILFORD AND
ASSOCIATES".
Verlag Gerd Hatje/Thames and Hudson
1994. Introductory Essay.
"AN EVOLVING DESIGN PHILOSOPHY
AND WORKING METHOD"
Wilford Stirling Wilford Exhibition (London)
Catalogue 1996. Introductory Essay.
BBC RADIO 3
Building for the Arts Programme 4,
26 October 1996 "Changing The Text"
Faculty of History Library,
Cambridge University
BBC RADIO 3
Building for the Arts Programme 6, 9
November 1996 "Everything Under One
Roof"—Arts Complexes, The Lowry, Salford
"DESIGN PHILOSOPHY"
Michael Wilford and Partners Exhibition
(Bilbao) Catalogue 1999. Introductory Essay.
BBC RADIO 3
"Bach and his Time" 26 March 2000

CLIENTS
United Nations, Museums, Universities,
Central and Local Governments, New Town
Corporations and Corporate Clients including
Bayer, Benchmark, B Braun, Chelsfield, City
Acre Investment Trust, Landesbank of Baden
Wurttemberg, Olivetti, Olympia and York,
Siemens and Sto, together with individual patrons
Rena Brion, Lord Palumbo and Baron Thyssen.

PHOTOGRAPHERS' CREDITS

RALPH APPELBAUM ASSOCIATES
p. 272 (except bottom right)

TILL BENATZKY
pp. 126 (top and bottom right), 127, 128 (top right),

FLORIAN BOLK
pp. 176 (left), 178 (left), 180 (left and bottom right)

B BRAUN AG
p. 115

ZOOEY BRAUN
p. 128 (left)

RICHARD BRYANT/ARCAID
pp. 38–41, 63–66, 94–99, 122 (top left, top middle and top right), 122–123, 130, 133–135, 176 (bottom right), 177, 179, 180 (top right), 242–251, 262, 264–265

CANADIAN CENTRE FOR ARCHITECTURE
pp. 171, 222

PETER COOK
pp. 176 (top right), 178 (top and bottom right), 181

PETER DE RUIG
pp. 141–145, 152–155

DP ARCHITECTS
p. 224

CHRIS EDGCOMBE
pp. 22, 24–25, 26, 31 (top left and top right), 35, 59, 84, 88, 106, 149, 156, 161, 174, 189, 191–192, 195, 210, 214–215, 240

ESTACION INTERMODAL DE ABANDO GESTION DEL PROJECTO S.A.
p. 20

DENNIS GILBERT
pp. 164, 165 (right and bottom left), 166–167

EUJIN GOH
pp. 227, 229

SIEGFRIED GRAGNATO
pp. 81, 82 (top left, bottom left and top right), 83

TIM GRIFFITH
pp. 226 (top left), 228

RALF GRÖMMINGER
pp. 126 (left), 128 (bottom right), 129

ROLAND HALBE
pp. 46 (bottom right), 50–51, 52 (top left, bottom middle and bottom left), 53, 111 (top left), 112 (top left and bottom left), 114 (top left and top right), 216–219, 284 (top and bottom right), 285 (top left and right)

HAYES DAVIDSON
pp. 260–261

PETER HYATT
pp. 200–203

WOLFRAM JANZER
p. 186

FAS KEUZENKAMP
pp. 138, 140

PROCTOR MATTHEWS
pp. 118, 120

MONIKA NIKOLIC
pp. 109–110, 111 (right), 112 (bottom middle and bottom right), 113 (top left, bottom left and bottom right), 114 (middle right, bottom left and bottom right)

DIE PHOTODESIGNER
p. 52 (top right and bottom right)

JONATHON ROSE
p. 226 (top right, bottom left and bottom right)

CITY OF SALFORD
p. 234

ALBRECHT IMANUEL SCHNABEL
pp. 284 (bottom left), 285 (bottom right), 287

STO AG
p. 31 (bottom left and bottom right)

MANFRED STORCK
pp. 67, 78 (bottom right), 283

MICHAEL WILFORD ARCHITECTS/CHRIS DYSON ARCHITECTS
pp. 272 (bottom right), 273

MICHAEL WILFORD ARCHITECTS/MUMA
pp. 204, 207–209

MICHAEL WILFORD AND PARTNERS
pp. 102–104, 122 (bottom left and bottom right)

WILFORD SCHUPP ARCHITEKTEN
p. 28, pp. 33 (bottom left and bottom right), 45, 46 (top right), 57, 73–74, 77, 78 (top right), 82 (bottom right), 102, 103, 124, 162, 165 (top right), 187, 232–233, 254–255, 276–277, 281, 285 (bottom left), 286

KIM ZWARTS
pp. 111 (bottom left), 112 (top middle and top right), 113 (top right),

IMAGES FROM THE JAMES STIRLING/ MICHAEL WILFORD FONDS GENEROUSLY PROVIDED BY THE CANADIAN CENTRE FOR ARCHITECTURE, MONTREAL.

Artifice books on architecture
10a Acton Street
London WC1X 9NG
United Kingdom

Tel: +44 (0)20 7713 5097
Fax: +44 (0)20 7713 8682
sales@artificebooksonline.com
www.artificebooksonline.com

British Library Cataloguing-in-Publication Data. A CIP record
for this book is available from the British Library.

ISBN 978 1 908967 05 3

Artifice books on architecture is an environmentally responsible
company. *Michael Wilford: with Michael Wilford and Partners,
Wilford Schupp Architekten and Others. Buildings and Projects
1992–2012* is printed on sustainably sourced paper.